The Law Commission
(LAW COM No 305)

PARTICIPATING IN CRIME

*Presented to the Parliament of the United Kingdom by the Lord Chancellor
and Secretary of State for Justice by Command of Her Majesty
May 2007*

Cm 7084   £32.50

The Law Commission was set up by the Law Commissions Act 1965 for the purpose of promoting the reform of the law.

The Law Commissioners are:

> The Honourable Mr Justice Etherton, *Chairman*
> Professor Hugh Beale QC, FBA
> Mr Stuart Bridge
> Professor Jeremy Horder
> Mr Kenneth Parker QC

The Chief Executive of the Law Commission is Mr Steve Humphreys.

The Law Commission is located at Conquest House, 37-38 John Street, Theobalds Road, London WC1N 2BQ.

The terms of this report were agreed on 28 February 2007.

The text of this report is available on the Internet at:

http://www.lawcom.gov.uk

THE LAW COMMISSION

PARTICIPATING IN CRIME

CONTENTS

THE LAW COMMISSION

PARTICIPATING IN CRIME

To the Right Honourable the Lord Falconer of Thoroton, Lord Chancellor and Secretary of State for Justice

PART 1
INTRODUCTION

1.1 This is the second of two reports in which we consider the circumstances in which a person ('D') ought to be criminally liable for assisting or encouraging another person ('P'), to commit an offence ('the principal offence').[1]

Example 1A

D and P agree to rob V. While D keeps watch, P approaches V with a knife.

(i) The police arrest P before he reaches V.

(ii) P robs V.

The conduct that the offence of robbery proscribes is the appropriation of property by the use or threatened use of force.[2] In example 1A, only P will engage in the proscribed conduct. P is the principal offender. However, by agreeing to the offence and by keeping watch, D will be participating in the offence.

1.2 In the first report,[3] we considered D's liability in cases like example 1A(i). We recommended that even if P does not subsequently commit the principal offence it still ought to be possible for D to be liable for assisting or encouraging its commission ('inchoate liability'). In contrast, this second report considers cases like example 1A(ii), focusing on the circumstances in which D ought to be held liable for the full offence should P commit or attempt to commit it ('secondary liability').[4] Secondary liability is a more serious form of liability than inchoate liability. If D is secondarily liable, D, as well as P, is convicted of the principal offence. D is labelled in the same way as P and may be subject to the same penalty as P.

---

[1] In this report we must also consider the circumstances in which D ought to be criminally liable for *agreeing* with P to commit an offence, and the offence is committed in consequence.

[2] The appropriation must be dishonest and it must be accompanied by an intention to permanently deprive V of his or her property: Theft Act 1968 s 8.

[3] Inchoate Liability for Assisting and Encouraging Crime (2006) Law Com No 300 ('the first report').

[4] In order to avoid wearisome repetition, any reference in this report to P committing a principal offence includes P attempting to commit the offence.

1.3 The concepts of inchoate liability and of secondary liability have long been recognised at common law. However, each is beset by problems. At common law the scope of inchoate liability is restricted to cases where D's conduct consists of encouraging, as opposed to assisting, P to commit a principal offence. This has had an impact on the scope of secondary liability. The common law has compensated for the limited scope of inchoate liability by over-extending the scope of secondary liability.[5] The primary recommendation of the first report is that inchoate liability should extend beyond encouragement to include acts of assistance as well. This recommendation now enables the problem of secondary liability's scope to be addressed along with problems that have arisen in relation to the very nature of such liability, without the distraction of a simultaneous concern with the nature and scope of inchoate liability.

1.4 Taken together, the recommendations contained in both reports would, if implemented, result in a scheme whereby inchoate and secondary liability will support and supplement each other in a way that is rational and fair.

THE PROBLEMS WITH THE CURRENT LAW OF SECONDARY LIABILITY

General problems

Parity of culpability

1.5 At the core of the doctrine of secondary liability is the notion that D can and should be convicted of the offence that P commits even though D has only "aided, abetted, counselled or procured"[6] P to commit the offence. It follows that if D is to be liable to the same stigma and penalty as P, D's culpability should be at least comparable to that of P. With this in mind, we now explain what we mean by 'parity of culpability'.

1.6 In the first report, we said that a criminal offence could consist of one or more of three external elements: conduct, the circumstances in which the conduct takes place and the consequences of the conduct.[7] Leaving aside cases of voluntary intoxication and cases where P can incur criminal liability by an omission, liability normally requires that P intended to perpetrate the *conduct* that constitutes the conduct element.

1.7 It might be thought, therefore, that if P's liability for a principal offence is dependent on his or her conduct being intended, D also ought to incur liability for the principal offence *only* if he or she also intended that P should engage in its conduct element. In the absence of such an intention on D's part, there is no parity of culpability.

---

[5] See further paras 1.8 and 1.9 below.

[6] The language of the Accessories and Abettors Act 1861, s 8 and the Magistrates' Courts Act 1980, s 44.

[7] R A Duff, *Criminal Attempts* (1996) p 13 believes that this way of distinguishing the different elements of an offence is problematic because it is relative to the way that we describe actions. Thus, if a rapist's action is described as "having sexual intercourse" the victim's non-consent is a circumstance of the rapist's action. If the rapist's action is described as "having non-consensual sexual intercourse" the victim's non-consent is part of the action itself rather than a circumstance. Despite this, we still feel that it is a helpful construct through which to explore secondary liability.

1.8   However, the present law, in order to overcome the problems caused by the limited scope of inchoate liability at common law, does not require this:

Example 1B

D works in a sports shop. P calls at the shop and decides to purchase a baseball bat. Overhearing the conversation between P and P's girlfriend, D believes that P is likely use the baseball bat not only to play baseball but also to assault V. Nevertheless, D sells the baseball bat to P. P uses the bat to assault V.

The case law suggests that D is guilty of assault despite the fact that he did not intend, desire or agree that P should attack V. D's belief that P is likely to use the bat to attack V is sufficient to render D complicit in and liable for P's offence.[8]

1.9   In sanctioning the conviction of D for assault in example 1B, the current law fails to afford proper weight to the principle that ought to underpin secondary liability, namely parity of culpability. P intended to attack V whereas D did not intend that V should be attacked.[9] In this report, we make recommendations which, if implemented, would prevent D in example 1B being convicted of assault unless D intended P to attack V. Instead, D would be convicted of an inchoate offence of assisting or encouraging assault.[10]

JOINT CRIMINAL VENTURES

1.10   In example 1B, D and P are not parties to a joint criminal venture. Joint criminal ventures are cases where D and P either agree to commit an offence or share with each other an intention to commit an offence and the offence is subsequently committed.[11] In example 1B, had D agreed with P that P should use the bat to assault V, D and P would have been parties to a joint criminal venture.

---

[8]   Some of the authorities hold that D can be convicted as a secondary party even if he or she merely believed that P *might* use the bat to commit robbery.

[9]   Neither did D agree that P should attack V.

[10] In the first report, we set out the state of mind required of D if he or she is to be held inchoately liable for encouraging or assisting the commission of a principal offence.

[11] If the offence is not subsequently committed, D may still be convicted of the offence of conspiracy - Criminal Law Act 1977, s 1.

1.11 This report also deals with joint criminal ventures. In such cases, the facts will often reveal that D intended that the conduct element of one or more principal offences should be committed. However, there will be cases where, pursuant to the joint criminal venture, P commits an offence that D did not intend P (or another participant in the joint venture) to commit. In the context of a joint criminal venture between D and P, it is our view that the principle of parity of culpability does not require that D actually intend the conduct element of a particular offence to be committed by P. D's agreement (or shared joint intention) to participate in the joint criminal venture itself provides a substantial element of culpability, meaning that there can be parity of culpability between D and P even if D did not in addition intend P to engage in the conduct element of an offence. There will be such parity of culpability if, for example, D foresaw that P might engage in the conduct element of a particular offence.[12] In such circumstances, it is acceptable to label and punish D and P in the same way.

A doctrine characterised by uncertainty and incoherence

1.12 The doctrine of secondary liability has developed haphazardly and is permeated with uncertainty. Crucially, these features affect not merely the margins of the doctrine but key concepts. Two examples are the fault element of secondary liability and the defences that are available to D. In the consultation paper published in 1993,[13] the Commission emphasised the unsatisfactory state of the law:

> It displays to a marked degree what is often the characteristic of an area of criminal law governed by the common law, that clear rules and agreed statements of principle are conspicuously lacking from it.[14]

More recently, Professor Ashworth has described the law as:

> … replete with uncertainties and conflict. It betrays the worst features of the common law: what some would regard as flexibility appears here as a succession of opportunistic decisions by the courts, often extending the law, and resulting in a body of jurisprudence that has little coherence.[15]

1.13 It must be remembered that the doctrine of secondary liability is itself of more than marginal importance. It is a doctrine of general application which determines the liability of secondary parties for all offences ranging from the most trivial to the most serious, namely murder. It is unacceptable that such an important basis of criminal liability should be characterised by the features referred to by Professor Ashworth.

---

[12] We set out our reasons in full in Part 3, paras 3.127 to 3.131.

[13] Assisting and Encouraging Crime (1993) Law Commission Consultation Paper No 131 ('the CP').

[14] Above, para 1.1.

[15] A J Ashworth, *Principles of Criminal Law* (4th ed 2003) 441.

Specific problems

1.14   Having referred to the general problems of parity of culpability, on the one hand, and of incoherence and uncertainty, on the other hand, we now seek to identify some of the specific problems which lie at the core of the doctrine of secondary liability.

D's state of mind in relation to the commission of the principal offence

1.15   D's state of mind in relation to the commission of the principal offence might be thought to be a fundamental issue. Yet, as Professor Glanville Williams has observed:

> The authorities do not state a consistent fault principle for accessories. Sometimes they require a purpose to bring about the crime; sometimes knowledge; sometimes an intention in a wider sense; sometimes they are satisfied with an intention to play some part in bringing it about; sometimes they use a formula which embraces recklessness.[16]

1.16   The failure to provide a clear and authoritative set of rules manifests itself in a number of ways:

(1)   There is uncertainty as to what state of mind D must have in relation to P committing the principal offence:

Example 1C

D sells P some petrol believing that P *may* use it to make a petrol bomb with which he *might* commit arson.

Example 1D

D lends his car to P so that P can drive his pregnant wife to the hospital. D believes that P has been drinking alcohol and is *probably* over the prescribed limit.

On this issue, the authorities are in impressive disarray. At common law, there is support for at least four different tests for determining D's liability.[17]

(2)   There is uncertainty as to the circumstances in which D can be secondarily liable for an offence committed by P which is different from the offence that D believed P would commit:

---

[16]   "Complicity, Purpose and the Draft Code: Part 1" [1990] *Criminal Law Review* 4.

[17]   See Part 2, para 2.65 and Appendix B, paras B.109 and B.117.

Example 1E

D helps P to take V's car without V's consent. D does so in the belief that P merely wants to use the car temporarily and that P will in due course return it to V. Instead, P decides to keep it.

Had D's belief been correct, P would have committed the offence of taking a motor vehicle without the authority of its owner.[18] Instead, the offence that P has committed is theft (of a motor vehicle).[19] On one view, whether D is guilty of theft depends on whether taking a motor vehicle without authority is an offence of the same 'type' as theft. There is no clear guidance to assist in determining whether offence *x* is an offence of the same 'type' as offence *y*.

> (3) The common law provides no clear answer as to the circumstances in which D is secondarily liable where the offence that P commits is the same type of offence that D believed P would commit, but is, in some manner, factually different:

Example 1F

D, a racist, encourages P to set fire to the local Afro-Caribbean community centre. P, finding blanket security at the centre, instead sets fire to a local public house that is frequented by people from the centre. Unbeknown to P, D's brother owns the public house.

> (4) It is unclear whether D's secondary liability can extend indefinitely on the basis of a single act of assistance or encouragement:

Example 1G

D and P agreed to commit a burglary in London in 2005. While D acted as lookout, P was to perpetrate the burglary using a jemmy provided by D. P fell ill and the enterprise was abandoned. D forgot to request the return of the jemmy. In 2007, P uses the jemmy to commit a string of burglaries in Liverpool.

In each of examples 1C to 1G, it is impossible to state with confidence whether or not, under the common law, D is secondarily liable for the offence committed by P.[20]

1.17 Professor Sullivan has captured the overall lack of a settled set of principles and rules in relation to the fault element of secondary liability:

---

[18] Contrary to the Theft Act 1968, s 12(1). The offence is punishable by a maximum term of six months imprisonment.

[19] Contrary to the Theft Act 1968, s 1. The offence, following conviction in a trial on indictment, is punishable by a maximum term of seven years imprisonment.

[20] For our recommendations in relation to the fault element of complicity, see Part 3 paras 3.68 to 3.169.

Arguably, under the current law, it *may* be enough for the prosecution to prove that D was no more than reckless in the sense of adverting to the possibility that P might be offending in his presence, or that he might in the future use assistance provided by D. If one then mixes in the attenuations that *may* be permissible under *particular* readings of Bainbridge and Maxwell, a proposition of impressive inculpatory sweep emerges. D, at present, *may* become an accomplice if he suspects that he may assist P in one of a number of offences that he contemplates P might commit, if the offence that P perpetrates turns out to be an offence which D had not contemplated P would commit, provided that it is an offence of the same "type" as one of the offences that D had contemplated P might commit.[21]

Liability for omissions

1.18   The circumstances in which a person can incur liability for an omission is an issue of constitutional and social importance. According to Professor Ashworth:

> … the key issue question in accessorial liability is simple to state: can a person be convicted as an accomplice merely for standing by and doing nothing while an offence is being committed?

Yet, the common law fails to provide clear rules for identifying the circumstances in which D can be secondarily liable for encouraging or assisting P to commit an offence by virtue of refraining from exercising an entitlement to control P's actions:

Example 1H

D decides to hold a party at his house. In the course of the evening, D is told that in the upstairs bedroom a guest, P, is about to rape another guest, V, who is the worse for drink. D decides to do nothing. P rapes V.

Under the present law, it is uncertain whether D can be convicted of rape.

Performing a legal duty

1.19   The common law appears to exempt D from secondary liability merely because D, in assisting P to commit the principal offence, performed a legal duty:

Example 1J

P lends D a jemmy. Later P demands the jemmy back. D knows that P intends to use the jemmy to burgle V's premises. D, who hates V, returns the jemmy so that P can commit the burglary. P commits the burglary.

---

[21]   G R Sullivan, "The Law Commission Consultation Paper on Complicity: (2) Fault Elements and Joint Enterprise" [1994] *Criminal Law Review* 252, 253 (emphasis added). The two cases that Professor Sullivan refers to are *Bainbridge* [1960] 1 QB 129 and *DPP for Northern Ireland v Maxwell* [1978] 1WLR 1350 (hereafter "*Maxwell*").

In *National Coal Board v Gamble ('NCB v Gamble')*[22] Devlin J said that D was not liable because by returning the jemmy D was refraining from committing the tort of detinue.[23] The appeal to civil law concepts is of dubious merit. Criminal liability then becomes dependent on complex civil law issues that attain an inflated and unwelcome significance.

Joint criminal ventures

1.20 The doctrine of secondary liability determines the circumstances in which D may be held criminally liable for a principal offence which he or she 'aids, abets, counsels or procures'[24] P to commit and which P does commit. In some, but not all, cases, D aids, abets or counsels P to commit an offence by virtue of being a party with P to a joint criminal venture.

1.21 Joint criminal ventures are cases where D and P agree to commit or share a common intention to commit an offence ('the agreed offence'):

Example 1K

D and P agree to burgle V's house. D gives P a jemmy and P commits the burglary.

Example 1L

D and P are in a group that is being abused by another group that includes V. Simultaneously, and without communicating, D and P chase V. D holds V down while P punches V.

In each example D and P are parties to a joint criminal venture. In example 1K, D and P have expressly agreed to commit an offence and they share a common intention to commit the agreed offence. In example 1L, although there is no express agreement and no communication between them, D and P share a common intention to assault V. There is a tacit and reciprocal understanding that V should be attacked.

---

[22] [1959] 1 QB 11.

[23] Above, 20. Detinue was a civil wrong which consisted of unlawfully detaining another person's property. Detinue was abolished by the Tort (Interference with Goods) Act 1977, s 2(1). See further Glanville Williams, "Obedience to Law as a Crime" (1990) 53(4) *Modern Law Review* 445.

[24] Accessories and Abettors Act 1861, s 8.

1.22　By contrast:

Example 1M

D is the process of attacking V. P, who does not know D, watches from a distance. P, who hates V, decides to join in when he sees that D has temporarily ceased his attack. P walks over and kicks V. [25]

Although both P and D each intend to assault V, they have not agreed to assault V and their common intention is not a shared intention. They are not parties to a joint criminal venture.

1.23　Provided that the only offence that P commits is the agreed offence, most cases of joint criminal venture pose no particular problems. Indeed, in one respect, such cases are likely to be less problematic than cases where D and P are not parties to a joint criminal venture. This is because the mere fact of agreement is sufficient to render D liable for the agreed offence, with no requirement that D does anything further by way of encouragement or assistance.[26] By contrast, where D and P are not parties to a joint criminal venture, there must be a discrete act of encouragement or assistance by D in order to render him or her liable as a secondary party.[27]

1.24　In addition to or instead of the agreed offence, P may commit another offence ('a collateral offence'):

Example 1N

D and P agree to commit a robbery against the first person, V, that they encounter. D knows that, should V be female, there is a real possibility that P will rape her. D urges P not to commit rape should V be female. In the event, they encounter V who is female. They commit the robbery and, despite D's protests, P rapes V.

As will become apparent, the courts have been greatly troubled in determining the circumstances in which and the extent to which D should be held liable for a collateral offence, particularly if the collateral offence is an unlawful homicide:

Example 1P

D and P agree to attack V by punches and kicks to the body. Unknown to D, P is armed with a knife. In the course of the attack, P fatally stabs V. P's intention was to kill V.

---

[25] A variation of the facts of *Petters and Parfitt* [1995] *Criminal Law Review* 501.

[26] Thus, in example 1K, D would be guilty of burglary even if he did not provide P with a jemmy.

[27] This difference is reflected in the contrasting requirements of clause 1 (non-joint venture) and clause 2 (joint criminal venture) of the draft Bill appended to this report.

1.25　The question that has greatly troubled the courts is this: if P and D are parties to a joint criminal venture which does not have as its object the killing of V,[28] to what extent, if any, should D be held responsible for V's death in the event that P kills V? The courts have addressed this question on a number of occasions but each case has created as many ambiguities as it has resolved. In Part 2, we provide a brief account of the relevant case law.[29] In this report, however, we do not set out our recommendations for reforming the law of complicity in relation to homicide. This is because we have already done so in our recent report on the law of homicide.[30]

1.26　There is also a wider doctrinal issue which is not confined to cases where the principal offence is a homicide offence. Some commentators maintain that the doctrine of secondary liability, properly applied, cannot determine D's liability for a collateral offence.[31] This is, it is said, because D has not 'aided, abetted, counselled or procured' P to commit the collateral offence.[32] Taking example 1N, the argument is that D cannot be said to have 'aided, abetted, counselled or procured' P to commit rape when D has expressed opposition to that offence being committed. On this view, secondary liability and criminal joint venture liability are distinct doctrines.[33] The doctrine of secondary liability governs D's liability for the agreed offence but a separate joint criminal venture doctrine governs D's liability for the collateral offence.[34] We consider the doctrinal issue in more detail below.[35]

1.27　Finally there is the issue, already referred to, concerning the principal of 'parity of culpability'.[36] For all offences committed pursuant to a joint criminal venture, we believe that there can be parity of culpability between D and P even in the exceptional case where, despite agreeing, D does not intend P to commit the principal offence. We set out our reasons in Part 3.[37]

---

[28]　If the agreed offence involves the use of violence which is *intended to kill* V, there is no difficulty. Should P kill V, P and D are each guilty of murder. This would be so even if the method that P employed to kill V was one that D had not foreseen and involved exceptional cruelty which sickens D.

[29]　Paras 2.66 to 2.80 and Appendix B, paras B.124 to B.132.

[30]　Murder, Manslaughter and Infanticide (2006) Law Com No 304, Part 4.

[31]　Simester and Sullivan, *Criminal Law Theory and Doctrine* (2nd ed 2003) pp 224 to 226.

[32]　See the speech of Lord Mustill in *Powell and Daniels, English* [1999] 1 AC 1, 11.

[33]　By contrast, Smith and Hogan, *Criminal Law* (11th ed 2005) pp 190 to 191 says that joint ventures "are governed by the ordinary principles of secondary participation". On this view, the doctrine of secondary liability governs D's liability for all offences committed by P in the course of a joint criminal venture.

[34]　Accordingly, Simester and Sullivan, *Criminal Law Theory and Doctrine* (2nd ed 2003) p 220 (n 159) states that if the only offence that P commits is the agreed offence, it is not a joint criminal venture.

[35]　See Part 3 paras 3.47 to 3.58.

[36]　Paras 1.5 to 1.11 above.

[37]　Paras 3.127 to 3.131.

The doctrine of innocent agency

1.28   The essence of the common law doctrine is that if D intentionally causes an innocent agent (X) to commit an offence, D is guilty of the offence as a principal offender.[38] However, under the current law uncertainty surrounds the contours of the common law doctrine.

1.29   The problem, actual or perceived, has arisen when the principal offence can be committed only by a person who meets a particular description and D does not meet that description. For example, where D, who is not married, causes X, who is married, to 'marry' V by falsely telling X that his wife has died. On one view, convicting D as a principal offender is illogical because the definition of bigamy stipulates that a principal offender can only commit the offence if he or she is already married.

Causing the commission of a no-fault offence

1.30   Under the current law, if D 'procures' the commission of a no-fault offence by P,[39] P is guilty of the offence as a principal offender and D is guilty of the offence as a secondary party. However, in our view, holding D liable for the offence as a secondary party does not accurately reflect the nature of D's wrongdoing. This is because in reality D commits the offence through P. In Part 4 we set out our recommendation for the creation of a new offence which would better reflect the nature of D's liability.[40]

THE COMMISSION'S PROPOSALS IN 1993

1.31   In the CP, the Commission recognised the problems that we have referred to above. The Commission's proposed solution was extremely radical. It entailed no less than the abolition of secondary liability. Instead, the Commission proposed that D's liability should always be inchoate.

The difference between inchoate liability and secondary liability

1.32   If D is secondarily liable, he or she is convicted of the principal offence that P commits. It follows that for D to be secondarily liable, P must commit the principal offence. In many cases, however, P does not go on to commit the principal offence that D has sought to assist or encourage. At common law, D can still be criminally liable provided that his or her conduct consisted of encouragement as opposed to assistance. For example, if D encourages P to commit burglary but P is arrested before he or she can commit the burglary, D is guilty of the common law inchoate offence of incitement (to commit burglary). By contrast, if D, in return for payment, provides P with a jemmy knowing that P intends to use it to commit burglary, D incurs no criminal liability if P is arrested before being able to commit the burglary.

---

[38]   For example, D gives a parcel containing a bomb to P and tells P to deliver it to V. D tells P that it is a birthday present for V. As D hoped, the bomb explodes killing V. D is guilty of murder as a principal offender.

[39]   A no-fault offence is one that P can commit without being at fault in relation to the circumstances element of the offence.

[40]   See paras 4.28 to 4.37 below.

The Commission's reasons for rejecting secondary liability

1.33 The Commission set out its reasons in the following passage:

> However, the conclusion that an accessory's liability is, *even in the present law*, essentially inchoate in nature springs directly from analysis of the conduct that founds that liability in law. An accessory's legal fault is complete as soon as his act of assistance is done, and acts thereafter by the *principal*, in particular in committing or not committing the crime assisted, cannot therefore add to or detract from that fault. Moreover, it is not the present law, and it is logically impossible that it should become the law, that the accessory must *cause* the commission of the principal crime; and for that reason also the actual occurrence of the principal crime is not taken into account in assessing the accessory's culpability. Even under the present law, therefore, where the principal crime has to be committed before accessory liability can attach, the conditions for the liability of the accessory should be, indeed can only be, assessed at the time of, and in relation to, that act of assistance.[41]

1.34 In place of secondary liability, the Commission, recognising that at common law there is no inchoate liability for assisting, as opposed to encouraging the commission of a principal offence, proposed that there should be two statutory inchoate offences:

    (1)   assisting P to commit an offence; and

    (2)   encouraging P to commit an offence.

1.35 Under the Commission's proposals in the CP, D's liability would always be inchoate even if P committed the principal offence. Accordingly, if D lent a firearm to P so that P could murder V and P used the firearm to murder V, D would no longer be guilty of murder (secondary liability) but of assisting murder (inchoate liability).

1.36 Although we agree that the scope of inchoate liability should be extended to cover assisting, we no longer support the view that secondary liability should be abolished. Instead, we are of the view that reform of inchoate liability for assisting and encouraging crime, rather than being a reason for dispensing with secondary liability, presents an opportunity for its reform. This leads us to consider the first report.

THE FIRST REPORT

1.37 The first report is pivotal to an understanding of the recommendations that we make in this report. This is for two reasons. First, in that report, we recommended that the doctrine of secondary liability should be retained. Secondly, we made recommendations for reform of inchoate liability for assisting and encouraging crime which, if implemented, would facilitate reform of secondary liability. We consider each of these in turn.

---

[41] Para 4.24 (emphasis in original).

Retaining the doctrine of secondary liability

1.38   In the first report, we said that we no longer favoured the abolition of secondary liability. Instead, D's liability for assisting or encouraging crime should be governed by a statutory scheme in which inchoate and secondary liability support and complement each other. There were two main reasons why we rejected the abolition of secondary liability. First, we said that there were cases where D's culpability was such that D would be insufficiently condemned and labelled if he or she were to be convicted of merely assisting or encouraging the commission of the principal offence rather than convicted of the offence itself. The obvious case, particularly if it is D who is the instigator, is where D assists or encourages P with the intention that P should commit the principal offence.

1.39   Secondly, the considerable forensic advantages associated with secondary liability would be jeopardised by a scheme that comprised only inchoate offences. By virtue of section 8 of the Accessories and Abettors Act 1861, a person who is an accessory can be charged, indicted and punished as a principal offender. This means that the prosecution can obtain a conviction even if it cannot be proved whether the accused was a principal offender or an accessory provided that he or she must have been one or the other.[42] For example, suppose that D1 and D2 are jointly charged with burglary. It is known that one of them entered the premises while the other kept watch. D1 and D2 can each be convicted of burglary despite the prosecution being unable to prove who entered the premises (the principal offender) and who kept watch (the accessory).[43]

1.40   This is of considerable assistance to the prosecution in cases where it is difficult or impossible to prove the precise role of the various parties. In addition, the prosecution does not have to specify in advance whether the allegation is that an accused was a principal offender or an accessory.[44] In *Mercer*[45] it was held that there is no violation of Article 6(3) of the European Convention on Human Rights and Fundamental Freedoms where the prosecution alleges that an accused is a party to an offence but cannot specify his or her precise role.[46] The scheme that we are recommending preserves the forensic advantages of secondary liability.

---

[42]   *Swindall v Osborne* (1864) 2 Car. & K. 230; *Du Cros v Lambourne* [1907] 1 KB 40; *Ramnath Mohan* [1967] 2 AC 187. D can properly be convicted even if some of the jury find that he or she was the principal offender and some find that he or she was the accessory – *Giannetto* [1997] 1 Cr App R 1 in which the Court of Appeal referred with approval to the decision of the Supreme Court of Canada in *Thatcher v R* (1987) 39 DLR (4th) 275.

[43]   In *Powell and Daniels* [1999] 1 AC 1 it could be proved that the accused was either the person (P) who murdered V or a person (D) who was on a joint criminal venture with P to buy drugs from V believing that P might shoot V with intent to cause serious harm. Accordingly, the accused could be convicted of murder.

[44]   The House of Lords has indicated that it is desirable, wherever possible, for the prosecution to specify whether the accused is alleged to be a principal offender or an accessory – *Maxwell* [1978] 1 WLR 1350.

[45]   [2001] EWCA Crim 638, (2001) WL 542166.

[46]   Article 6(3) provides, amongst other things, that everybody charged with a criminal offence has the right "to be informed promptly, in a language which he understands and in detail, of the nature and cause of the accusation against him".

Reform of inchoate liability for assisting and encouraging crime

1.41   In the first report, we said that the major defect of the current law is that the scope of inchoate liability for assisting or encouraging the commission of an offence is limited. This is because, at common law, D can be inchoately liable only if his or her conduct consists of encouraging P to commit an offence. If D does so with the requisite fault element, D is guilty of the common law inchoate offence of incitement.[47] By contrast, if D *assists* (but does not encourage) P to commit a principal offence that P does not subsequently commit, D incurs no liability. Admittedly, Parliament has enacted a considerable number of statutory offences that criminalise particular instances of inchoate assistance.[48] However, there are no statutory inchoate offences in relation to some of the most serious offences, including murder, robbery, burglary and blackmail. This has had an adverse knock-on effect on the scope of secondary liability. The common law has compensated for the limited scope of inchoate liability at common law by over-extending the scope of secondary liability.[49]

1.42   Accordingly, in the first report, we recommended the creation of two general statutory inchoate offences. They would replace the common law offence of incitement and fill the gap at common law caused by the lack of any inchoate liability where D assists but does not encourage the commission of an offence that P does not subsequently commit. The scheme of inchoate liability that we have recommended would consist of two core inchoate offences:

   (1)   doing an act capable of encouraging or assisting P to commit an offence *intending* that P should be encouraged or assisted to commit the offence ('the clause 1 inchoate offence'):

Example 1Q

D pays P £20000 so that P will murder V who is D's wife. P is arrested in connection with another matter before he can murder V.

---

   (2)   doing an act capable of encouraging or assisting P to commit an offence *believing* that it *will* encourage or assist P to commit the offence and believing that P *will* commit the offence ('the clause 2 inchoate offence'):

Example 1R

D, in return for payment, provides P with the address of V. D believes that P will murder V. D, however, having been paid, is indifferent as to whether or not P murders V. P is arrested in connection with another matter before he can murder V.[50]

---

[47]   Incitement is a free-standing offence but always relates to the principal offence incited. Accordingly, D is charged with incitement to rob or incitement to steal as opposed to simply 'incitement'.

[48]   Examples include Prison Act 1952, s 39; Forgery and Counterfeiting Act 1981, s 17(1); Computer Misuse Act 1990, s 2(1)(b) and 2(3); Terrorism Act 2000 s 12(2) and 17; Asylum and Immigration (Treatment of Claimants, etc) Act 2004, s 4(2).

[49]   See para 1.8 above.

[50]   D incurs no liability under the current law because he has assisted but not encouraged P.

Under our recommendations, in example 1Q, D would be guilty of the clause 1 inchoate offence because he intended that P should commit murder. In example 1R, D would be guilty of the clause 2 inchoate offence because he believed that P would commit murder. Both the clause 1 inchoate offence and the clause 2 inchoate offence would enable D to be held inchoately liable for assisting P to commit a principal offence even if P, as in the two examples, did not go on to commit it.

1.43   In addition, the clause 2 inchoate offence has important implications for reform of secondary liability:

> **Example 1S**
>
> The same facts as in example 1R except that P murders V.

Under the current law, D is guilty of murder as a secondary party. However, although we consider that D's conduct is undoubtedly deserving of censure and punishment, we do not believe that D is fairly labelled as a murderer. D's culpability is not comparable to that of P. D did not *intend* that P should attack, let alone murder, V.

1.44   However, the current law does not reflect our normative claim that, in example 1S, D ought not to be convicted of murder because he did not intend P to engage in the conduct element of the principal offence. At common law, D is guilty of murder. It is easy to understand why. As long as there is no inchoate liability for assisting the commission of an offence, the common law is faced with a stark choice on the facts of example 1S – convict D of murder (as a secondary party) or exonerate D.

1.45   The clause 2 inchoate offence would transform the landscape. It would perform a dual role. It would not only capture D's conduct in example 1R where P does not commit the principal offence. It would also capture D's conduct in example 1S where P does commit the principal offence. In cases where D believes that P will commit the principal offence and P does so, there would no longer be the stark choice between convicting D of murder or exonerating D. In example 1S, it would be possible to convict D of assisting and encouraging murder (inchoate liability) just as it would be in example 1R where P does not commit the principal offence. Accordingly, in cases where D and P are not parties to a joint criminal venture, it would be possible to limit the scope of secondary liability to those cases where D intended that P should engage in the conduct element of the principal offence. In doing so, the principle of 'parity of culpability' would be honoured.

AN OUTLINE OF THE SCHEME THAT WE ARE RECOMMENDING IN THIS REPORT

The overall structure

1.46   In place of the common law rules of secondary liability and innocent agency, we are recommending a statutory scheme. The scheme is contained in two draft Bills that accompany this report – Participating in Crime Bill ('the Bill') and Participating in Crime (Jurisdiction, Procedure and Consequential Provisions) Bill ('the Supplementary Bill'). The scheme consists of three conceptually distinct forms of liability:

Type 1: secondary liability

1.47 The Bill subcategorises this type of liability under two headings. First, D would be liable, provided he or she satisfies the requisite fault element, for an offence that P commits with D's encouragement or assistance (clause 1 of the Bill). Secondly, D would be liable, provided he or she satisfies the requisite fault element, for any offences committed pursuant to a joint criminal venture (clause 2 of the Bill).

CLAUSE 1 OF THE BILL

1.48 Under clause 1 of the Bill, D would be liable for a principal offence committed by P if D assisted or encouraged P to perpetrate the conduct element of the principal offence and *intended* that the conduct element should be perpetrated. This would have the effect of narrowing the scope of secondary liability in cases where D and P are not parties to a joint criminal venture.

1.49 For the purposes of clause 1, D 'intends' only if he or she acts in order that the conduct element of the principal offence is perpetrated. In our use and understanding of the word 'intention', we adopt the common law meaning. This means that if D foresaw as a virtual certainty P engaging in the conduct element of the offence, that would be evidence from which the jury or magistrates could (but would not have to) find that D intended the perpetration of the conduct element.[51]

CLAUSE 2 OF THE BILL

1.50 Clause 2 would govern D's liability where D and P have formed a joint criminal venture. This will cover both agreed offences and collateral offences committed by P in the course of the joint criminal venture.

1.51 In relation to clause 2, D would be liable for any offence committed by P provided that its commission fell within the scope of the joint venture. A joint criminal venture is formed when the parties agree to commit an offence or when they share with each other a common intention to commit an offence.[52] D would be liable for any offence (agreed or collateral) that he or she foresaw might be committed as a possible result of the venture. The mere fact that D was not present when the offence was committed or that he or she would rather that it was not committed would not in itself preclude a jury finding that the offence fell within the scope of the joint venture.[53]

---

[51] See Part 3, paras 3.84 to 3.93.

[52] See example 1L above as an illustration of D and P sharing with each other a common intention despite the fact that there is no communication between them.

[53] Clause 2(4) of the Bill.

Type 2: innocent agency

1.52   We are recommending that the common law doctrine of innocent agency should be replaced by a statutory regime.[54] D would be liable for an offence as a principal offender if he or she intentionally caused P, an innocent agent, to commit the conduct element of an offence but P does not commit the offence because P:

(1)   is under the age of 10 years;

(2)   has a defence of insanity; or

(3)   acts without the fault required to be convicted of the offence;[55]

1.53   Our recommendations would ensure that D could be convicted of a principal offence as a principal offender even if the offence can only be committed by a person who meets a particular description and D does not fit that description.

Type 3: causing the commission of a no-fault offence

1.54   We are recommending the creation of a new statutory offence of causing another person to commit a no-fault offence. Accordingly, under this form of liability, D would be convicted as a principal offender rather than, as under the current law, a secondary party to the no-fault offence committed by P.[56]

Summary

1.55   Much more so than at common law, the scheme emphasises the derivative nature of secondary liability. Subject to a very limited number of exceptions, D would incur secondary liability only if P commits a principal offence. The exceptions relate to where P does not commit an offence because he or she has a complete defence, for example duress, or a partial defence to murder, for example provocation.

1.56   Our scheme confines secondary liability to cases where D has assisted or encouraged P and/or has formed a joint criminal venture with P. Under the current law, D can incur secondary liability by 'procuring' P to commit an offence. Under our recommendations, 'procuring' will cease to be a basis of secondary liability. Instead, procuring in the sense of intentionally causing a person to do a criminal act will result in D incurring liability as a principal offender.

---

[54]   Clause 8(b) of the Supplementary Bill abolishes the common law rules in relation to innocent agency.

[55]   Clause 4 of the Bill.

[56]   Clause 5 of the Bill.

Limitations on liability and defences[57]

The Tyrrell exemption

1.57   Under the current law, if an offence is enacted to protect a category of persons and D falls within that category, D cannot be convicted of committing the offence as a secondary party (or of inciting P to commit the offence). This is known as the *Tyrrell*[58] exemption. In *Tyrrell*, P, an adult, had unlawful sexual intercourse with D, a child aged between 13 and 16.[59] It was alleged that D had encouraged P to commit the offence. Despite this, the court held that D could not be liable as a secondary party because the primary offence was intended to protect "victims from themselves".[60] Our scheme preserves and refines the common law *Tyrrell* exemption.

1.58   We are recommending that D should not be held liable as a secondary party or as a principal offender by virtue of innocent agency if:

(1)   the principal offence is one that exists for the protection of a particular category of person;

(2)   D falls within that category; and

(3)   D is the victim of the principal offence.[61]

Acting to prevent the commission of an offence or to prevent or limit the occurrence of harm

1.59   We are recommending that if D is charged with committing an offence as a secondary party, it should be a defence if D proves on the balance of probabilities that he or she acted in order to prevent the commission of an offence or the occurrence of harm and that it was reasonable to act as D did:

Example 1T

D and P are at a pub after a football match and meet a rival gang of supporters. P, along with some others, plan to attack the rival gang and stab their most vocal member (V). D, who does not want V to be harmed, manages to persuade P and the others to damage an item of V's property instead. D is charged with encouraging P to commit criminal damage.

---

[57]   See further Part 5.

[58]   [1894] 1 QB 710.

[59]   Contrary to the Criminal Law Amendment Act 1885, s 5.

[60]   [1894] 1 QB 710, Lord Coleridge at p 712.

[61]   Clause 6 of the Bill.

D has encouraged P to commit criminal damage. He has done so in order to prevent the commission of a serious offence against the person. It would be for a jury to decide whether in doing so D had acted reasonably in all the circumstances. The jury would be entitled to take into account the seriousness of the harm that D was seeking to prevent and also whether or not there were any lawful steps that were available to D, for example, whether in example 1T D should have alerted the police. However, if the jury conclude that D did act reasonably in encouraging the offence, we believe that the defence should be available.

AN OVERVIEW OF INCHOATE AND SECONDARY LIABILITY FOR ASSISTING AND ENCOURAGING CRIME

1.60 It is important that the recommendations in this report are read in the light of the recommendations that we made in the first report. In this section, we provide a brief outline of the overall scheme.

D's liability where P does not commit the principal offence

1.61 D's liability would always be inchoate. D would commit an inchoate offence of encouraging or assisting P to commit an offence:

    (1)   if D does an act capable of encouraging or assisting P to commit an offence:

        (a)   intending to assist or encourage P to perpetrate the conduct element of the offence ('the clause 1 inchoate offence'); or

        (b)   believing that his or her act will assist or encourage P to perpetrate the conduct element and that P will perpetrate it ('the clause 2 inchoate offence');

AND

    (2)   if the principal offence requires proof of fault:

        (a)   D believes that P will perpetrate the conduct element with the fault element required to be convicted of the offence; or

        (b)   D's own state of mind is such that were he to perpetrate the conduct element, he would do so with the requisite fault.

Specific defences

1.62 Where D's liability is grounded on the clause 2 inchoate offence, it would be a defence if D acted reasonably in the circumstances. The burden of proof would be on D to demonstrate that he or she had acted reasonably. The defence would not be available to the clause 1 inchoate offence.

D's liability where P does commit the principal offence

Clause 1

1.63 Beyond inchoate liability, D would be liable for P's offence as a secondary party provided that D intended P to engage in the conduct element of the offence and:

(1)   D believed that P would perpetrate the conduct element with the fault required to be convicted of the offence; or

(2)   D's state of mind was such that, had he or she perpetrated the conduct element, it would have been with the fault required for conviction of the offence.

1.64   Accordingly, if D indifferently assisted or encouraged P to commit an offence, D would no longer be a secondary party to P's offence. However, if D believed that P would commit the principal offence, D would commit the clause 2 inchoate offence of assisting or encouraging P to commit the principal offence believing D would commit it.[62]

1.65   Accordingly, there is scope for the clause 2 inchoate offence to apply even if P does commit or attempt to commit the principal offence. However, for the clause 2 inchoate offence to apply, D must believe that P *will* commit the principal offence. This means that if D believes that P might commit the principal offence, D will not incur either secondary or inchoate liability in respect of the principal offence.

Clause 2

1.66   D would be liable for any offence committed by P that was within the scope of the joint criminal venture. It would be a question of fact and degree whether the offence committed by P was within the scope of the venture. The fact that D was opposed to the commission of the offence would not in itself prevent the tribunal of fact from finding that the offence was within the scope of the venture.[63]

General defences

1.67   There would be two defences to both inchoate and secondary liability. The first would be where D acted reasonably in order to prevent the commission of an offence or to limit the occurrence of harm. The burden of proof would be on D to establish the defence. The second would be where the principal offence was one which existed for the protection of a particular category of person and D was both a member of that category and the victim of the offence (or would have been had the principal offence been committed).

---

[62] This is subject to one qualification. If the jury find that D believed that P would commit the principal offence in the sense of believing that it was 'virtually certain' that P would do so, they would be entitled to find that D 'intended' to commit the offence. D would then be liable as a secondary party.

[63] It will be an exceptional case where D is opposed to the commission of the agreed offence. However, it will not be an unusual occurrence for D to be opposed to the commission of a collateral offence.

THE STRUCTURE OF THIS REPORT

1.68 In Part 2 we provide a summary of the current law.

1.69 In Part 3 we set out and explain our recommendations for a statutory scheme of secondary liability.

1.70 In Part 4 we set out and explain our recommendations for a statutory scheme of innocent agency and for a new offence of causing the commission of a no fault offence.

1.71 In Part 5 we consider defences and exemptions.

1.72 In Part 6 we consider extra-territorial jurisdiction.

1.73 In Part 7 we set out our recommendations.

1.74 Appendix A contains the draft Participating in Crime Bill and the draft Participating in Crime (Jurisdiction, Procedure and Consequential Provisions) Bill. It also includes a commentary to the Participating in Crime Bills.

1.75 Appendix B contains a more expansive and detailed account of the current law than that contained in Part 2.

PART 2
A SUMMARY OF THE CURRENT LAW

INTRODUCTION

2.1 In this Part we provide a summary of the present law. We would normally set out the current law in the consultation paper that precedes a final report. However, in this instance, the CP pre-dates this report by a substantial period of time during which a number of important developments have occurred.[1] It is for this reason that we are providing a summary of the current law in this report. However, it is only a summary of what is a very complex and difficult area of the criminal law. We recognise that some readers would prefer a more expansive account of the current law. This is to be found at Appendix B.

SECONDARY LIABILITY

A common law doctrine

2.2 The primary statutory source of the modern law of complicity is section 8 of the Accessories and Abettors Act 1861. It provides that anyone who 'shall aid, abet, counsel or procure the commission of any indictable offence ... shall be liable to be tried, indicted and punished as a principal offender'.[2] However, the fundamental principle that section 8 embodies is a common law principle, namely that aiding, abetting, counselling or procuring another person to commit an offence is not a distinct offence. Rather, a person who, with the requisite state of mind, aids, abets, counsels or procures another person to commit an offence is him or herself guilty of that offence (provided that the offence is subsequently committed). Accordingly, D is liable to the same stigma and penalties as P.

A doctrine of general application

2.3 In *Powell and Daniels, English*,[3] Lord Steyn referred to a particular feature of secondary liability:

> But there is no special rule governing the criminal liability of accessories in cases of murder. The principle governing the criminal liability of accessories applies across the spectrum of most criminal offences.[4]

Lord Steyn was highlighting a crucial distinction between primary and secondary liability. Offences are generally defined with reference to P. The definition of an offence will stipulate what it is that P must do, in what circumstances, with what consequences and with what state of mind. The rules that govern P's liability for a particular offence are unique to that offence.

---

[1] Eg, the decisions of the Court of Appeal in *Rook* [1993] 2 All ER 955; *Reardon* [1999] *Criminal Law Review* 392; *Bryce* [2004] EWCA Crim 1231; [2004] 2 Cr App R 35; *Webster* [2006] EWCA Crim 415, [2006] 2 Cr App R 6; *Rahman* [2007] EWCA Crim 342 and the decision of the House of Lords in *Powell and Daniels, English* [1999] 1 AC 1.

[2] The corresponding provision for summary offences is Magistrates' Courts Act 1980, s 44.

[3] [1999] 1 AC 1.

[4] Above, 12.

2.4   By contrast, secondary liability is a common law doctrine the rules of which are generally the same irrespective of the context in which D provides encouragement or assistance and regardless of the seriousness of the principal offence. Accordingly, the rules governing D1's liability for robbery are the same as those governing D2's liability for the lesser offence of theft.

The forensic advantages of secondary liability

2.5   Section 8 preserves another fundamental feature of the common law. In *Swindall and Osborne*,[5] D and P encouraged each other to race their respective carts along a road. One of the carts struck V who died. D and P were each charged with manslaughter. At their trial, it was submitted that neither could be convicted of manslaughter because the prosecution was unable to prove whose cart had struck V. Chief Baron Pollock rejected the submission. As a result, the case is authority for the proposition that the mere fact that the prosecution cannot prove whether a person participated in an offence as a principal offender or as a secondary party does not preclude that person being convicted of the offence.

2.6   Accordingly, a participant in an offence can be convicted of it even if the prosecution is unable to prove his or her precise role. It suffices that participation itself, whether as a principal offender or as a secondary party, can be proven.[6] This is of considerable benefit to the prosecution in cases of joint criminal ventures where it can be difficult to pinpoint the precise nature of D's role in the commission of the principal offence.

The parameters of the doctrine of secondary liability

The derivative theory of secondary liability

2.7   According to the derivative theory of secondary liability, D's liability for 'aiding, abetting, counselling or procuring' P to commit an offence derives from and is dependent upon the liability of P. It should follow that, in order for D to be held liable, P must have committed a principal offence. Thus, if D prepares and hands a syringe containing heroin to P who self-injects and dies as a result, D is not criminally liable for P's death as a secondary party because P did not commit an offence by self-injecting.[7] However, a description of D's liability as being necessarily dependent upon the commission of a principal offence requires refinement if it is accurately to reflect the way the law has developed.

---

[5]   (1846) 2 C & K 230, 175 ER 95.

[6]   *Swindall and Osborne* (1846) 2 C & K 230, 175 ER 95; *Du Cros v Lambourne* [1907] 1 KB 40; *Mohan v R* [1967] 2 AC 187. In *Giannetto* [1997] 1 Cr App R 1 the Court of Appeal held that D could properly be convicted even if some of the jury thought that he or she was a principal offender and some thought that he or she was a secondary party.

[7]   *Dias* [2001] EWCA Crim 2986; [2002] 2 Cr App R 5. In recent decisions where D has assisted P to self-inject, the Court of Appeal has held that D can be convicted of manslaughter as a principal offender - *Rogers (Stephen)* [2003] EWCA Crim 945; [2003] 1 WLR 1374; *Finlay* [2003] EWCA Crim 3868, [2003] WL 23145128; *Kennedy (Simon)* [2005] EWCA Crim 685, [2005] 1 WLR 2159.

Exceptions to the derivative theory

2.8   There are a number of circumstances in which P, despite satisfying the external elements of a principal offence, does not commit the offence:[8]

(1)   P is a person who cannot incur criminal responsibility either because he or she is aged under 10 years[9] or is legally insane; or

(2)   P is a person who is capable of incurring criminal responsibility but lacks the requisite fault element to be convicted of the principal offence.

(3)   P, although able to incur criminal responsibility and satisfying the fault element of the offence, has a complete defence, for example duress.[10]

2.9   In those cases, if the derivative theory of secondary liability were to be rigorously applied, D would not be criminally liable for an offence that he or she had sought to assist or encourage. This would give rise to some very unsatisfactory results:

Example 2A

D gives P, aged 9, a loaded gun knowing that P wants to use it to cause serious harm to V. P shoots at V causing serious harm.

Example 2B

D encourages P to 'collect' an item from V's house and bring it to D's house. D, lying, tells P that V has consented to this.[11] P fetches the item.

Example 2C

D encourages P to commit theft and says that if P does not do so, D will cut off the fingers of P's child. P commits the theft.

---

[8]   By external elements, we mean those elements of an offence that come within the term 'actus reus', namely conduct, circumstance and consequence.

[9]   The minimum age of criminal responsibility - Children and Young Persons Act 1933, s 50.

[10]   Apart from murder, attempted murder and, possibly, some forms of treason, duress is available as a complete defence if a person commits what would otherwise be an offence as a result of being threatened with death or serious injury if a reasonable person might have responded to the threat as D did. However, although a complete defence, duress does not negate the fault element of the offence. In our report Murder, Manslaughter and Infanticide (2006) Law Com No 304 we recommended that there should be two separate offences, namely first degree murder and second degree murder. We also recommended that duress should be capable of being of a complete defence to both offences (and attempted murder).

[11]   The external elements of the offence of burglary are satisfied. D has entered V's property as a trespasser and taken an item of property without V's consent – Theft Act 1968, s 9(1)(b). However, P has not satisfied the fault element of the offence because P believed that P had consented to the property being taken.

In each example, P has not committed an offence. Accordingly, in each example, a strict application of the derivative theory would prevent D being convicted of the principal offence. It is true that in examples 2B and 2C, D would not escape all criminal liability. It would be possible to convict D of the common law offences of incitement to commit burglary and incitement to commit theft respectively. However, that is not the same as convicting D of burglary or theft.[12]

2.10 In such cases, the common law has resorted to two mechanisms in order to hold D criminally liable for the principal offence. The first of these is the doctrine of innocent agency by virtue of which D is convicted as a principal offender rather than as a secondary party. The second is to hold D liable as a secondary party on the basis that, although no principal offence has been committed, D has 'procured' the commission of the conduct element of the offence. On one occasion, the Court of Criminal Appeal upheld D's conviction on both bases.[13]

THE DOCTRINE OF INNOCENT AGENCY

2.11 The underlying idea is simple. The doctrine serves "to convert, in effect, an apparent 'accessory' into a [perpetrator]".[14] If D uses an innocent agent to commit an offence, D is considered to have committed the offence as a principal offender:

> **Example 2D**
>
> D asks P to deliver a package to V. Unknown to P, the package contains a bomb. P delivers the package and, as D had hoped, the bomb explodes. V is killed.

D is guilty of murder as a principal offender.

2.12 The apparent simplicity of the doctrine conceals some difficult issues. First, it should not be possible to employ the doctrine if the principal offence is one that as a matter of law can only be perpetrated by those who meet a particular description and D does not meet that description:

> **Example 2E**
>
> D, a bachelor, untruthfully but on reasonable grounds, persuades P that P's estranged wife died three years ago. D encourages P to 'marry' V. In consequence P does so.[15]

---

[12] In example 2A, D's conduct consists of assistance and not encouragement and, therefore, D cannot be convicted of incitement to cause grievous bodily harm. There is no equivalent common law inchoate offence to capture cases where D's conduct consists only of assistance. The recommendations in the first report would fill this gap in the law.

[13] *Cogan and Leak* [1976] QB 217.

[14] K J M Smith, *A Modern Treatise on the Law of Criminal Complicity* (1991) p 94.

[15] An example provided by Professor K J M Smith, *A Modern Treatise on the Law of Criminal Complicity* (1991) p 106.

P has not committed the offence of bigamy[16] because he reasonably believed that his estranged wife was dead.[17] Equally, it ought not to be possible to convict D of bigamy on the basis of innocent agency because as a matter of law only those who are married can commit bigamy as a principal offender.[18]

2.13 Secondly, in the view of some commentators,[19] certain offences appear to require that their conduct element be personally performed:

> **Example 2F**
>
> D encourages P to have sexual intercourse with his daughter V, aged 16. D has previously told V that he will cause her serious bodily harm if she does not let P have sexual intercourse with her. Terrified, V allows P to have intercourse with her. P is unaware of the threats and reasonably believes that V is freely consenting.

P is not guilty of rape since he believed on reasonable grounds that V was consenting to intercourse.[20] In *Cogan and Leak*,[21] the Court of Criminal Appeal held that in similar circumstances D could be convicted of rape as a principal offender by virtue of the doctrine of innocent agency. Yet, on one view, to hold D guilty of rape as a principal offender is a "violent wrench of the English language"[22] because it was P, not D, who had sexual intercourse with V.[23]

---

[16] Offences against the Person Act 1861, s 57.

[17] *Tolson* (1889) LR 23 QBD 168.

[18] However, in *Cogan and Leak* [1976] QB 217 the Court of Appeal applied the doctrine when upholding the conviction of D for raping his wife notwithstanding that as the law then stood a husband could not as a matter of law rape a wife with whom he was cohabiting.

[19] Eg, Glanville Williams, *Textbook of Criminal Law* (2nd ed 1983) p 371.

[20] Sexual Offences Act 2003, s 1(1)(c).

[21] [1976] QB 217.

[22] Glanville Williams, *Textbook of Criminal Law* (2nd ed 1983) p 371.

[23] In *DPP v K & B* [1997] 1 Cr App R 36 counsel for the prosecution submitted that a woman could be convicted of rape as a principal offender by virtue of the doctrine of innocent agency. The court did not have to decide whether the submission was correct.

2.14   The second means by which the courts have striven to render D criminally liable despite the absence of a principal offence has been by resorting to the concept of 'procuring'. As a basis of secondary liability, 'procuring' is an anomaly. Whereas D can 'aid, abet or counsel' P to commit an offence without causing P to commit the offence, 'procuring' implies a special kind of causal link between D's conduct and P's commission of the principal offence.[24] Normally, a person who causes a proscribed outcome is liable as a principal offender. However, it is clear that, in the context of no-fault offences,[25] D is secondarily liable for causing P to commit a no-fault offence:

Example 2G

D 'laces' P's non-alcoholic drink with the result that P unwittingly drives while in excess of the prescribed limit.

D is guilty of the no-fault offence of driving with excess alcohol[26] but as a secondary party and not as a principal offender.

2.15   As Professor Ashworth has observed, cases like example 2G:

> represent the high-water mark of causal connection among the various types of accessorial conduct … in which there is no meeting of minds between principal and accomplice.[27]

Nevertheless, if D procures P to commit a no-fault offence, it is at least understandable that D should be convicted of the offence as a secondary party rather than as a principal offender. After all, it is P who has committed the offence and it is inappropriate and inaccurate to describe D and P as joint principals.[28]

---

[24]   *A-G's Reference (No 1 of 1975)* [1975] QB 773.

[25]   A no-fault offence is one that P can commit without being at fault in relation to the circumstances element of the offence.

[26]   Road Traffic Act 1988, s 5(1). It is a no-fault offence because P can commit the offence even though he does not know or believe that he or she is driving with excess alcohol.

[27]   A J Ashworth, *Principles of Criminal Law* (4th ed 2003) p 423.

[28]   After all, only P has driven the motor vehicle. As will become apparent, however, we believe that in such circumstances D ought to be convicted as a principal offender, albeit not of the principal offence that P commits but rather of the new offence that we are recommending, namely causing P to commit a no-fault offence – see Part 4 paras 4.28 to 4.37 below.

2.16 However, the courts have gone further by extending 'procuring' as a basis of secondary liability to offences that do require proof of fault. The courts have done so in order to ensure that D is held criminally liable in cases where, although P has not committed an offence, D has acted reprehensibly. In cases where, by lies, threats or other underhand behaviour, D has brought about the commission by P of the conduct element of a principal offence, the courts have held that D can be convicted of the offence as a secondary party although, because P lacks the fault to be convicted or has a defence, there is no principal offender.[29]

2.17 The result is not necessarily unsatisfactory. As Professor Ashworth has commented:

> [D] has done all that he or she intended to do in order to further [P's] crime and, considered in isolation, D is surely no less culpable than if [P] had been found guilty.[30]

However, whatever the practical benefits, the outcome represents a significant dilution of the derivative theory and is achieved only by affording an enhanced scope to what was already an anomalous form of secondary liability.

Secondary liability for a more serious offence than that committed by P

2.18 A strict application of the derivative theory of secondary liability poses a particular problem where P does commit a principal offence but it is a lesser offence than the one that D intended P to commit:

Example 2H

D wants V to die. D hands a gun to P saying that it contains blank ammunition when D knows that it contains live bullets. D then encourages P to shoot at V, ostensibly in order to frighten V. P, who knows that V suffers from a serious heart condition, shoots at and kills V with the live ammunition.[31]

Although D's state of mind justifies a conviction for murder, application of the derivative theory of secondary liability should result, instead, in D being convicted of the offence that P has committed, namely manslaughter. This approach was accepted by the Court of Appeal in *Richards*.[32]

---

[29] *Cogan and Leak* [1976] QB 217; *Millward* [1994] *Criminal Law Review* 527; *DPP v K and B* [1997] 1 CR App R 36.

[30] *Principles of Criminal Law*, (4th ed 2003) p 435.

[31] P is not guilty of murder because it was not P's intention to kill or cause really serious harm. However, P is guilty of manslaughter by virtue of having done an unlawful and dangerous act that caused V's death. The act was dangerous, even on P's belief that he was firing blanks, because P was aware of V's heart condition – *Dawson* (1985) 81 Cr App R 150; *Watson* [1989] 1 WLR 684.

[32] [1974] QB 776.

2.19   This approach can, however, lead to the result that, in example 2H, D is guilty of manslaughter and not murder despite intending that P should kill V and playing a key causal role in bringing about V's death. Accordingly, in *Howe*,[33] the House of Lords disapproved *Richards* thereby making it possible to convict D of murder in example 2H.[34]

THE CONDUCT ELEMENT OF SECONDARY LIABILITY

Assistance and encouragement

2.20   Section 8 of the Accessories and Abettors Act 1861 provides that a person who 'aid[s], abet[s], counsel[s] or procure[s]' the commission of an offence shall be liable to be tried, indicted and punished as a principal offender.[35]

2.21   Disregarding 'procuring', it is generally accepted that these specified modes of involvement cover two types of conduct on the part of D, namely the provision of assistance and the provision of encouragement.

2.22   It is doubtful if all cases of 'procuring' can be described properly as involving the provision of assistance or encouragement. For example, D adds alcohol to P's non-alcoholic drink without P's knowledge. As a result, P commits the no-fault offence of driving with excess alcohol.[36] To describe D's conduct as assisting or encouraging P to commit the offence disregards the fact that it was D, not P, who was responsible for the circumstance element of the offence (having excess alcohol in his blood).

Voluntary presence at the scene of an offence

2.23   While it is clear that words and gestures can constitute encouragement, a more difficult question is whether voluntary presence, unaccompanied by any words or gestures, can constitute encouragement. It is clear that D does not encourage P if D does no more than remain at the scene of an offence the commission of which D had no forewarning. For example, D is sitting on a bus when a passenger, P, suddenly attacks the driver. D is under no obligation either to intervene or to leave the bus.

2.24   It is different where D voluntarily goes to a place knowing or believing that an offence is taking or will take place. The authorities suggest that D's conduct is capable of constituting encouragement.[37] However, in addition, D must intend that his or her presence should encourage P and P must in fact be encouraged by D's presence.[38]

---

[33]   [1987] AC 417.

[34]   The converse situation is where P commits a more serious offence than the offence that D intended or believed that P would commit. It does not offend the derivative theory of liability to hold D liable for the lesser offence.

[35]   Section 8 applies to indictable offences. The corresponding provision for summary offences is the Magistrates' Courts Act 1980, s 44.

[36]   *A-G's Reference (No 1 of 1975)* [1975] QB 773.

[37]   *Coney* (1882) 8 QBD 534; *Allan* [1965] 1 QB 130; *Clarkson* [1971] 1 WLR 1402.

[38]   Above.

Omissions

2.25 The common law is reluctant to impose criminal liability for omissions. In general, an omission to act does not fix D with secondary liability. Arguably, however, there are two categories of cases which are exceptions to the general rule.

FAILURE TO DISCHARGE A LEGAL DUTY

2.26 If D is under a legal duty to act, failure to discharge the duty is capable of constituting assistance or encouragement.[39] Examples are a security guard who deliberately omits to lock a door to enable burglars to enter the premises, and a store detective who deliberately ignores acts of theft committed by customers. In each case, the duty to act emanates from their contracts of employment.[40]

FAILURE TO EXERCISE AN ENTITLEMENT TO CONTROL THE ACTIONS OF P

2.27 The common law has recognised that if D fails to exercise an entitlement to control the actions of P, he or she may be liable for an offence that P commits as a result. Thus, in *Du Cros v Lam*bourne[41] it was proved that D's car had been driven dangerously at a time when D and P were both in it. However, it could not be proven whether it was P or D who was driving. D's conviction was upheld because, even if not the driver, he was a secondary party as he had the power to prevent P driving or continuing to drive in a dangerous manner.

2.28 The entitlement to control exception is significant because it represents a potentially extensive departure from the general rule that D cannot be convicted by virtue of an omission to act. It has been applied to the licensee of a public house who allowed customers to drink alcohol outside the permitted hours,[42] to the supervisor of a learner driver[43] and to a company for omitting to take steps to prevent its drivers from falsifying their tachograph records.[44]

---

[39] Simester and Sullivan, *Criminal Law Theory and Doctrine* (2nd ed 2003) p 204 suggest that where there is a failure to take reasonable steps to discharge a legal duty, the failure in itself constitutes assistance and not merely evidence of encouragement.

[40] In each example, the fact that the burglars and the customers may be unaware of D's assistance is irrelevant.

[41] [1907] 1KB 40.

[42] *Tuck v Robson* [1970] 1 WLR 741.

[43] *Rubie v Faulkner* [1940] 1 KB 571.

[44] *J F Alford Transport Ltd* [1997] 2 Cr App R 326. However, on the facts the conviction was quashed because of the trial judge's misdirection to the jury. See also *Gaunt* [2003] EWCA Crim 3925, [2004] 2 Cr App R (s) 37 where D, a manager, failed to take steps to prevent his employees, P, racially harassing another employee, V.

2.29 However, the ambit of the exception is unclear and it is questionable whether it represents a general principle. If D holds a party at his house and knows that one guest is about to rape another guest, is D liable if he, although able to intervene, decides not to? Alternatively, in the middle of the night, D is awoken by screams in his garden. D gets up and sees that P is about to assault V. Although able to intervene safely and effectively, D goes back to bed. Does it make any difference that, in the former case, P is an invitee whereas in the latter P is a trespasser? The common law provides no clear answer to these questions.[45]

Causation, connection and secondary liability

Introduction

2.30 In this section we consider what effect, if any, D's assistance or encouragement must have in relation to P's commission of the principal offence if D is to incur liability for the offence as a secondary party.

D's conduct need not cause P to commit the principal offence and need not make any difference to the outcome

2.31 Apart from cases where D is alleged to have 'procured' P to commit an offence, D's conduct need not cause P to commit the principal offence in the sense that 'but for' D's conduct, P would not have committed the offence.[46] However, according to Professor K J M Smith, although D's conduct does not have to cause P to commit the principal offence in the 'but for' sense:

> It has always been implied in the concept of complicity that [D's] involvement … did make some difference to the outcome and as a consequence of this, accessories have been implicitly linked to the harm element in the principal offence.[47]

2.32 However, it is clear that D can be convicted as a secondary party despite the fact that his or her assistance or encouragement has made no material difference to the 'outcome':

Example 2J

P has made up his mind to murder V. He plans to do so by stabbing V with his kitchen knife. However, D, who has his own reasons for wanting to see V murdered, provides P with an identical kitchen knife. P uses D's knife to murder V.

---

[45] For our answers and recommendations, see Part 3, paras 3.39 to 3.41.

[46] In the nineteenth century, Stephen thought that 'counselling' incorporated a requirement of 'but for' causation – *Digest* (4th ed) Art 39. Dicta in *Assistant Recorder of Kingston-upon-Hull ex parte Morgan* [1969] 2 QB 58, 61 can be interpreted as support for Stephen's view. However, in *Calhaem* [1985] QB 808 the Court of Appeal held that there did not have to be any causal connection between the counselling and the commission of the offence. See also *Bryce* [2004] EWCA Crim 1231, [2004] 2 Cr App R 35.

[47] Professor K J M Smith *A Modern Treatise on the Law of Criminal Complicity* (1991), p 19.

D's act of assistance has made no material difference to the outcome but D is guilty of murder. What matters is that D's assistance or encouragement has some impact on the course of conduct that ends in the commission of the offence. In this example, D's assistance does have such an impact because V is killed with D's knife and not with P's.

2.33 The authorities speak of there having to be "a connection"[48] between D's conduct and P committing the principal offence. In *A-G v Able*,[49] Mr Justice Woolf said that that there has to be a "sufficient" connection.[50] However, the precise nature of this sufficient connection is elusive. It is best understood, at least where D's conduct consists of assistance, as meaning that D's conduct has made a contribution to the commission of the offence. This is why D is guilty of murder in example 2J. D, by providing P with the knife which P used to murder V, has contributed to the outcome. By contrast, if P had decided to use his own knife to murder V, D would not have been guilty of murder because his assistance would have made no contribution to the commission of the offence.[51]

2.34 P does not have to know that he or she is being assisted by D:

> **Example 2K**
>
> P plans a robbery intending to use his own gun. D is aware of this. The day before the robbery, D notices that P's own gun is missing from the drawer. Without telling P, he places his own gun, a similar kind to P's, in the drawer for P to use. P commits the robbery using D's gun.[52]

D is guilty of robbery because he has contributed to the robbery by virtue of the fact that it was his gun which P used to commit the robbery.[53]

---

[48] *Calhaem* [1985] 1 QB 808, 813.

[49] [1984] 1 QB 795.

[50] Above, p 812.

[51] However, under the recommendations in the first report, D would be guilty of the inchoate offence of intentionally assisting or encouraging P to commit murder.

[52] The example is provided by Simester and Sullivan, *Criminal Law Theory and Doctrine* (2nd ed 2003) p 200.

[53] See also *State v Tally* (1894) 102 Ala 25 where D, who knew that P was planning to murder V, prevented T from warning V. This facilitated the killing of V by P who was unaware of what D had done.

2.35   In example 2K, D provided assistance. Cases where D encourages but does not assist P are more difficult. As with assistance, D can be liable as a secondary party even if D's encouragement makes no material difference to the outcome, for example if P has already irrevocably made up his or her mind to commit the principal offence.[54] However, in contrast to assistance, encouragement must have the capacity to act on P's mind and, therefore, P should have to be aware of D's encouragement.[55] Thus, D cannot be convicted of an offence as a secondary party if he or she shouts encouragement to P who is deaf and therefore unaware of D's encouragement.

2.36   In most cases, there will be no issue as to whether P was aware of D's encouragement. Occasionally, however, the circumstances will be such that the prosecution would have to provide proof on the issue:

> **Example 2L**
>
> D is at a football match attended by a large crowd. There is an altercation between two players, P and V, who are thirty yards away from D. D shouts out to P 'knock his block off'. At that moment, P punches V in the face.

Given the distance between D and P together with the noise generated by the crowd, there is a reasonable possibility that P was unaware of D's encouragement. In such a case, the prosecution would have to prove that P was aware of the encouragement.

Presumed encouragement

2.37   In addition, it might be thought that the prosecution would have to prove that P was in fact encouraged by D's behaviour. However, although not explicit in the case law, there appears to be a presumption that, if D acts in a manner that is capable of encouraging P, not only was P aware of the encouragement but also that it operated on P's mind. Thus, if D, seeing P with a knife in his hand chasing V, shouts out 'stab him' and P does so, it is presumed not only that P heard D's words but also that they operated on P's mind and, thereby, contributed to the commission of the offence.

2.38   The presumption is clearly demonstrated where the conduct that is alleged to constitute the encouragement consists of D's voluntary presence at the scene of an offence:

---

[54] As in *Giannetto* (1997) 1 Cr App R 1 where the Court of Appeal noted, without disapproval, the trial judge's direction that D could be convicted of murder if, on P saying that he was going to kill D's wife, D had patted P on the back and said "Oh goody".

[55] *Caelham* [1985] 1 QB 808.

> **Example 2M**
>
> D, a critic, attends a concert. One of the performers is P. By performing at the concert, P is committing an offence because he does not have a work permit. D is aware of this.[56]

D's presence at the concert has made little difference to the outcome but it is presumed, by virtue of D being part of an audience for whom P is playing, that P is inspired to perform by D's presence as part of the audience.

2.39 In theory, English law has not been prepared to dispense with the dual requirements that P must have been aware of D's encouragement and must have been encouraged by it. However, in its presumption of actual encouragement, English law reflects the concerns of Chief Justice Eichelbaum who, in delivering the judgment of the New Zealand Court of Appeal, said:

> … where violence is inflicted or sexual offending perpetrated in the presence of others, it would be a manifest nonsense to require proof that [P] were aware of the encouragement provided by each individual.[57]

Rebutting the presumption

2.40 If D can adduce evidence that realistically suggests that P might not have been aware of D's encouragement or might not have been encouraged by it, the prosecution must prove that D was aware of it and was in fact encouraged by it. Professor Keith Smith provides this example:

> **Example 2N**
>
> D comes across P and V in the middle of a fierce argument. D, a congenital troublemaker, urges P to punch V. Just before striking V, P tells D to 'mind his own business'.[58]

The presumption that D's words of encouragement made a contribution to P's assault on V is rebutted by the evidence of what P said to D.

2.41 The presumption can be rebutted even if there is a meeting of minds between P and D:

> **Example 2P**
>
> D encourages P to murder V. P attends a football match at which, unknown to P, V is present. There is a riot in the course of which P murders an unknown person who turns out to be V.[59]

---

[56] The facts are those of *Wilcox v Jeffery* [1951] 1 All ER 464.

[57] R v *Schriek* [1997] 2 NZLR 139, 150.

[58] K J M Smith, "The Law Commission Consultation Paper on Complicity: (1) A Blueprint for Rationalism" [1994] *Criminal Law Review* 239, 244. (footnote)

D is not an accessory to V's murder because the act of P was not done "within the scope of [D's] authority or advice."[60] It was pure coincidence that the victim turned out to be V.

Procuring

2.42 Where D's contribution consists of 'procuring' P to commit an offence, there is authority that there has to be a causal link between D's conduct and P's commission of the principal offence. In *A-G's Reference (No 1 of 1975)*[61] the Court of Appeal said:

> To procure means to produce by endeavour. ... Causation here is important. You cannot procure an offence unless there is a causal link between what you do and the commission of the offence....[62]

Thus, the prosecution must prove that P would not have committed the offence but for D's conduct.[63]

THE FAULT ELEMENT OF SECONDARY LIABILITY

Introduction

2.43 If D lends P a hammer which P uses to commit burglary, D has assisted the commission of the offence. However, if D neither knew nor believed that P would or might use the hammer to commit burglary, it might be thought that D is not morally culpable and ought not to be held criminally responsible for the burglary. English law reflects this view. It does so by stipulating that D must be at fault in relation to the principal offence. In the following paragraphs, we summarise what it means to say that D must be at fault in relation to the principal offence.

---

[59] The example is taken from the Court of Appeal's judgment in *Calhaem* [1985] QB 808, 813.

[60] Above. In *Calhaem* the Court of Appeal upheld D's conviction for 'counselling' P to murder V. At his trial, P had testified that, although hired by D to murder V, he originally had never intended to murder V. He said that he did so only when V screamed and he panicked. The court held that the murder of V had been done within the 'scope of the authority or advice' of D.

[61] [1975] QB 773.

[62] Above, 779 to 780.

[63] It is true that in *Blakely and Sutton v DPP* [1991] RTR 405 the Divisional Court thought that D 'procured' a result if he or she contemplated it as a possible consequence of his act. However, the observation was not necessary to the decision.

D's state of mind in relation to his or her own act of assistance or encouragement

Intending the act of assistance or encouragement

2.44   D must intend to do the act of assistance or encouragement. For example, D, following a day's grouse shooting, forgets to return his shotgun to the secure cupboard where he keeps his firearms. P, finding the shotgun in D's kitchen, uses it to murder V. D is not guilty of murder because, although his conduct has assisted P to murder V, he did not intentionally leave the shotgun where P could find and use it to kill someone.

Intention to assist or encourage

2.45   There are dicta which support the view that, in addition to intentionally doing the act of assistance or encouragement, to be convicted of the same offence as P, D must intend to assist or encourage P in the sense of acting in order to do so.[64] However, the preferred view is that the prosecution only have to prove that D acted in order to assist or encourage P if either there is an evidential basis supporting a claim by D that he or she acted in order to hinder or obstruct rather than assist P, or, arguably, in cases where D is alleged to have encouraged P by virtue of nothing more than his or her presence at the commission of the offence.

Belief as to whether one's conduct will in fact assist or encourage

2.46   Although D must believe that his or her conduct has the capacity to assist or encourage P to commit the principal offence, it is unclear whether D must also believe that it will in fact assist or encourage P to commit the offence. For example, D, knowing that P intends to burgle 10 Acacia Avenue, leaves a ladder outside the premises to facilitate P's entry. In doing so, D believes that P is far more likely to use other means to secure entry. In the event, P does use the ladder to gain entry.[65]

D's state of mind in relation to the commission of the principal offence

D's attitude towards the commission of the principal offence

2.47   D can be convicted of the principal offence even though he or she does not intend that P should commit it. Accordingly if a shopkeeper (D) sells P a baseball bat which P uses to assault V, the mere fact that D did not intend to assist or encourage P, nor intend that the offence should be committed, does not in itself exonerate D. D's liability turns on his knowledge or belief as to whether P will or might assault V.[66]

---

[64]   *Clarkson* [1971] 1 WLR 1402; *National Coal Board v Gamble* [1959] 1 QB 11, 20; *Maxwell v DPP for Northern Island* [1978] 1 WLR 13570; *Bryce* [2004] EWCA 1231, [2004] 2 CR App R 35 [71].

[65]   Our recommendations will resolve this confusion. See Part 3, para 3.75 to 3.83.

[66]   See, for example, *Johnson v Youden* [1950] 1 KB 544.

Knowing the essential matters of the principal offence

2.48　In a leading authority,[67] it was said that D must 'know the essential matters which constitute the principal offence'.[68] There are two central issues: what are 'essential matters' and what is meant by 'know'?

WHAT ARE THE ESSENTIAL MATTERS?

2.49　The following proposition serves as a starting point: the essential matters of an offence include all the external elements of the offence. A criminal offence can consist of one or more of three external elements: conduct, the circumstances in which the conduct takes place and the consequences of the conduct.[69]

2.50　Although an offence can comprise all three elements, not all three are integral to the definition of every offence. Whether one, two or all three elements are part of the definition of an offence varies a good deal. For the purpose of determining D's liability, it is essential to identify accurately each external element of the principal offence that P commits.

The conduct element

2.51　The conduct element is always an essential matter that D must 'know'. For example, if D sells P petrol and P uses it to set fire to V's house, D has assisted P to commit arson. However, if D believed that the petrol was only going to be used for standard domestic purposes, then it would be inappropriate to punish him for the act of assistance.

2.52　In general, although the conduct element is an essential matter, the details of the conduct element are not. For example, D lends P a jemmy which P uses to commit a burglary. The conduct element of burglary is entering a building or part of a building as a trespasser. D must 'know' that P is going to enter a building as a trespasser but D does not have to know which building or the date and time.

2.53　Sometimes, however, D may specify a particular person or item of property. Thus, D may pay P £1000 to burn down a particular building or to murder a particular person. There is a line of authority which suggests that in such cases the particular building or person is no mere detail but is an essential matter. On this view, if D deliberately commits the offence against a different building or person, D is not liable for P's offence because he or she did not 'know' that building or person.[70] By contrast, D is liable for P's offence if P accidentally or by mistake commits the offence against a different item of property or a different person. An example would be where D hands P a broken glass and encourages P to strike V1. P aims at V1 but accidentally strikes V2.

---

[67]　*Johnson v Youden* [1950] 1 KB 544.

[68]　Above, 546.

[69]　See Part 1, para 1.6.

[70]　*Leahy* [1985] WL 310719 (Crown Court); *Reardon* [1999] *Criminal Law Review* 392.

2.54 The scope of the deliberate variation in performance rule is unclear. If D encourages P to steal V's Rolls Royce, is D guilty of theft if, instead, D steals V's Bentley? If D, a racist, encourages P to set fire to the local Afro-Caribbean community centre, is D guilty of arson if P, finding blanket security at the centre, instead sets fire to a local public house which is frequented by people from the centre. In each case, D, despite the variation in performance, is unlikely to be discontented with the outcome.[71]

2.55 In addition, there is a more fundamental problem. In a leading authority,[72] it was said that D must know that "a crime of the type in question was intended".[73] This has opened up the prospect of D being convicted of an offence the conduct element of which is different from that of the offence which D believed P was intending to commit. For example, D provides a stolen credit card to P believing that P will use it to obtain property by deception. Instead, P uses it to commit burglary by slipping the latch on V's door, entering V's property and stealing V's video recorder.

2.56 On one view, obtaining property by deception and burglary are offences of the same 'type' because they are both offences under the Theft Act 1968. On this view, the fact that their respective conduct elements are different is of no consequence.

2.57 In our view, for D's liability to be dependent on whether the offence committed by P is of the same 'type' as that which P commits is unsatisfactory. 'Type' is too amorphous a term to found a secure foundation for attributing liability as a secondary party.

The circumstance element

2.58 The circumstance element is always an essential matter of which D must 'know'. For example, D sells petrol to P believing that P is going to make a petrol bomb with which to set fire to P's isolated country cottage, with a view to making a false insurance claim. P does use the petrol to make a bomb but instead uses it to set fire to the house of his enemy, V. P has committed arson.[74] However, D is not guilty of arson because, believing that P would set fire to his own property, D did not 'know' that the circumstance element of arson – that the property belongs to another person - would be satisfied.

2.59 The circumstance element is an essential matter even if the principal offence is a no-fault offence, that is one that P can commit without being at fault in relation to its circumstance element.[75]

---

[71] For our discussion and recommendations on this topic in Part 3, see paras 3.153 to 3.166.

[72] *Bainbridge* [1960] 1 QB 129.

[73] Above, 132.

[74] Criminal Damage Act 1971, s 1(3).

[75] *Callow v Tillstone* (1900) 83 LT 411.

The consequence element

2.60   The general rule is that the consequence element is an essential matter of which D must 'know'. There are, however, some offences that P can commit without being at fault in relation to their consequence element. These are known as constructive liability offences and they include some of the most serious offences – murder, manslaughter, unlawful and malicious wounding and causing death by dangerous driving. The rule is therefore that D, like P, is not required to 'know' the consequence element if the principal offence is one of constructive liability.

2.61   However, this exception in relation to constructive liability offences appeared to be called into question by the decision of the House of Lords in *Powell and Daniels, English*.[76] The certified questions before the House of Lords referred to D realising that P might kill V. Lord Steyn referred to 'a secondary party who foresees that the primary party might *kill* with the intent sufficient of murder....'[77] Lord Hutton said that it was sufficient to found a conviction for murder for D to have realised that P "might *kill* with intent to do so or with intent to cause grievous bodily harm".[78] It is arguable, therefore, that the House of Lords is of the view that D had to foresee not only that P might attack V intending to kill or cause serious harm but also that P might in fact kill V.

2.62   The suggestion that D had to have contemplated that V might die ran counter to earlier authorities.[79] The issue was resolved by the Court of Appeal in *Neary*[80] where it was held that it suffices if D foresees that P might attack V intending to kill or to cause serious harm, even if D did not realise that V might die.

'The fault element of the principle offence'

2.63   Another essential matter is the fault element required by P in relation to the principal offence. For P to be convicted of murder he or she must have intended to kill or cause serious harm to V. Thus, if P with D's assistance murders V, D cannot be convicted of murder unless he or she 'knew' that P intended to kill or cause serious harm to V.

WHAT IS MEANT BY 'KNOWING' THE ESSENTIAL MATTERS?

No joint criminal venture[81]

2.64   If D has to 'know' the essential matters of the principal offence, it might be thought that D must know or believe that:

        (1)   P is committing or *will* commit the conduct element; and

---

[76]   [1991] AC 1.

[77]   Above, at 14.

[78]   Above, at 27.

[79]   *Chan Wing-siu* [1985] 1 AC 168; *Hyde* [1991] 1 QB 134.

[80]   [2002] EWCA Crim 1736 referred to with approval by the Court of Appeal in *Rahman* [2007] EWCA Crim 342.

[81]   For our discussion and recommendations on this topic in Part 3, see paras 3.70 to 3.122.

(2)   P is doing or *will* do so in the circumstances and with the consequences (unless the offence is a constructive liability offence) proof of which is required for conviction of the offence.

2.65   However, the courts have demonstrated a readiness to dilute the stringent fault requirement of knowledge. With regard to the conduct element of the principal offence, there are authorities that can be cited in support of no less than four different tests, each of which requires something less than a belief that P will commit the conduct element. The tests are:

(1)   belief that P might commit the conduct element;[82]

(2)   foresight of the risk of a strong possibility that P will commit it;[83]

(3)   contemplation of the risk of a real possibility that P will commit it;[84] and

(4)   foresight that it is likely that P will commit it.[85]

Joint criminal ventures[86]

2.66   We explained in Part 1 that joint criminal ventures are cases where D and P share a common intention to commit an offence – the agreed offence. It might be thought that the requirement that D must 'know' the essential matters of the principal offence would be unproblematic where the principal offence that P commits is the agreed offence. It will be an exceptional case where D does not intend that P (or another party to the venture) will commit the conduct element in the circumstances and with the consequences proof of which is required for conviction of the offence.

2.67   An example of the exceptional case is *Rook*[87] where D was involved in a plan to murder V. However, at his trial, D claimed that it had never been his intention that V should be killed. D claimed that he thought that if, having been paid, he absented himself on the day of the murder, P would desist from murdering V. In the event, P did murder V. The trial judge directed the jury that D was guilty of murder if he intended to assist P to commit a murder "which he knew would probably be committed." D was convicted of murder.

---

[82]   *Blakely and Sutton v DPP* [1991] RTR 405.

[83]   *Reardon* [1999] *Criminal Law Review* 392.

[84]   *Bryce* [2004] EWCA Crim 1231, [2004] 2 Cr App R 35.

[85]   *Webster* [2006] EWCA Crim 415, [2006] 2 Cr App R 6.

[86]   For our discussion and recommendations on this topic in Part 3, see paras 3.123 to 3.169.

[87]   [1993] 2 All ER 955.

2.68   In upholding D's conviction, the Court of Appeal said that the judge's direction
        had been too generous to D. D was guilty of murder if he foresaw that P *might*
        attack V intending to kill or cause serious harm to V. In doing so, the Court of
        Appeal applied to agreed offences the rule that had already been established by
        the case of *Chan Wing-siu*[88] in relation to collateral offences. In *Chan Wing-siu*
        the agreed offence was robbery. In the course of the robbery, P committed a
        collateral offence of murder by fatally stabbing V. The trial judge directed the jury
        that they could convict D of murder if D foresaw that P might stab V intending to
        cause serious harm. The Privy Council upheld D's conviction for murder.

2.69   Accordingly, the general principle is that D is guilty of any offence committed in
        the course of a joint criminal venture if he or she foresaw that P might commit the
        conduct element of the offence in the circumstances (if any) and with the fault
        required to be convicted of the offence. If the principal offence is not a
        constructive liability offence, D must also foresee that in committing the conduct
        element D might also bring about the consequence element (if any) of the
        offence.[89]

Particular problems with the law of homicide

INTRODUCTION

2.70   The agreed offence in *Rook* and the collateral offence in *Chan Wing-siu* was
        murder. As indicated above, murder and manslaughter are constructive liability
        offences. P can be convicted of either offence despite neither having intended to
        kill V nor foreseeing the possibility that V might be killed.

2.71   In determining D's liability for a homicide offence committed by P, the courts have
        over the years grappled with the following issue. If D and P are parties to a joint
        criminal venture which, as far as D is concerned, does not involve the intentional
        killing of V, to what extent, if any, should D be held responsible for V's death in
        the event that P kills V?

THE LAW BEFORE 1997

2.72   Initially, the question fell for consideration in two ways. The following example
        illustrates the first way in which the question arose:

Example 2Q

D and P agree to commit burglary at V's premises. D foresees that if V disturbs
them, P might attack V intending to kill or cause serious harm to V. D begs P not
to use any violence against V. As D feared, V does disturb them and P murders
her.

---

[88] [1985] 1 AC 168.

[89] The principle is not confined to cases of homicide. For example, in *Chan Wing-Siu* had D
      foreseen that, in the course of the robbery, P might rape V and had P done so, D would
      have been guilty of rape.

The issue is whether, despite not intending that V should be killed or suffer serious harm, D should be convicted of murder because he or she foresaw that P might attack V intending to kill or cause serious harm to V? Relevant features of example 2Q are:

(1)   D and P agreed to commit an offence which did not involve the use or threatened use of *serious* violence against V; and

(2)   D did foresee that P might attack V intending to kill or to cause serious harm to V.

2.73   As noted above, the courts have held that D is guilty of murder on the grounds that, having chosen to participate in a joint criminal venture, D ought to be convicted of murder if he or she foresaw that P might attack V with the fault element of murder.[90] It matters not that D was opposed to the commission of the offence.

2.74   The following example illustrates the second way that the question arose:

Example 2R

D and P agree to inflict less than serious harm on V by punching him. In the course of assaulting V, P pulls out a knife, which D was unaware that P had, and fatally stabs V. P is charged with murder, and D is charged with manslaughter.

The relevant features of this example are:

(1)   D and P had agreed to commit an offence which did not involve the use or threatened use of *serious* violence against V; and

(2)   unlike the previous example, D did not foresee that P might do an act intending to kill or cause serious bodily harm to V.

2.75   D will not be guilty of murder in this example because he does not intend or foresee that death or serious harm may be inflicted by P. The issue is whether D should be convicted of manslaughter or excused liability for V's death.[91] Before 1997 the Court of Appeal was unable to take a consistent line on the issue. In some cases it upheld D's conviction for manslaughter[92] while in others it quashed D's conviction.[93]

---

[90]   *Chan Wing-siu* [1985] 1 AC 168; *Rook* [1993] 2 All ER 955; *Powell and Daniels, English* [1999] 1 AC 1.

[91]   Regardless of whether D was liable for V's death, D would be liable for the offence that he or she had agreed with P to commit (assuming that it had been committed).

[92]   *Betty* (1963) 48 Cr App R 6; *Reid* (1975) 62 Cr App R 109; *Stewart and Schofield* [1995] 3 All ER 159.

[93]   *Lovesey and Petersen* (1969) 53 Cr App R 461; *Dunbar* [1988] *Criminal Law Review* 693.

POWELL AND DANIELS, ENGLISH[94]

2.76 On one view, the rule established in *Chan Wing-siu*, namely that D is guilty of murder if, participating in a joint criminal venture, he foresees that P might attack V intending to kill or cause serious bodily harm to V, is severe on D. On this view, it is particularly severe if D foresees that P might attack V not with the intention of killing V but with the intention of causing serious but non-lethal harm to V. The problem arose in 1997 in the conjoined appeals of *Powell and Daniels, English*.[95]

2.77 In *Powell and Daniels* D and P went to V's house to buy drugs. On arrival, P shot and killed V. The trial judge directed the jury that D was guilty of murder if D foresaw that P might intentionally kill or cause serious harm to V. D was convicted of murder as a secondary party. The House of Lords, following *Chan Wing-siu*, upheld D's conviction.

2.78 In *English*, D and P agreed to attack V by assaulting V with wooden posts. As far as D was concerned, the shared intention was to cause injury to, but not to kill, V. In the course of the attack, P pulled out a knife, which D maintained he was unaware that P had, and killed V. The trial judge, in accordance with *Hyde*[96] directed the jury that they could convict D of murder if he had foreseen that P might attack V intending to kill or cause serious injury to V. As such, the direction enabled the jury to convict D irrespective of what particular act he foresaw P might perpetrate provided that they were sure that D had foreseen that P might attack V intending to kill or cause serious bodily harm. D was convicted of murder.[97]

2.79 It was possible that, following the judge's direction, the jury convicted D on the basis that he had intended or foreseen that P might attack V with a wooden post (but not a knife) intending to cause V serious bodily harm (but not to kill V). The certified question for the House of Lords assumed that it was on that basis that the jury had convicted D. The House of Lords quashed D's conviction. In doing so, Lord Hutton made it clear that D is liable if he or she foresaw the act causing V's death as a possible incident of the joint criminal venture unless he or she dismissed the risk as negligible.

2.80 Lord Hutton, delivering the leading speech, said that he agreed with the submission made on behalf of English that:

> … to be guilty under the principle stated in Chan Wing-siu v R [D] must foresee an *act* of the *type* which [P] committed, and that in the present case the use of the knife was *fundamentally different* to the use of a wooden post.[98]

---

[94] [1999] 1 AC 1.

[95] Above.

[96] [1991] 1 QB 134.

[97] It is not known whether the jury found that, in stabbing V, P intended to kill V or merely intended to cause serious bodily harm.

[98] *Powell and Daniels, English* [1999] 1 AC 1, 28 (emphasis added).

D was not guilty of murder because although he had intended or foreseen that P might attack V intending to cause serious harm, the act that killed V was 'fundamentally different' from the act that D had anticipated. P's lethal act was outside the scope of the joint criminal venture. Since it was outside the scope of the joint criminal venture, not only was D not guilty of murder but, according to Lord Hutton, he was also not guilty of manslaughter.

The issues arising from Powell and Daniels, English

DISTINGUISHING ACTIONS FROM THE INTENTIONS WITH WHICH THEY ARE DONE?

2.81   In *Van Hoogstraten*,[99] Sir Stephen Mitchell said that '...foresight defines the scope of the joint enterprise'. In that regard, he set out a two-step test to determine whether D is liable for the killing of V by P. First, the task of the trial judge is to identify correctly the act of P that caused V's death. It is then for the jury to determine whether or not D foresaw that P might do that act. If the jury is not sure that D did so foresee, they should acquit D of both murder and manslaughter.

2.82   Secondly, and by way of contrast, if the jury is sure that D *did* so foresee, the extent of D's liability for V's death will then depend on whether the jury is also sure that D foresaw that P might do the act with the necessary intent for murder. If they are sure, the verdict is murder. Otherwise, D is guilty of manslaughter.

2.83   Sir Stephen's approach has much to commend it, not least because it simplifies the task of the jury. The jury is not required to consider whether the act that caused V's death was 'fundamentally different' from that foreseen by D, but only whether it was foreseen by D as a possibility. Nevertheless, in *Attorney-General's Reference (No 3 of 2004)*[100], which followed *Van Hoogstraten*, the Court of Appeal, whilst upholding Sir Stephen's ruling, approached the case in a manner which better reflected Lord Hutton's speech in *English*.

2.84   Although some passages suggest that Lord Hutton was endorsing an approach similar to Sir Stephen's, the better view is that he was not. Accordingly, following *English,* if the act of P that caused V's death was not foreseen by D, D is not criminally responsible for V's death provided that the lethal act was 'fundamentally different' from that foreseen by D. If the lethal act was not 'fundamentally different', the mere fact that it was not foreseen by D will be of no avail. On this approach, the jury must decide what was the act that killed V, did D foresee it, and was it fundamentally different.

THE SCOPE OF THE 'FUNDAMENTALLY DIFFERENT ACT' RULE

2.85   Under the *Chan Wing-siu* principle, there are a number of different ways in which D can be convicted of murder in the event of P killing V:

> (1)   D foresaw that P might kill V intending to kill V, and P does kill V with that intent. In principle, both D and P have committed murder;

[99]   2 December 2003, unreported.

[100]   [2005] EWCA Crim 1882.

(2)   D foresaw that P might kill V intending to cause V serious bodily harm. An example would be if D foresaw that P might knee-cap V intending to cause serious harm but not to kill. Nevertheless, D realised that the knee-capping might result in V's death. P intentionally kills V in some other way. In principle, both D and P have committed murder; and

(3)   D foresaw that P might cause serious harm to V intending to cause serious harm to V. D intentionally kills V. In principle, both D and P have committed murder.

2.86   In *English*, the issue of D's liability for a "fundamentally different" lethal act was confined to (3). Subsequently, the Court of Appeal in *Rahman*[101] has held that in (1), D cannot take advantage of the "fundamentally different" rule. Thus, if D foresees that P might kick V to the head intending to kill V and, instead, P murders V by stabbing V, D is guilty of murder. By contrast, the Court of Appeal also said that in (2), D can take advantage of the "fundamentally different" rule.[102]

2.87   In addition to this difference over the scope of the 'fundamentally different act' rule, there have been differences of opinion between courts over how to determine whether the lethal act is 'fundamentally different'. This has centred on two key issues.

2.88   The first is the relevance of P's state of mind, in perpetrating the lethal act, to the question of whether that act was 'fundamentally different' to what D anticipated might happen. In *Attorney General's Reference (No 3 of 2004)*[103] the prosecution submitted that *as a matter of law* a lethal act perpetrated by P cannot be 'fundamentally different' if the only difference between it and the act foreseen by D was P's state of mind in perpetrating it. The Court of Appeal rejected the submission. However, in *Gilmore*[104] the Court of Appeal of Northern Ireland said that it was 'conceivable that in some cases the nature of the principal's [state of mind] may change the nature of the act committed by him....'[105]

---

[101] [2007] EWCA Crim 342.

[102] The 'fundamental difference' rule will also apply to cases where the question is whether D is guilty of *manslaughter* or of no homicide offence. An example would be where D foresaw that P might cause less than serious harm to V intending to cause less than serious harm to V and P killed V. There is no doubt that on such facts D can take advantage of the 'fundamental difference' rule: *Attorney General's Reference (No 3 of 2004)* [2005] EWCA Crim 1882.

[103] [2005] EWCA Crim 1882.

[104] [2000] 2 Cr App R 407.

[105] Above, 415.

2.89   The second is the relevance of the fact that P used a weapon to perpetrate the lethal act different from the one that D anticipated that P might use. Assuming that D did not foresee that P might attack V intending to *kill,* if P kills V by employing a weapon that D did not contemplate, or by using it in a way that D did not contemplate, it will be a question of fact whether the use of the weapon was a 'fundamentally different act'. However, there has been very little in the way of guidance for juries.[106]

2.90   The case of *Gilmore*[107] illustrates the problem. D had driven P to the house knowing that the house was occupied and that P intended to petrol bomb it. However, D believed the petrol bomb to be much smaller than was the case. D believed that the bomb would damage the property and cause fear to the occupants but would not harm them. P, well aware of the size of the petrol bomb, threw it into the house. The occupants were killed. P and D were convicted of murder. The Court of Appeal of Northern Ireland quashed D's conviction for murder in the light of D's belief as to the size and impact of the bomb. However, it substituted a conviction of manslaughter because the act carried out by P (the throwing of a petrol bomb into an occupied property) was the very act contemplated by D. The fact that the bomb used was much larger than the one contemplated by D was beside the point.

2.91   In *Van Hoogstraten*, Sir Stephen Mitchell doubted the correctness of *Gilmore*. This is because, employing Sir Stephen's approach, the definition of the 'relevant act' is likely to have included the fact that the petrol bomb was very large and that it would be thrown with the intention to kill. If the relevant act was defined in such terms, the defendant in *Gilmore* is likely to have escaped liability for manslaughter as well as murder. This comparison not only demonstrates the central importance of the definition of the 'relevant act', but also how different interpretations would effect a defendant like the one in *Gilmore*.

The most recent guidance

2.92   The most recent decision is that of the Court of Appeal in *Rahman*.[108] Lord Justice Hooper said that the proper approach is reflected in the four following questions:

>   "1. What was P's act which caused the death of V? (eg, stabbing, shooting, kicking, beating).[109]
>
>   2. Did D realise that one of the attackers might do <u>this</u> act? If yes, guilty of murder. If no go to the next question.
>
>   3. What act or acts did D realise that one of the attackers might do to cause V really serious injury?

---

[106] The current Judicial Studies Board direction refers, without any elaboration, to an act that is 'fundamentally different'.

[107] [2000] 2 Cr App R 407.

[108] [2007] EWCA Crim 342.

[109] On this view, the focus is on the physical act of P and not on P's intention in doing the act (our footnote).

4. Is this act or are these acts which D realise that one of the attackers might do, of a fundamentally different nature to P's act which caused the death of V? If yes, not guilty of murder. If no, guilty of murder."

2.93 The provision of this guidance is welcome.[110] However, the guidance brings into focus two weaknesses within the current law.

2.94 In one respect the law may now be too harsh on D. This may happen when the act done by P is the one D anticipated, but P intended the act to be lethal, whereas D anticipated only that P might intend it to cause serious harm. In such a case, D will be guilty of murder in spite of the fact that he or she did not anticipate the use of lethal force.

2.95 In another respect, the law may be too generous to D. This may happen when the act done by P is not the one anticipated by D, yet D appreciated not only that P might act with the intent to do serious harm, but also that V might die as a result. In such a case, D may escape liability for murder, in spite of the fact that he or she did anticipate the use of lethal force if, for example, P uses a weapon that D did not anticipate P using.

2.96 In both such cases, it is not clear that the 'fundamental difference' rule produces the right results.

NO LIABILITY FOR NOT ONLY MURDER BUT ALSO MANSLAUGHTER

2.97 *English* clearly decides that if the act that caused V's death was fundamentally different and therefore one for which D is not responsible, as well as being not guilty of murder, D is not guilty of manslaughter. There is no halfway house as far as liability for V's death is concerned.[111] The decision opens up the prospect of D escaping all liability for V's death even in cases where D's intention was that V should suffer serious, albeit non-lethal, harm. Lord Hutton made no reference to the line of authority[112] which had previously held that, if D is a party to a joint criminal venture involving the use or threatened use of unlawful violence against V, D can be convicted of manslaughter even though he or she had not foreseen the lethal act. The status of that line of authority is, therefore, uncertain.[113] However, subsequent cases have confirmed that D is not guilty of either murder or manslaughter.

---

[110] We have already pointed out that we believe this guidance is more generous to the accused than the guidance provided in *Powell and Daniels*, para 2.86 above.

[111] D may be convicted of other offences, for example causing grievous bodily harm with intent, assault occasioning actual bodily harm and conspiracy to cause such harm.

[112] *Anderson and Morris* [1996] 2 QB 110, n 158.

[113] *Crooks* [1999] NI 226; *Uddin* [1999] QB 431; *A-G's Reference (No 3 of 2004)* [2005] EWCA Crim 1882.

PART 3
A STATUTORY SCHEME OF SECONDARY LIABILITY

INTRODUCTION

3.1 Under the scheme that we are recommending, D's liability could take one of three forms:

(1) secondary liability for an offence that P commits;[1]

(2) liability as a principal offender for an offence that P does not commit because P is an innocent agent;[2] and

(3) liability as a principal offender for causing P to commit a no-fault offence.[3]

In this Part we focus on secondary liability. We begin by briefly outlining what would be the main features of secondary liability if our recommendations were implemented. We then set out and explain our recommendations for reforming the conduct element of secondary liability. Finally, we consider what should be the fault element of secondary liability.[4]

Preserving the forensic advantages of secondary liability

3.2 In Part 2, we identified a "fundamental feature of the common law".[5] D can be convicted of the principal offence even if the prosecution cannot prove whether, in participating in the offence, D was a principal offender or a secondary party (provided that it can be proved that he or she must have been one or other). The forensic advantages to the prosecution are inestimable because, in joint criminal ventures, the prosecution will often be unable to prove who was the principal offender and who was the accessory. In this respect, our scheme would preserve the common law.[6]

Reflecting the derivative theory of secondary liability

3.3 In Part 2, we also explained how the common law has to some extent departed from the derivative theory of secondary liability.[7] The courts have distanced themselves from the derivative theory:

---

[1] There will be a small number of cases where D is secondarily liable for a principal offence despite P not committing the offence - see Part 4 paras 4.11 to 4.13.

[2] See Part 4 paras 4.8 to 4.27.

[3] See Part 4 paras 4.28 to 4.37.

[4] In Part 5, we consider what defences there should be to secondary liability.

[5] Para 2.5. See also Appendix B, paras B.6 and B.7.

[6] Clause 5 of the Supplementary Bill.

[7] Paras 2.8 to 2.19 and Appendix B, paras B.14 to B.27.

(1)   by holding D liable for a principal offence as a secondary party in circumstances where D procures P to commit the conduct element of the offence but P does not commit the offence because he or she acts without the fault required to be convicted of the offence;[8]

(2)   by holding D liable for a principal offence that is more serious than the offence that P commits;[9] and

(3)   by holding D liable for a principal offence that P does not commit because, despite satisfying both the external and fault elements of the principal offence, P has a complete or, if the principal offence is murder, a partial defence.[10]

3.4   In Part 4, we will set out our recommendations for replacing the common law doctrine of innocent agency with a statutory regime. As will become apparent, the concept of innocent agency that we are recommending would not be constrained by features of the doctrine that currently confine its scope at common law. As a result, in cases within (1) and (2) above, it would be possible to convict D as a principal offender (rather than by a fiction that D is a secondary party) despite P not having committed the principal offence. We have considered whether, in cases within (3) above, it should also be possible to convict D as a principal offender by virtue of P being an innocent agent. However, for reasons that we explain in Part 4,[11] we do not believe that it would be right to do so. Such cases, therefore, would remain exceptions to the derivative theory of secondary liability.[12]

Narrowing the scope of secondary liability

3.5   We believe that D should only be convicted of the principal offence if his or her culpability is comparable to P's. Accordingly, we are recommending that, apart from offences committed pursuant to a joint criminal venture, D must intend that P should engage in the conduct element of the principal offence.

3.6   Thus, if P uses a baseball bat to murder V, a shopkeeper, D, who sold the bat to P, would not be liable for the murder even though he or she believed that P was likely to use the bat to murder V. D would only be guilty of murder if he or she intended P to use the bat to attack V (and also believed that P would do so intending to kill or cause serious harm to V).

---

[8]   See Part 2, paras 2.16 to 2.17 and Appendix B, paras B.21 to B.24.

[9]   See Part 2, paras 2.18 to 2.19 and Appendix B, paras B.25 to B.27.

[10] See Part 2, para 2.8 (3) and Appendix B, para B.14 (1).

[11] See Part 4, paras 4.11 to 4.13.

[12] The mechanism for retaining this exception to the derivative theory is cl 10 of the Bill. It provides that, for the purposes of determining whether D is guilty of an offence as a secondary party, P commits an offence if P acts with the fault required for conviction of the offence, is of or over the age of 10 and does not have a defence of insanity. If so, P commits an offence even if he or she has another defence, for example duress, provocation or diminished responsibility.

3.7　It might be said that narrowing the scope of secondary liability in this way will result in the doctrine being confined to joint criminal ventures. The argument runs that if D, as well as P, has to intend the commission of the conduct element of the principal, they are inevitably parties to a joint criminal venture. However, this is to overlook the fact that, for D and P to be parties to a joint criminal venture, they must share a common intention to commit an offence. They must each have the same intention and each must know that the other has the same intention. It is not enough that coincidentally they both intend that the same criminal act should be committed:

Example 3A

D observes P amongst a group of youths who are about to attack V. D is pleased because he hates V. On leaving the scene, D is approached by two police officers. They say that they are looking for a group of youths who they have reason to believe are about to carry out an assault. D deliberately points the officers in the wrong direction. Meanwhile P begins to assault V.

Example 3B

D, who does not know P, sees P assaulting D's enemy, V. V tries to run away but D trips him up. P continues the assault on V.

Example 3C

D writes and distributes a racist pamphlet encouraging his readers to attack anyone who is not white skinned. P, a racist himself, is encouraged by the pamphlet and assaults V.

In these examples, D's intention is to assist or encourage P to assault V. However, D and P are not parties to a joint criminal venture because they do not share, either expressly or tacitly, a common intention. It just so happens that both have the same intention that V should be assaulted.

Retaining the doctrine of extended common purpose

3.8　In Part 2, we referred to *Chan Wing-siu*[13] where the Privy Council held that, where D and P are parties to a joint criminal venture, D can be convicted of a collateral offence committed by P if D foresaw the possibility of P committing the offence. We are aware that some commentators believe that this is very severe on D, particularly if the collateral offence is murder as it was in *Chan Wing-siu*. However, we believe, both as a matter of principle and on policy grounds, that convicting D on the basis of foresight of a possibility can be justified. We set out our reasons below.[14]

---

[13]　[1985] 1 AC 168.

[14]　Paras 3.132 to 3.152 below.

THE CONDUCT ELEMENT

Clause 1: 'assisting' and 'encouraging'

3.9   Under the present law, by virtue of section 8 of the Accessories and Abettors Act a person who 'aids, abets, counsels or procures' the commission of a principal offence can be tried, convicted and punished for the offence in the same way as the principal offender. We agree with the view expressed in the CP that it would be simpler and clearer if the language of section 8 was replaced by 'assisting' and 'encouraging'. The words capture what is the core of D's conduct, namely helping and seeking to influence P to commit an offence. As explained by Professor Kadish:

> Two kinds of action render [D] liable for the criminal actions of [P]: intentionally influencing the decision of [P] to commit a crime and intentionally helping [P] to commit the crime, where the helping actions themselves constitute no part of the actions prohibited by the definition of the crime."[15]

Recommendation

3.10   **We recommend that section 8 of the Accessories and Abettors Act 1861 and section 44(1) of the Magistrates' Courts Act 1980 should be repealed[16] and replaced by a statutory provision which describes the conduct element as 'assisting or encouraging'.[17]**

The meaning of 'encouraging'

3.11   There are two issues. One is identifying what conduct ought to be capable of amounting to encouraging. The other is whether it is necessary or desirable to provide a statutory definition of encouraging.

---

[15] "Complicity, cause and blame – a study in the interpretation of doctrine" (1985) 73(2) *California Law Review* 323, 342.

[16] Clause 9(1) and (2) of the Supplementary Bill.

[17] Clause 1 of the Bill.

EMBOLDENING P TO COMMIT AN OFFENCE

3.12 As we stated in the first report, we believe that encouraging should have the same broad meaning that 'inciting' has in the context of the common law inchoate offence of incitement.[18] In particular, we agree with the provisional view expressed in the CP that encouraging should encompass not only instigating and persuading but also conduct that emboldens a person who has already decided to commit an offence.[19] We do so because, as the Commission said in the CP, to embolden P in his or her intention to commit an offence may not only make it less likely that P will desist but is undesirable conduct that conflicts with the citizen's duty to respect legal obligations.[20] We also agree that to make D's liability depend on whether he or she in fact instigated the commission of an offence would result in infinite room for argument.[21]

3.13 Further, as will become apparent, we are recommending that if D is not a party with P to a joint criminal venture, he or she should be liable for the principal offence only if he or she intended that P should engage in the conduct element of the principal offence. If D has that intention, we do not believe that it would be unreasonable for D to be held liable for the principal offence even though his or her behaviour does no more than embolden P to engage in or continue to engage in conduct that P was already minded to engage in.

MAKING THREATS OR EXERTING PRESSURE

3.14 It is clear that at common law incitement can consist of threats and pressure.[22] Although it might be thought to be linguistically inappropriate to describe threatening or coercing as 'encouraging', such conduct ought to be and is caught by the offences that we are recommending.[23] As Simester and Sullivan point out,[24] there is no reason why an employer who persuades an employee to commit an offence by threatening redundancy should be in a better position than an employer whose persuasive technique is to offer a pay rise.

Recommendation

3.15 **We recommend that 'encouraging' a person to do an act should include doing so by emboldening, threatening or pressurising another person to do a criminal act.[25]**

---

[18] In *Goldman* [2001] EWCA Crim 1684, [2001] WL 825029 it was held that 'incitement' covered a suggestion, proposal, persuasion or inducement. In *Giannetto* [1997] 1 Cr App R 1 the trial judge directed the jury that D would be liable as an accessory to the murder of V if P had suggested murdering V and D had replied 'Oh goody'. The Court of Appeal did not criticise the direction, saying that "mere encouragement … would suffice" (p 13).

[19] Para 4.148.

[20] Para 4.150.

[21] Para 4.149.

[22] *Applin v Race Relations Board* [1973] QB 815.

[23] Clause 8(1) of the Bill.

[24] *Criminal Law Theory and Doctrine* (2nd ed 2003) p 266.

[25] Clause 8(1) of the Bill.

DEFINING 'ENCOURAGING'

3.16 The draft Criminal Code did not expand on the meaning of 'incite'. Likewise, we believe that it is unnecessary to expand on the meaning of 'encourage'. It is a word in common usage and, if anything, is more familiar to juries and magistrates than 'incite'.

3.17 We are strengthened in our view by the fact that the meaning of incite has rarely troubled the courts. It is true that in the CP the Commission suggested[26] that there was uncertainty as to whether there had to be an element of persuasion or pressure. If there was any uncertainty,[27] it is now clear that there is no such requirement.[28]

The meaning of 'assisting'

3.18 Unlike 'encouraging', in the CP the Commission had no common law inchoate offence to draw upon when considering the meaning of 'assisting'. It said that assisting in its normal sense "extends to any conduct on the part of D that, as a matter of fact, makes it easier for P to commit the principal offence".[29] Having concluded that assisting is a "sufficient and satisfactory concept",[30] it suggested that assistance should include the giving of advice as to how to commit an offence and advice as to how P might avoid detection or apprehension.[31] The Commission invited comment on whether acts of insubstantial assistance should be excluded from the scope of the offence.[32]

ADVICE AS ASSISTANCE

3.19 In *A-G v Able*[33] the High Court held that the giving of advice was conduct capable of 'aiding and abetting' for the purposes of secondary liability. This can mean that D commits an offence each time a person relies on the advice irrespective of how many persons do so. In the CP the Commission noted that the law had been strongly criticised in this respect because it:

---

[26] Para 2.133.

[27] The Commission itself said that specific authority for the view that there had to be persuasion or pressure was 'notably sparse' - para 2.132.

[28] *Marlow* [1998] 1 Cr App R (s) 273; *Goldman* [2001] EWCA Crim 1684, [2001] WL 825029.

[29] Para 4.71.

[30] Para 4.48.

[31] Para 4.99(2).

[32] Para 5.2.(6.2).

[33] [1984] QB 795. The case involved the distribution of a leaflet describing ways of committing suicide. It was a civil case in which the Attorney-General sought a declaration that publication of the booklet would constitute an offence because it would 'aid and abet' suicide contrary to s 2(1) of the Suicide Act 1961.

gives too great an extension to criminal complicity. If the writer of the letter was guilty the first time his information was used, he would be guilty the nth time, which is absurd.[34]

3.20 Despite the criticism of *A-G v Able*, in the CP the Commission proposed that providing advice should be conduct capable of amounting to assisting. No respondent to the CP disagreed with the proposal that providing advice should be conduct that is capable of assisting. We continue to believe that it should be so regarded.

ACTS OF INSUBSTANTIAL ASSISTANCE

3.21 In the CP, the Commission said that if it was D's purpose to facilitate the commission of an offence, D should be liable whether or not the assistance was substantial.[35] We invited comment on whether liability should be limited to substantial assistance if the fault elements of the inchoate offence of assisting crime were to be extended beyond purpose or intention.[36] The majority of respondents thought that it should be irrelevant whether the assistance was substantial. We agree.

3.22 We think that to introduce such a requirement would lead to uncertainty and difficulty. It would require juries and magistrates to 'seek to assess how extensive a contribution the assistance would have been (or was) in bringing about the principal offence'.[37] Further, as we said when discussing the meaning of 'encouraging', we are recommending that if D is not a party with P to a joint criminal venture, he or she should be liable for the principal offence only if he or she intended that P should engage in its conduct element. If D has that intention, we do not believe that it should be necessary that his or her conduct amounts to substantial or direct assistance. Accordingly, D should be liable if his or her act assists or encourages to any extent. The marginal nature of any assistance or encouragement can be reflected in the sentence or, in cases of murder, the length of the minimum term set by the trial judge.

3.23 We are reinforced in our thinking by research that shows the tendency of group activity to lead individual members of the group to see their own acts of assistance as being of lesser consequence, in the context of the group's activity as a whole. This can lead to a greater lack of restraint and to less of a willingness to accept responsibility for actions, than would be the case had those actions formed a part of a single individual's criminal plan. As Professor Katyal has argued:

---

[34] Para 4.53 quoting Glanville Williams, *Criminal Law: The General Part* (2nd ed 1960) p 381 criticising the New Zealand case of *Baker* (1909) 28 NZLR 536 where D was held liable as a party to an offence because he had written a letter describing in general terms techniques for safe-breaking. It should be noted that the problem that Professor Williams adverted to is not confined to advice. For example, a jemmy can be used to commit numerous burglaries.

[35] Para 4.66.

[36] Para 4.67.

[37] Professor K J M Smith, "The Law Commission Consultation Paper on Complicity Part 1: A Blueprint for Rationalism" [1994] *Criminal Law Review* 239, 247.

Specialisation also permits *crimes of diffusion*, where the responsibility for a single crime is spread over many persons... diffusion can... remove internal restraints to crime. ... a person who drives a person from Point A to Point B may not feel that he is doing something gravely immoral, even when the driver is driving away from the scene of the crime... the forces of morality and social norms are thus subverted through strategies that disaggregate human behaviour, playing on the idea that little bad acts are excusable.[38]

'Actual' encouragement or assistance

3.24 In order for D to be held liable for the principal offence, his or her conduct would have in fact to have encouraged or assisted P at the time that P engaged in the conduct element of the principal offence.[39] The burden of proof would be on the prosecution to prove that P was assisted or encouraged. However, whether P was in fact assisted or encouraged should only be an issue if there is evidence before the court, as in example 2N,[40] realistically to suggest that P might not have been.

Omissions as acts capable of encouraging or assisting

3.25 In the first report, we said that determining the circumstances in which a person should incur criminal liability for an omission involves difficult policy issues. In the context of secondary liability, Professor Ashworth says that 'the key question is simple to state: can a person be convicted as an accomplice merely for standing by and doing nothing when an offence is being committed?'[41]

3.26 The general rule at common law is that a person incurs no criminal liability for standing by and doing nothing. The reluctance of the law to impose criminal liability for omissions is attributable to a number of reasons of which perhaps the most significant is that:

> The prohibition of omissions is far more intrusive upon the individuals' autonomy and freedom than is the prohibition of acts, which is why the systematic imposition of (criminal or civil) liability for failures to act is to be resisted.[42]

3.27 However, the general rule of common law is subject to an important exception. Provided an offence is capable of being committed by inaction, a person may commit the offence if he or she is under a duty to act but refrains from doing so.[43] In the context of secondary liability, the law has focused on three issues:

---

[38] Neal Kumar Katyal "Conspiracy Theory" 112 *Yale Law Journal* (2003) 101 at 116 and 117 (emphasis in original).

[39] Clause 1(1)(c) of the Bill.

[40] See Part 2, para 2.40. See also, Appendix B, para B.62.

[41] *Principles of Criminal Law* (4th ed 2003) p 418.

[42] Simester and Brookbanks, *Principles of Criminal Law* (2nd ed 2002) p 46.

[43] *Gibbins and Proctor* (1918) 13 Cr App R 134; *Pittwood* (1902) 19 TLR 37.

(1)   the extent to which and the circumstances in which D can incur secondary liability by virtue of mere presence when P commits an offence;

(2)   whether D can incur secondary liability by failing to take steps to discharge a duty;[44] and

(3)   whether D can incur secondary liability by failing to exercise an entitlement to prevent or control the actions of P.[45]

3.28   The law in relation to (1) is reasonably clear:

Example 3D

D is on a bus when a passenger P starts to assault another passenger V. D remains in his seat and continues to read his newspaper.

D, provided that he takes no positive action to encourage or assist P, is not an accessory to the assault because he is under no legal obligation to act in order to prevent P assaulting V.

Example 3E

D comes across P who is about to rape V. V pleads for D to help her but D passes by. P rapes V.

Again, D incurs no criminal liability for declining to go to V's aid. By contrast, if D takes the positive step of stopping in order to watch P rape V, D will be guilty of rape if the jury find that D intended to encourage P to commit rape and that P was in fact encouraged by D's presence.[46]

3.29   The law in relation to (2) is also reasonably clear. If D is under a duty to act, then D can incur secondary liability for an offence committed by P as a result of D failing to take steps to discharge the duty, provided that P is thereby assisted or encouraged to commit the offence:

Example 3F

D and P are the parents of V. P tells D, who is watching television, that he is going to drown V in the bath. D continues to watch television while P drowns V.

---

[44]   A parent is under a legal duty to act in order to ensure the health and safety of his or her child. A police officer is under a similar duty towards those whom he or she has arrested or who are in his or her custody. A legal duty to act may arise because of a contractual relationship, eg employer and employee.

[45]   The owner of a motor car is entitled to control the actions of those whom he or she allows to drive the car – *Du Cros v Lambourne* [1907] 1 KB 40. An owner of premises or land is entitled to control the actions of those who are on the premises or land.

[46]   The relevant authorities are *Coney* (1882) 8 QBD 534; *Wilcox v Jeffery* [1951] 1 All ER 464; *Allan* [1965] 1 QB 130; *Smith v Baker* [1971] 1 RTR 350; *Clarkson* [1971] 1 WLR 1402; *Allen v Ireland* [1984] 1 WLR 903; *Bland* [1988] *Criminal Law Review* 41.

D is guilty of murder if he intended V to be drowned by P because, by omitting to intervene, he failed to take appropriate steps to discharge his parental duty to secure the safety of V.

3.30 The law in relation to (3) is far less clear. There have been specific instances where the courts have held D to be secondarily liable for failing to control the actions of others.[47] However, it is open to question whether any general principle can be derived from those cases.[48]

THE PROPOSALS IN THE CP

3.31 In the CP, the Commission distinguished encouraging, on the one hand, and assisting, on the other. It provisionally concluded that it ought not to be possible to *assist* crime by failing to discharge a duty or by failing to exercise an entitlement to prevent or control the actions of P.[49] The justification for this limitation was threefold. First, it would bring certainty. Secondly, it would prevent the scope of the offence being unreasonably wide. Finally, it would mean that liability for encouraging and assisting would be in line with the general principles of the criminal law.

3.32 By contrast, the Commission provisionally concluded that the proposed inchoate offence of *encouraging* crime could be committed by inaction.[50] The Commission thought that it would neither be unreasonable nor make the law dangerously wide if encouraging encompassed omissions.

RESPONSES TO THE PROPOSALS IN THE CP

3.33 The majority of respondents who addressed this issue did not accept the proposition that failing to discharge a duty to prevent or control P's actions should *never* be regarded as 'assisting'. Respondents accepted that an unqualified criminalisation of omissions that assist crime would unreasonably widen the law, for example the view that failing to assist a constable to prevent a breach of the peace should represent assisting a breach of the peace.[51] However, they believed that a blanket rule that omissions can never constitute 'assistance' would result in greater injustice.

---

[47] *Du Cros v Lambourne* [1907] 1 KB 40; *Tuck v Robson* [1970] 1 WLR 741 where a publican permitted customers to consume alcohol on the licensed premises outside the permitted hours; *JF Alford Transport* [1997] 2 Cr App R 326 where a company did nothing to prevent its employees falsifying their tachograph records; *Gaunt* [2003] EWCA Crim 3925, [2004] 2 Cr App R (s) 37.

[48] Previously the Commission has taken the view that there is such a general principle – clause 27(3) of the Draft Criminal Code Bill and commentary in A Criminal Code for England and Wales, vol 2 Commentary on Draft Criminal Code Bill (1989) Law Com No 177 para 9.22. See Professor Glanville Williams, "Which of you did it?" (1989) 52(2) *Modern Law Review* 179 and, by the same author, "What should the Code do about Omissions" (1987) 7(1) *Legal Studies* 92.

[49] Paras 4.69 to 4.75.

[50] Para 4.158.

[51] See paras 3.37 and 3.38 below.

CONCLUSIONS AND RECOMMENDATIONS

Failure to discharge a duty

3.34   In principle, we believe that it should be possible for D to incur secondary liability by virtue of inaction on the part of D that consists of refraining from taking reasonable steps to discharge a duty. Confining liability to positive acts would result in D incurring no criminal liability in situations where he or she ought to, for example D, a disgruntled security guard, who fails to turn on a burglar alarm with the intention of assisting P to burgle the premises of D's employer.

3.35   It would be for the trial judge to rule whether D was under a duty. The question whether D had failed to take reasonable steps to discharge his or her duty would be one of fact for the jury.

Recommendation

3.36   **We recommend that encouraging or assisting a person to do a criminal act should include doing so by failing to take reasonable steps to discharge a duty.[52]**

Failure to assist a constable to prevent a breach of the peace

3.37   At common law every citizen is under a duty to respond to a constable's request for assistance to prevent a breach of the peace.[53] We do not believe that it would be thought to be either desirable or acceptable for citizens to incur inchoate liability merely for failing to respond to such a request.

Recommendation

3.38   **We recommend that a person failing to respond to a constable's request for assistance in preventing a breach of the peace should not be regarded as encouraging or assisting a person to do a criminal act.[54]**

Failure to exercise an entitlement to prevent or control the actions of P

3.39   We said in the first report that it would be an over-extension of the criminal law if D could be inchoately liable on the basis that he or she had refrained from exercising an entitlement to prevent or control P's actions.[55] We emphasised that the new offences that we were recommending were inchoate offences capable of being committed even if the principal offence is not committed.

3.40   Every citizen is entitled to use reasonable force to control the actions of P in order to prevent P committing an offence.[56] However, we do not think it would be acceptable if D could be criminally liable for encouraging or assisting P to commit a crime merely because D failed to take action to prevent P committing the crime.

---

[52]   Clause 8(2)(b) of the Bill.

[53]   *Brown* (1841) Car & M 312, 172 ER 522.

[54]   Clause 8(3) of the Bill.

[55]   Paras 5.68 to 5.70.

[56]   Criminal Law Act 1967, s 3(1).

3.41   The entitlement that everyone has to control the actions of others in order to prevent the commission of an offence is an illustration of a general power. In addition, D may have a specific entitlement to control P's activities regardless of whether P is committing or is about to commit an offence. For example, the owner of land is entitled to control the actions of others on the land:

Example 3G

D, who has a telephone, is awoken by a noise coming from his garden. Opening the window, D asks P what he is doing. P replies 'go back to bed'. D, although believing that P is about to commit an assault on V, goes back to bed. P, encouraged by D's non-intervention, proceeds to assault V.

It might be thought that D's conduct is callous and displays a lack of empathy for V. In itself, this is not to justify the imposition of criminal liability. In this kind of example, if D could be made criminally liable for his failure to intervene, it would be a case of imposing liability because D was not being a good samaritan or 'busy body'. That is potentially far too harsh a consequence in such cases of non-intervention.[57]

Clause 2: Joint criminal ventures

'Agreed' offences

3.42   It is generally accepted that D is liable for an 'agreed' offence because, with the requisite state of mind, he or she has assisted or encouraged its commission. In the great majority of cases, this is a satisfactory explanation of D's liability for an agreed offence. In many cases, so far as assistance is concerned, if D and P agree to commit an offence which P subsequently commits, it will be possible to point to some discrete act on D's part pursuant to the agreement which constitutes assistance:

Example 3H

D and P agree to commit a burglary at V's premises. D drives P to the premises and keeps watch while P enters V's property and steals her jewellery.

D's conduct has assisted P to commit burglary.

3.43   Further, even if it is not possible to identify a discrete act of assistance, it will usually be the case that the agreement itself emboldens and therefore (mutually) *encourages* both D and P. However, exceptionally, D may be able to adduce evidence indicating that the agreement has neither assisted nor encouraged P to commit the agreed offence. An example is where P testifies that, although he or she agreed with D to commit the offence, the agreement did not act as any kind of encouragement.

---

[57]   See the discussion in Simester and Sullivan, *Criminal Law Theory and Doctrine* (2nd ed 2003) pp 73 to 74.

3.44 Under our recommendations, the fact that P testified that he or she was not encouraged by the agreement with D to commit the agreed offence would not be relevant. The conduct element of clause 2 would be satisfied by an agreement or shared intention between D and P to commit the agreed offence and would not require the prosecution to demonstrate actual assistance or encouragement.

3.45 Promises and agreements are forms of social and normative practice, entry into which in and of itself creates obligations, commitments and expectations as to future conduct (here, playing some part in the offence, even just by 'making up the numbers'). It is the creation of these obligations, commitments and expectations through simple agreement or shared intention that provides a basis for finding D liable under clause 2.[58] When D engages in the normative practice, by agreeing to commit the offence or sharing an intention to commit an offence, he or she should not be heard to say later that his or her agreement or shared intention did not have the normative significance it would ordinarily have in terms of obligations, commitments and expectations created. D can no more escape liability in this way than, in the civil law, someone can say that no contractual liability was ever created by a binding agreement simply because no one expected the contract to be fulfilled or relied on.

'Collateral' offences

3.46 We have said above that, in relation to the agreed offence, the conduct element should be satisfied by virtue of D having entered into an agreement or sharing an intention with P to commit the agreed offence. We are recommending that in relation to collateral offences, the conduct element should also be satisfied by virtue of D having entered into an agreement or sharing an intention with P to commit the agreed offence. We acknowledge that such a recommendation, in as much as it relates to collateral offences, has to be seen against the background of a debate amongst judges and commentators concerning the doctrinal basis of secondary liability. We now consider the doctrinal issue.

THE DOCTRINAL ISSUE

3.47 One view holds that it is doctrinally unsound to seek to base D's liability for a collateral offence on D having assisted or encouraged P to commit it. In the CP, the Commission inclined to this view. It thought that the 'ordinary rules of secondary liability do not wholly overlap with joint enterprise cases'.[59] The Commission's reasoning was that the basis of secondary liability is 'actual acts of assistance and encouragement'[60] but that in the case of a collateral offence D does not in fact assist or encourage P to commit that offence:

---

[58] In the case of a promise by D to assist, not forming part of a joint venture, if the promise emboldened P to commit the offence, D would be guilty of the offence by virtue of clause 1.

[59] Para 2.120. In the CP, the Commission used the term 'joint enterprise' rather than 'joint criminal venture'.

[60] Above.

> **Example 3J**
>
> P and D agree to supply X with a class A drug (heroin). D knows that P has dealt in illicit pornography and anticipates that should X ask for child pornography, there is a real risk that P will supply it. D urges P not to do so. P agrees not to, but D still has his concerns. Nevertheless, D proceeds with the venture. As D feared, X asks for the child pornography and P supplies it.

On the Commission's view, as set out in the CP, although D had assisted or encouraged P to supply a class A drug, D had not assisted or encouraged the supply of the pornography. Indeed, D had sought to discourage it. Yet, D is guilty of supplying child pornography.[61]

3.48   Some commentators take the same view. According to Simester and Sullivan:

> ... the actus reus requirements of joint enterprise liability *differ* from those applying to participation by assistance or encouragement. There is no need to show a common purpose in standard cases of aiding and abetting. But it is [D]'s commitment to that common unlawful purpose (to commit crime A) which justifies the law's requiring only that [D] must foresee the possibility of crime B, rather than demanding that [D] must *help* or *encourage* crime B ... .[62]

3.49   We do not understand Simester and Sullivan to be saying that P's commission of a collateral offence *necessarily* involves no assistance or encouragement on D's part. It is clear that in many instances where P commits a collateral offence, D will have assisted or encouraged its commission even if D expressed opposition to P committing the offence:

> **Example 3K**
>
> D and P have agreed to commit a burglary. D realises that there is a possibility that P might also murder the householder, V, should V disturb them. D tells P in the strongest terms that P should not do so. D drives them to V's house where in the course of committing the burglary they are disturbed by V. In order to ensure that they are not identified, and despite D's protestations, P murders V.

It is true that D did not intend that P should murder V or that P should be assisted or encouraged to do so. However, whether or not P is in fact assisted or encouraged by D's conduct is not dependent on D's attitude towards the commission of the collateral offence. By driving P to the house, D has assisted P to commit not only burglary but also murder.

---

[61]   Contrary to the Protection of Children Act 1978, s1(1)(b).

[62]   *Criminal Law Theory and Doctrine* (2nd ed 2003) p 225 (emphasis in original). See also G R Sullivan, "Complicity for First Degree Murder and Complicity in an Unlawful Killing" [2006] *Criminal Law Review* 502, 508 to 509.

3.50 Rather, the point that Simester and Sullivan are seeking to emphasise is that in some cases where P commits a collateral offence it is impossible to identify any conduct on D's part which has assisted or encouraged P to commit the offence. In example 3K, it could easily have been P who drove the car. D could have been downstairs unaware that P was murdering V upstairs.

3.51 More recently, Professor Simester has defended the view that D's liability for a collateral offence is not grounded upon actual assistance or encouragement:

> Through entering into a joint [criminal venture], [D] changes her normative position. [D] becomes, by her deliberate choice, a participant in a group action to commit a crime. Moreover her new status has moral significance: she associates herself with the conduct of the other members of the group in a way that the mere aider and abettor, who remains an independent character throughout the episode does not. Whereas aiding and abetting doctrines are grounded in [D's] contribution to another's crime, joint [criminal venture] is grounded in *affiliation*. [D] voluntarily subscribes to a co-operative endeavour, one that is identified by its shared criminal purpose. As such, joint [criminal venture] doctrines impose a form of collective responsibility, predicated on membership of the unlawful concert... By offering allegiance to the enterprise, [D] implicitly condones its furtherance.[63]

3.52 In our view, Professor Simester's theory explains D's liability for some but not all collateral offences. He sets limits to the circumstances in which D can be regarded as affiliating him or herself to crimes committed in the course of a joint venture:

> "she [S] accepts responsibility for the wrongs perpetrated in realising... that [common] purpose. Her responsibility for incidental offences is not unlimited: S can not be said to accept the risk of wrongs by P that she does not foresee, or which depart radically from their shared enterprise, and joint enterprise liability rightly does not extend to such cases."[64]

3.53 We agree that D should not be liable for radical departures on the part of P from the joint criminal venture.[65] However, we do not accept that the only collateral offences for which D may be made liable are those "perpetrated in realising" or that "grow out of"[66] the agreed offence. In our view, it ought to be possible to hold D liable for a collateral offence committed by P, even when the offence did nothing to further the joint criminal venture, if D was aware that the commission of that offence was just the sort of thing that P might do.

---

[63] A P Simester, "The Mental Element in Complicity" (2006) 122 *Law Quarterly Review* 578, 598 to 600 (our emphasis).

[64] Above, 599.

[65] See paras 3.153 to 3.166 below.

[66] A P Simester, "The Mental Element in Complicity" (2006) 122 *Law Quarterly Review* 578, 600.

> **Example 3L**
>
> D commits burglaries with P, even though D knows that P has convictions for raping householders. D has said to P that he (D) wants nothing to do with any rape. In the course of one of their burglaries, unknown to D, P commits rape. [67]

3.54 By contrast, Smith and Hogan maintain that:

> The only peculiarity of joint [venture] cases is that, once a common purpose to commit the offence in question is proved, there is no need to look further for evidence of assisting and encouraging. The act of combining to commit the offence satisfies these requirements of aiding and abetting. Frequently it will be acts of encouragement which provide the evidence of the common purpose. It is simply necessary to apply the ordinary principles of secondary liability to the joint [venture] … . [68]

3.55 On this view, D's liability for a collateral offence is always grounded on the fact that D has assisted or encouraged P to commit the collateral offence. Unlike Simester and Sullivan, Smith and Hogan believe that the collateral offence can always be traced back to the initial agreement, and, therefore, the initial encouragement which is provided by this agreement remains active.

3.56 Ultimately, however, the differences between these accounts of D's liability for a collateral offence committed by P, while real enough, do not produce sufficiently significant differences in practice for it to be important for us to choose between them. In fact, we doubt whether each theory satisfactorily explains all the possible scenarios. As we have already acknowledged above,[69] the vast majority of agreed offences will be committed by P in circumstances where there can be no argument that there has been some degree of assistance or encouragement on the part of D. Likewise, there will be many collateral offences committed by P in circumstances where it is clear that D has assisted or encouraged P to commit the offence. However, unlike Smith and Hogan, we acknowledge the viability of the view that offences committed pursuant to a joint criminal venture can be committed without any actual assistance or encouragement by D.

---

[67] It is true that there are authorities which suggest that, in this example, D is not guilty of rape because he did not 'authorise' its commission – see *Anderson and Morris* [1966] 2 QB 110, 118 to 119. However, *Chan Wing-siu* [1985] AC 168, *Hui Chi-Ming* [1992] 1 AC 34 and *Powell and Daniels, English* [1999] 1 AC 1 establish that D is liable for a collateral offence if he or she foresaw that it might be committed as a possible incident of the joint criminal venture.

[68] *Criminal Law* (11th ed 2005) p 191.

[69] See paras 3.42 and 3.43.

3.57 In our view, D's liability for a collateral offence should not be dependent on whether his or her conduct is classified as 'assistance' or 'encouragement'. Under our recommendation, the conduct element would be satisfied by the agreement itself without the need to look beyond it. What is important is that the agreement must be one which involves the commission of an offence. D is involved not merely in a joint venture but in a joint *criminal* venture. The criminal law would exceed its brief were it to hold D liable for offences arising from D participating in a joint venture that is not criminal, for example an agreement to embark on a 'pub crawl'.

3.58 Moreover, we note that the broader justification that Professor Simester gives for imposing liability for a collateral offence is strikingly similar to both Smith and Hogan and our preferred justification. He says:

> Criminal associations tend to encourage and escalate criminality. They present a threat to public safety that ordinary criminal prohibitions, addressed to individual actors, do not entirely address.[70]

We agree. The truth of this observation is what, on our view, justifies holding that the act of agreeing to participate in a joint criminal venture should suffice to satisfy the conduct element of secondary liability for all offences arising from that venture.

Recommendation

3.59 **We recommend that, for D to satisfy the conduct element of clause 2, he or she must either:**

(1) **agree with P to commit an offence; or**

(2) **share a common intention with P to commit an offence.**

Negating the effect of assistance, encouragement or agreements pursuant to a joint criminal venture

3.60 Under the recommendations in our first report, as soon as D does an act capable of assisting or encouraging P to commit the principal offence, he or she would be inchoately liable for assisting or encouraging P to commit the offence.[71] Under the current law and under the recommendations in this report, D would be secondarily liable if P goes on to commit the principal offence.[72] It would not avail D that he or she either regretted his or her act of assistance or encouragement, or, in the case of joint criminal ventures, no longer considered him or herself to be part of the venture.

---

[70] A P Simester, "The Mental Element in Complicity" (2006) 122 *Law Quarterly Review* 578, 599.

[71] Provided that D satisfied the requisite fault element.

[72] Provided that D satisfies the fault element that we are recommending – see paras 3.68 to 3.169 below.

3.61 However, we believe that the law would be too harsh if it did not allow for the possibility of D negating the effect of his or her conduct before the principal offence is committed. If successful in negating the effect of his or her conduct, D should still be inchoately liable but, even if P does commit the principal offence, D should not be guilty of the principal offence as a secondary party.

3.62 To take advantage of this, D should have to demonstrate that he or she had successfully negated the effect of his or her conduct. We consider an example involving assistance:

Example 3M

D, seeing P attacking V, hands P a baseball bat. Mid fight, P does not realise that it was D that handed him the bat, but is happy to make use of it. However, regretting his act, D quickly takes the bat back before P can use it in the assault. P continues the assult on V.

In this example, it should be open to D to argue that, by taking back the bat before it was used in the assault, he successfully negated the effect of his conduct: the assistance.

3.63 Let us consider an example involving a joint criminal venture:

Example 3N

D and P agree to commit robbery the following week. They agree to meet at the scene of the crime and that D will bring weapons. The following day D has second thoughts and leaves the country without telling P. P arrives at the place where the robbery is to take place. Finding that D is absent, P nevertheless goes on to commit the robbery.

In this example, as in example 3M above, it should be open to D to contend that he negated the effect of his assistance (in this case by not providing weapons). However, D has not negated the effect of his agreement with P to take part in a joint criminal venture. Under the current law and under the recommendations in this report, D would therefore be guilty of robbery.[73] The law regards P as deriving tacit support from the fact that (so far as P knows) D is still 'in on it' and D has done nothing to withdraw or 'neutralise the effect'[74] of his previous agreement/support. Although D may have withdrawn his assistance, D is still to be regarded as part of the joint criminal venture.

---

[73] *Rook* (1993) 97 Cr App R 327.

[74] *Jones* [2006] SASC 189, [157].

3.64   As examples 3M and 3N above demonstrate, it is likely to be harder for D to successfully countermand the effect of his or her conduct in cases of joint criminal ventures. This is because, as well as negating any assistance or encouragement provided, D must also negate the effect of his or her agreement with P to commit an offence.[75]

3.65   The ultimate decision of whether D has managed to negate the effect of his or her conduct will be for the jury. Each case will vary on its facts and we do not believe that there should be any fixed rules about what D has to do to negate the effect of his or her conduct. It would be artificial in the case of a joint criminal venture, for example, for D to have to notify each and every participant that he or she (D) will be taking no further part in it. It is not equivalent to severing a joint tenancy. However, it might be too generous to D to say that it always suffices if D has done all that he or she can reasonably do to negate the effect of his or her conduct.

3.66   The guiding principle should be that, the greater D's encouragement or assistance, and the closer D's purported withdrawal is to the commission of the offence, the harder it should be for D to claim that he or she successfully negated the effect of his or her conduct.

Recommendation

3.67   **We recommend that D should be able to avoid liability as a secondary party if he or she is able to demonstrate that he or she had negated the effect of his or her acts of assistance, encouragement or agreement before the principle offence was committed.**

THE FAULT ELEMENT

3.68   In this section, we set out our recommendations for the fault element of secondary liability. Our treatment of the fault element reflects the fact that we believe that there is an important normative difference between cases where D and P are parties to a joint criminal venture and those where they are not. The draft Participating in Crime Bill appended to this report reflects this view in that clause 1 addresses D's liability in cases where D and P are not parties to a joint criminal venture whereas clause 2 deals with joint criminal ventures.[76] As will become apparent, clause 1 consists of more stringent fault requirements than clause 2.

3.69   The order of treatment of the issues is as follows:

        (1)   Clause 1: assisting and encouraging an offence.

               (a)   D's state of mind in relation to the conduct element of the principal offence (paragraphs 3.70 to 3.97).

---

[75]   Although only in limited circumstances, the law should allow for the possibility of D negating the effect of his agreement to take part in a joint criminal venture. In example 3N, D may have been successful on this point if, prior to the robbery, he had told P that he no longer wanted to play any part in it.

[76]   For the possible application of clause 1 to joint criminal ventures, see para 3.124 below.

(b)   D's fault in relation to elements of the principal offence other than the conduct element (paragraphs 3.98 to 3.122).

(2)   Clause 2: participating in a joint criminal venture.

    (a)   Introduction, and why a distinct clause 2 is necessary (paragraphs 3.123 to 3.126).

    (b)   D's state of mind in relation to the conduct element of the principal offence (paragraphs 3.127 to 3.152).

    (c)   When P's conduct is outside the scope of the venture (paragraphs 3.153 to 3.166).

    (d)   D's fault in relation to elements of the principal offence other than the conduct element (paragraphs 3.167 to 3.169).

Clause 1: assisting or encouraging an offence

D's state of mind in relation to the conduct element of the principal offence

THE CURRENT LAW

3.70   In Part 2,[77] we observed that the preponderance of common law authority suggests that D may be convicted of the principal offence as a secondary party even if:

    (1)   it was not D's purpose to encourage or assist P to commit the principal offence; and

    (2)   it was not D's intention that the principal offence should be committed.

3.71   Accordingly, at common law, D can be guilty of a principal offence despite not intending that the offence, including its conduct element, be committed:

Example 3P

P, a local teenage boy, enters D's shop to buy a kitchen knife. D knows that P has a number of previous convictions for robbery, and although she does not want him to, she believes that he will use the knife for another robbery. Nevertheless, D sells P the knife, which P subsequently uses in a robbery.

At common law, D is guilty of robbery despite not intending that P should commit the offence.

---

[77] Paras 2.45 and 2.47. See also Appendix B, paras B.70 to B.74 and B.77 to B.78.

3.72   As a result, under the current law, the doctrine of secondary liability has the potential to capture those engaging in ostensibly innocent conduct including, for example, shopkeepers selling their merchandise, employees acting in the course of their employment and hosts dispensing alcohol to guests who will be driving home. On one view, such a broad concept is appropriate because, in order to protect the potential victims of crime, traders, employees and hosts should ensure that they do not encourage or assist P to commit offences. Professor Ashworth says that this view "criminalises the shopkeeper as an accomplice in every case where the customer's intention to commit that kind of offence is known"[78] and he describes the current law as supporting "a more social and less individualistic notion of responsibility".[79]

3.73   The contrary view is that, for example, a shopkeeper should be liable for an offence as a secondary party only if it was his or her intention to further the customer's offence. According to Professor Ashworth:

>   This stresses the notions of free trade and individual autonomy, treating the shopkeeper as a mere trader rather than as a fellow citizen's keeper.[80]

3.74   The contrasting views described by Professor Ashworth expose the stark policy choice that presently must be made because at common law there is no inchoate liability for assisting the commission of an offence. Those who by their ostensibly innocent conduct assist, without encouraging, others to commit an offence must either be convicted of the principal offence or be completely exonerated. The common law has come down on the side of convicting D of the principal offence. It has done so by holding that D's attitude towards the commission of the principal offence, including its conduct element, is irrelevant. D can be convicted of the principal offence if he or she knew or believed that P intended to commit it or even, according to some authorities, if he or she believed that P might commit it. This is a very broad doctrine of secondary liability.

A NEW APPROACH

3.75   In the first report,[81] we recommended the creation of inchoate offences to punish conduct that assists (or encourages) others to commit offences. In particular, we recommended that there should be an inchoate offence of assisting (or encouraging) P to commit a principal offence if D believed that P would commit the offence with D's assistance (or encouragement). The enactment of such offences would mean that, in cases of assistance, the present limited choice between either convicting D of the principal offence or exonerating D could be replaced by a more nuanced scheme of liability. Under such a scheme, the choices would lie between convicting D of the principal offence (secondary liability), convicting D of assisting or encouraging the principal offence (inchoate liability) or exonerating D. The middle option would permit the conviction of D in example 3P while still recognising that his culpability is not equivalent to that of P.

---

[78]   A J Ashworth, *Principles of Criminal Law* (4th ed 2003) p 421.

[79]   Above, 426.

[80]   Above, 421.

[81]   Inchoate Liability for Assisting and Encouraging Crime (2006) Law Com No 300.

3.76   Such a scheme needs to address two fundamental questions:

   (1)   what *attitude* must D have towards the commission of the principal offence before he or she can properly be convicted of *that* offence and, thereby, liable to the same stigma and penalties as P?

   (2)   what degree of *knowledge or belief* as to P's intention to commit the principal offence must D have before he or she can properly be convicted of that offence?

THE ATTITUDE OF D TOWARDS THE COMMISSION OF THE PRINCIPAL OFFENCE

Intending P to engage in the conduct element of the principal offence

3.77   It is important to acknowledge that, where D and P are not parties to a joint criminal venture, the conduct of D that constitutes assistance or encouragement may not be inherently wrong or harmful.[82] In example 3P, there is nothing inherently wrong or harmful in D selling a kitchen knife to P. Therefore, if P uses the knife to rob V, D ought not, without more, to be held responsible for the attack on V.

3.78   If D, when selling the knife, believed that P *might* use it to attack V, it might be thought that D's behaviour was morally objectionable and culpable. However, as Professor Simester observes:

> The most a secondary party does is assist or encourage a crime, not perpetrate it. Since this is [a] far less stringent contribution than is required of the perpetrator, it is insufficient in itself to involve [D] in P's crime. D's conduct is, by itself, innocent and not a wrong at all – she does something that is permitted, e.g. lend or sell P a knife, say, or a jemmy – something that we may do innocently in ordinary life. Conduct of this sort has no inherent or necessary connection to crime.

> When computer manufacturers make and sell computers, there is a recognised chance that their customers will use the machines to download and copy music illegally. Yet no one would say that those manufacturers are responsible for the illegal copying. Simply put: if my action is lawful and not wrong, someone else's crime does not become my lookout – and should not be my moral or legal responsibility – simply because I foresee its *possibility*. Something more is required.[83]

We agree. The issue is what the "something more" should consist of.

---

[82]   We acknowledge that there may be isolated instances where an act of assistance or encouragement is inherently wrong or harmful. An example would be where D sells P an illegal firearm.

[83]   A P Simester, "The Mental Element in Complicity" (2006) 122 *Law Quarterly Review* 578, 589 to 590.

3.79 On one view, it ought to be possible to convict D of the principal offence if D knows or believes that P *will* commit the principal offence. We agree that it ought to be possible to hold D criminally liable if he or she assists or encourages P in the knowledge or belief that P will commit the principal offence. However, D ought to be held inchoately liable and not secondarily liable, that is, D should be convicted of assisting and encouraging P to commit the principal offence rather than convicted of the principal offence itself. The recommendations that we made in the first report would enable D to be held inchoately liable.[84] However, if D is to be convicted of the principal offence, something further should be required.

3.80 If D is to be convicted of the principal offence and labelled in the same way as P, his or her culpability should be comparable to that of P. D's culpability is not comparable to that of P merely because D believes that P will commit the principal offence. Generally speaking, for P to be convicted of a principal offence he or she must have *intended* to commit its *conduct element*. Accordingly, if D and P are not parties to a criminal joint venture, D's culpability ought not to be considered comparable to that of P unless D likewise intends the commission of the conduct element of the principal offence. D, in rendering assistance or encouragement to P, should have to intend that P commit the conduct element.

3.81 A requirement that D must intend P to commit the conduct element of the principal offence is not tantamount to requiring that D must intend that P should commit the offence. The following example illustrates the distinction between D intending that the principal offence be committed, on the one hand, and D intending that P should commit its conduct element, on the other hand. It also shows how D's culpability can be comparable to that of P even though D does not intend P to commit the principal offence:

Example 3Q

D sees that P is about to throw a small stone at V. X is about to shout a warning to V. However, D, who dislikes V, puts his hand over X's mouth to stifle the warning. P throws the stone at V. P, who is unaware of D's presence and intervention, believes that V may suffer a minor injury as a result of being hit by the stone. Neither D nor P intend or foresee a risk of V suffering serious injury. Unfortunately, as P throws the stone, V ducks and the stone hits V in the eye. V suffers a serious injury.

P has committed the principal offence of unlawfully and maliciously inflicting grievous bodily harm.[85] It is a constructive liability offence because P can be convicted of the offence despite only intending or foreseeing that V might suffer *some* bodily harm. The fact that P neither intended nor foresaw that V would or might suffer *serious* bodily harm is irrelevant.[86]

---

[84] The proposed legislative response to our recommendations can be found in Part 2 of the Serious Crime Bill (introduced into Parliament on 16 January 2007).

[85] Offences against the Person Act 1861, s 20.

[86] *Mowatt* [1968] 1 QB 421; *Savage and Parmenter* [1992] 1 AC 699.

3.82   In example 3Q, D did not intend (or foresee) that P should commit the principal offence of unlawfully and maliciously inflicting grievous bodily harm because, like P, he did not intend (or foresee) that V would suffer serious bodily harm. However, if P can commit the principal offence without intending (or foreseeing) the consequence element of the offence, parity of culpability does not require that D must have intended (or foreseen) that V might suffer serious bodily harm. It should suffice that D, foreseeing that V might suffer a minor injury, intended P to engage in the conduct element of the principal offence, namely throwing a stone.[87]

3.83   It is for this reason that clause 1 of the draft Bill, rather than requiring D to intend P to commit an offence, states that D must intend a person to do a 'criminal act'. 'Criminal act' in reference to a principal offence means any act that falls within the definition of the conduct element that must be proved in order for a person to be convicted of a principal offence.[88] A simple example is the offence of rape where the conduct element consists of penile penetration of the vagina, anus or mouth.[89]

The meaning of 'intent'

3.84   For the purposes of determining the liability of P, the common law has provided a partial definition of intention: a person 'intends' a result if he or she acts in order to bring it about. Transposing this partial definition to the context of secondary liability, D 'intends' that P should engage in the conduct of the element of the principal offence if D's act of assistance or encouragement is in order that P should do so. Put another way, D 'intends' P to commit the conduct element if it is D's 'purpose' that P should commit the conduct element. In some instances, although it may not be D's purpose that P should engage in the conduct element of the principal offence, D may nevertheless believe that it is 'virtually certain' that P will do so. Thus, in example 3P, D may have sold the knife to P not merely believing that P would use the knife to commit a robbery, but in the belief that P would be 'virtually certain' to do so.

3.85   Consider this further example:

Example 3R

P enters D's shop and asks to buy a baseball bat. P tells D that he has just discovered his wife, V, in bed with the lodger and that he intends to use the bat to 'teach her a lesson that she will never forget'. D has no doubt that P will use the bat to attack V. However, D decides to sell P the bat. P uses it to attack V.

---

[87]   In example 3Q, D believed that there was a risk that V might suffer some, albeit minor, bodily harm. A quite distinct issue is whether D ought to be convicted of the principal offence of unlawfully and maliciously inflicting grievous bodily harm if when he handed the stone to P he did not believe that the stone would or might cause *any* injury to V – see paras 3.96 and 3.97 below.

[88]   Clause 11(2) of the Bill.

[89]   Sexual Offences Act 2003, s 1(1)(a).

The facts of example 3R can be fleshed out in different ways. D, with no financial pressures, decided to sell the bat simply because he was indifferent as to whether P used it to attack V. Alternatively, D may even have hoped that P would use it to attack V because V had previously been having an affair with D which she ended in order to have one with the lodger. In such circumstances, a jury might consider D's culpability to be greater than that of P. On the other hand, suppose that D had just received a final demand concerning a mortgage payment, which threatened eviction. D's role can now be (potentially) reinterpreted as an individual under financial pressure who may not want P to commit the offence but who is unwilling to turn down a profitable transaction. In such circumstances, a jury may consider D's conduct to be blameworthy, but not comparable to that of P.

3.86 In the context of the law of murder, the common law has developed a special rule for determining the liability of P in cases where P, although not having acted in order to bring about a result (death of a human being), nevertheless had an especially high level of culpability. The rule is that a jury may - but are not compelled to – find that P intended a result if he or she believed that it would be a certain consequence (barring some extraordinary intervention) of his or her actions irrespective of whether it was a desired consequence.[90]

3.87 Following our review of the law of homicide, we have recently published a report[91] in which we have recommended that the existing law in relation to the meaning of 'intention' should be codified. A jury should be directed that an intention to bring about a result may be found if it is shown that the defendant believed that the result was a virtually certain consequence of his or her action.[92]

3.88 We believe that a similar rule should apply for the purposes of determining D's liability for a principal offence committed by P, murder or otherwise. For the purposes of this rule, the intended 'result' is the commission by P of the conduct element of the principal offence. Accordingly, if a jury found that D believed that, with his or her assistance or encouragement, it was 'virtually certain' that P would engage in the conduct element of the principal offence, they would be entitled - but not compelled - to find that D 'intended' that P should do so. As with determining P's liability, foresight of virtual certainty is a basis for finding 'intent' but it is not a substitute for 'intent'.[93]

3.89 Effectively, this would enable the jury to find or not to find 'intention' according to the totality of the evidence presented to them. Thus, in example 3R, whether a jury found 'intention' would depend on consideration of all the circumstances surrounding the sale of the bat to P.

---

[90] *Woollin* [1999] 1 AC 82.

[91] Murder, Manslaughter and Infanticide (2006) Law Com No 304.

[92] Above, para 3.27

[93] This is consistent with the meaning of 'intention' set out in cl 18 of the Crime (Encouraging and Assisting) Bill appended to the first report. See also para A.100 of the first report.

3.90   The recommendations that we made in the first report would cater for cases where a jury, despite being of the view that D believed that it was 'virtually certain' that P would commit the conduct element of the principal offence, declined to make a finding of 'intent'. As we indicated above,[94] our recommendations would enable D to be held inchoately liable for assisting or encouraging P to commit the principal offence.

Recommendation

3.91   **We recommend that, in cases prosecuted under clause 1, for D to be liable for a principal offence committed by P, D must intend P to commit the conduct element of that offence.**

3.92   The following example illustrates how the recommendation would apply:

Example 3S

D's neighbour, V, is away for the weekend. D, who hates V, leaves a note pinned to a side gate of V's house saying that there is a valuable lawnmower that is in V's garden. D does so in the hope that somebody will steal it. P sees the note and enters V's garden. However, there is no lawnmower. P notices a garden shed and goes in. The lawnmower is there and P takes it.

P is guilty of burglary. The conduct element of burglary is entering a building as a trespasser, and the garden shed is a building. As it was not D's intention that P should enter the shed D is not guilty of burglary. However, D is guilty of theft. The conduct element of theft is the appropriation of property and it was D's intention that P should appropriate the lawnmower.

3.93   Our recommendation would provide a more focused and precise means of determining D's liability than the common law *Bainbridge*[95] test. If the *Bainbridge* test was applied to example 3S, the issue would be whether burglary and theft were offences of the same 'type'. Under our recommendation, it is immediately apparent that P's act of entering the shed falls outside the conduct element of the offence that D was seeking to assist P to commit.

Must D intend that it should be P, as opposed to some other person, who commits the conduct element?

3.94   We do not believe that it should have to be D's intention that the conduct element of the principal offence should be perpetrated by P as opposed to some other person:

Example 3T

In return for payment, D lends a gun to X so that X can shoot V, a local paedophile. X falls ill and, instead, it is his brother P who uses D's gun to murder V.

---

[94]   See para 3.75 above.

[95]   [1960] 1 QB 129. See Part 2, paras 2.55 to 2.57. See also Appendix B, paras B.82 to B.87.

> **Example 3U**
>
> D hires X, a freelance assassin to murder V, a rival gang leader. X is offered a more lucrative contract to murder Z. X decides to sub-contract the murder of V to P, another freelance assassin. P carries out the murder.

In each example, D ought to be liable as a secondary party. D is as culpable as he or she would have been had X not fallen ill or not been offered a more lucrative assignment.

Recommendation

3.95 **We recommend that, although D must intend that the conduct element of the principal offence should be committed, D need not intend that it should be P who commits it.[96]**

D'S KNOWLEDGE OR BELIEF AS TO WHETHER P (OR ANOTHER PERSON) WILL COMMIT THE CONDUCT ELEMENT

3.96 D ought not to escape liability for the principal offence merely because he or she, although intending P to commit the conduct element, harbours doubts as to whether P will do so:

> **Example 3V**
>
> D provides P with a gun intending that P should use it to murder V. However, D believes that P lacks the 'bottle' to murder V. In the event, P murders V.

D intended P to commit murder. It ought not to be open to D to submit that he or she should be exonerated merely because of doubts as to whether P would act on D's assistance or encouragement.

Recommendation

3.97 **We recommend that, if D intends P (or another person) to commit the conduct element, D need not believe that it will be committed.**

The fault required of D in relation to the essential elements of the principal offence other than the conduct element

3.98 Up to this point, we have recommended that for D to incur liability as a secondary party for a principal offence, D must intend P to commit the conduct element of the offence. We have focused on the conduct element because it is common to so many offences and is, therefore, of primary importance.

3.99 However, although fault in relation to the conduct element of P's offence is a necessary condition of D's liability, it is not a sufficient condition. If it were a sufficient condition, absurd consequences would follow. For example, D would be guilty of rape if he or she encouraged P to have consensual sexual intercourse with V but, instead, P had intercourse with V without his or her consent. In this example, the lack of consent is the circumstance element of the principal offence.

---

[96] Clause 1(1)(a) of the Bill.

3.100   The example in the preceding paragraph illustrates how fault can also be relevant to the circumstance and consequence elements of an offence. In addition, there are offences in which there are fault elements besides those that relate to the circumstance and consequence elements. Theft is an example. Theft is an offence consisting of a conduct element (appropriating property) and a circumstance element (the property must belong to another person). In addition, however, for P to be liable he or she must appropriate the property 'dishonestly' and with intent to permanently deprive the owner of the property. Again, unduly harsh consequences would follow if the focus were exclusively on D's state of mind in relation to the conduct element. For example, D would be guilty of theft if P dishonestly took property from a shop without paying for it after D had encouraged P to take the property but to pay for it.

3.101   Further, it would sometimes be impossible to determine accurately D's liability where the conduct that P perpetrates satisfies the conduct element of two or more offences:

Example 3W

In return for payment, D agrees to act as lookout while P takes V's vehicle. P takes the vehicle.

If P intends to permanently deprive V of the vehicle, P commits theft.[97] By contrast, if there is no intention to permanently deprive, P is guilty of taking a motor vehicle without the authority of its owner.[98] In order to determine accurately of which principal offence D ought to be convicted, it is essential to consider D's knowledge or belief as to whether P intended to permanently deprive V of the property.[99]

3.102   Accordingly, in addition to having to intend P to commit the conduct element of an offence, D should have to be at fault in relation to the other elements of the principal offence (circumstance, consequence and, if appropriate, P's state of mind).

3.103   In due course, we will consider the more complex issue of D's fault in relation to those elements. Before doing so, it would be helpful to provide a brief outline of what the law has to say regarding *P's* fault in relation to those elements.

---

[97] An offence contrary to Theft Act 1968, s 1 and punishable, following conviction on indictment, by a maximum term of imprisonment of seven years.

[98] A summary offence contrary to Theft Act 1968, s 12(1) and punishable by a maximum term of imprisonment of six months.

[99] Unless the view was taken that D should always be guilty of the less serious offence. However, we believe that this would not be a satisfactory conclusion.

FAULT IN RELATION TO P'S LIABILITY

3.104 The starting point in determining whether P is guilty of an offence is to identify the external elements of the offence and then to establish if they are satisfied. Thus, if P is charged with criminal damage, P can only be convicted of the offence if property has been damaged or destroyed (consequence) by an act of P (conduct) and the property belongs to another person (circumstance). The next step is to determine whether P has to satisfy a fault element in relation to each external element and, if so, in what that fault element consists. Finally, there is the issue of whether P satisfies each fault element.

3.105 The criminal law recognises different fault elements, the most important of which are intention, knowledge, recklessness and negligence. Broadly speaking, since the decision in *G*,[100] the first three involve consideration of P's state of mind. By contrast, P's state of mind may not be relevant to negligence. Thus, if an offence requires that P, in order to avoid conviction, must reasonably believe in the existence of a circumstance, for example that V is of or over a specified age, P will not escape liability if a reasonable person would not have believed V to be of that age even if P honestly believed that V was of that age.

3.106 It is always open to Parliament to enact an offence consisting of external elements in relation to which P does not have to be at fault. The offence of driving with excess alcohol is an example. P commits the offence if he or she drives (conduct) with a level of alcohol in excess of the prescribed limit (circumstance). The fact that P did not know or believe that he or she was over the prescribed limit is irrelevant as is the fact that a reasonable person would not have known or believed that P was over the limit.

3.107 However, in two recent decisions,[101] the House of Lords, when considering the circumstance elements of statutory offences has emphasised that there is a presumption that in order to be convicted of a statutory offence, P must be at fault in relation to its circumstance element. Lord Nicholls referred to:

> … the established common law presumption that a mental element, traditionally labelled mens rea, is an essential ingredient unless Parliament has indicated a contrary intention either expressly or by necessary implication.[102]

---

[100] [2003] UKHL 50, [2004] AC 1034.

[101] *B (A Minor) v DPP* [2000] 2 AC 428; *K* [2001] UKHL 41, [2002] 1 AC 462.

[102] *B (A Minor) v DPP* [2000] 2 AC 428, 460 by Lord Nicholls.

3.108   However, judicial enthusiasm for a fault element has not extended to constructive liability offences. These are offences where P can be convicted despite not being at fault in relation to the *consequence* element of the offence. Thus, P can be convicted of murder without having to intend or foresee a risk of death. It suffices if he or she intended to cause serious bodily harm. Likewise, P can be convicted of unlawfully and maliciously inflicting grievous bodily harm[103] without having to intend or foresee a risk of grievous bodily harm. It suffices if P foresaw the risk of inflicting some harm.[104]

FAULT IN RELATION TO D'S LIABILITY

3.109   There are three possible approaches:

(1)   there should be a more demanding fault element for D than P;

(2)   D must satisfy the same fault element as P;

(3)   D must believe that P, in committing the conduct element of a principal offence, would be committing the offence.

A more demanding fault element for D than P

3.110   The argument in favour of this approach is that it would reflect the respective contributions of P and D to the commission of the principal offence. On this argument, as P perpetrates the offence while D merely assists or encourages P to perpetrate it, there should a more demanding fault requirement for D than for P. This approach would also reflect the current law in relation to no-fault offences where D, unlike P, must be at fault in relation to the circumstance element of the offence:

Example 3X

P tells D that he is going to a party which V will be attending. P tells D that he is very attracted to V. D, who has never met V, encourages P to have consensual sexual intercourse with her. V tells P that she is aged 15 but, in fact, she is aged 12. With V's consent, P has sexual intercourse with her.

P has committed the offence of rape of a child under 13.[105] The offence is a no-fault offence and the fact that V consented to sexual intercourse and that P believed that V was 15 is irrelevant. By way of contrast, under the current law, D would be liable only if he or she knew or believed that V was probably under 13. That would continue to be the case under this approach.

---

[103] Offences Against the Person Act 1861, s 20.

[104] *Mowatt* [1968] 1 QB 421; *Savage* [1992] 1 AC 699.

[105] Sexual Offences Act 2003, s 5.

3.111 In other respects, however, this approach would represent a radical departure from the current law. First, D, unlike P, would have to be at fault in relation to the consequence element of a constructive liability offence. Thus, if D was charged with assault occasioning actual bodily harm, it would have to be proved that D intended that V should suffer actual bodily harm or foresaw a risk that V might suffer actual bodily harm whereas P could be convicted without intending or foreseeing a risk of actual bodily harm. Likewise, if D were charged with murder, it would have to be proved that D intended that V should die whereas P could be convicted if he or she had merely intended to cause grievous bodily harm.

3.112 We acknowledge that there is a substantial body of opinion that holds that constructive liability is wrong in principle. On this view, it might be said that such liability should be restricted to principal offenders. However, we believe that requiring that D, but not P, must intend or foresee the risk of the consequence would in fact compound the problem:

> **Example 3Y**
>
> D, a gang leader, orders one of his minions, P, to pay a visit to V who both D and P know suffers from a serious heart condition. The intention of the visit is to put 'the frighteners' on V. V is so frightened by the visit that he has a heart attack and dies.

P is guilty of manslaughter.[106] If P is guilty of manslaughter, it is right that the (in a broad sense) more culpable party, D, should also be convicted of the offence.

3.113 Secondly, in relation to offences where P can be convicted if he or she intends or is *reckless* as to the consequence element, D would have to intend the consequence. For example, if D and P were charged with criminal damage, P could be convicted if he or she foresaw a risk of damage or destruction while D would have to have intended damage or destruction.

The same fault element for D and P

3.114 While not so radical, this approach would represent a major departure from the common law in two respects. First, there are some offences of which P can only be convicted if he or she intended to bring about the consequence element:

> **Example 3Z**
>
> D gives P the address of V knowing that P wants to assault V. D dislikes V and hopes that P will attack V but merely so as to cause V less than serious harm. However, D believes that P intends to cause V serious bodily harm. P attacks V and, as D anticipated, intentionally causes V serious bodily harm.

---

[106] *Dawson* (1985) 81 Cr App R 150; *Watson* [1989] 1 WLR 684.

P is guilty of causing grievous bodily harm with intent.[107] Under the current law, D is also guilty of the offence because, although it was not D's intention that V should suffer serious bodily harm, he believed that it was P's intention to cause serious bodily harm. However, if D's fault had to be the same as P's, D would no longer be liable because he did not intend that V should suffer serious bodily harm.

3.115 In example 3Z, we believe that D should continue to be liable for causing V grievous bodily harm with intent. D's culpability is sufficiently comparable to that of P to merit such a conviction. It is true that D did not intend that V should suffer serious bodily harm. However, D did intend that P should attack V and D also believed that, in attacking V, P *would* do so intending that V should suffer serious harm.

3.116 Secondly, by contrast with the first approach, D, like P, could under this second approach be convicted of a no-fault offence even if he or she was not at fault in relation to its circumstance element.

D must believe that P, in committing the conduct element of an offence, would commit the offence[108]

3.117 This is the approach to the fault element that we favour. The following examples illustrates how this approach would apply:

Example 3AA

In return for payment, D acts as lookout while P takes V's car without V's consent. P intends to permanently deprive V of the car.

P has committed theft. D ought to be guilty of theft provided he or she believed that P, in taking the car, intended to permanently deprive V of it. However, if D believed that P did not intend to permanently deprive, D ought not to be guilty of theft but, rather, of taking a motor vehicle without the authority of its owner.

Example 3BB

D provides P with a baseball bat that P uses to intentionally cause grievous bodily harm to V.

In this example, D ought to be guilty of causing grievous bodily harm with intent provided that, when giving V the baseball bat, he believed that P, in using it to attack V, would do so with the intention of causing V serious bodily harm. D ought not to be guilty of the offence if he believed that P intended to inflict less than serious harm. In such a case D would be guilty of assault occasioning actual bodily harm, a lesser offence included within the greater offence, because D believed that P would attack V with the fault required to be convicted of that offence.

---

[107] Contrary to Offences against the Person Act 1861, s 18.

[108] It must be kept in mind in this discussion that, due to our previous recommendation, D's liability is already restricted by the need for D to intend that P commit the conduct element. Accordingly, in the examples that follow, it is assumed that D intends P to commit the conduct element.

3.118   By contrast,

> **Example 3CC**
>
> D and P live in a village 20 miles from the nearest hospital. D's wife is in labour and D is disqualified from driving. D knows that P had also been disqualified from driving but believes that P's disqualification has expired. D offers P £100 to drive D's wife to the hospital. P agrees to do so believing wrongly that his disqualification has expired.

In this example, P has committed the no-fault offence of driving while disqualified. However, D ought not to be guilty of driving while disqualified because he did not believe that P was committing the offence.

3.119   We acknowledge that in one respect, this might be thought to be too generous to D. In examples 3X and 3CC, P is guilty of a no-fault offence but D would not be. Nevertheless, we do not wish to see the scope of no-fault liability extended to secondary parties. As we state in Appendix B,[109] typically where an offence consists of a conduct and a circumstance element, the conduct element consists of an activity that in itself the law has no reason to punish. We acknowledge that there can be legitimate policy reasons for holding the perpetrator of the conduct liable despite he or she not being at fault in relation to the circumstance element. However, we are not persuaded that the same reasons apply with equal force to those whose conduct has only assisted or encouraged the perpetrator of the conduct.

3.120   In particular, while it will not *always* be the case, we believe that there will be many cases where P will be better placed than D to assess the circumstances in which his or her conduct takes place. Thus, in example 3X, it is P not D who knows V and can form an opinion as to her age. In example 3CC, P is far better placed to know if his disqualification has expired.

3.121   There will be occasions where D does not believe that P, in committing the conduct element, will be committing the principal offence but D's own state of mind is such that were he or she committing the conduct element, the offence would be committed:

> **Example 3DD**
>
> D and his daughter P, aged 16, are walking in the town when D sees V drop a £20 note. P then asks D if she may pick up and keep the note. D says 'yes go on' even though he realises that the note could easily be returned to V who is still standing nearby, because he thinks that P believes the note is lost and the owner untraceable. In fact, P did see V drop the note and is aware that V is still nearby.

---

[109] Para B.96.

In this example, P is almost certainly guilty of theft because she realised that the £20 note could easily be returned to its owner.[110] However, D thinks that P would *not* be acting with the fault element for theft, because D mistakenly thinks that P herself is acting in an honest way in picking up the note. So clause 1(2) would not be satisfied in this example because P does not think 'a person doing the act would commit the offence'. Nonetheless, clause 1(3) is satisfied because D's state of mind is such that had he done the act he would have committed the offence. Had D pocketed the note, he would have done so realising that it could easily be returned to its owner and that (barring exceptional circumstances) satisfies the test for dishonesty in theft. Accordingly, by virtue of clause 1(3), D participates in the theft committed by P.

Recommendation

3.122   **We recommend that for D to be convicted of a principal offence that P commits:**

(1)   **D must believe that P, in committing the conduct of the offence, would be committing the offence; or**

(2)   **D's state of mind is such that, were he or she committing the conduct element of the offence, he or she would commit the offence.**

Clause 2: participating in a joint criminal venture

Introduction

3.123   In Part 1, we explained that a joint criminal venture involves an agreement or a shared common intention between P and D to commit an offence – the agreed offence. In addition to or instead of the agreed offence, P may commit a collateral offence.

3.124   In the great majority of cases where the principal offence committed by P is the agreed offence rather than a collateral offence, the Bill makes it possible to convict D by virtue of clause 1 as well as clause 2. This is because if D and P have agreed to commit offence x, it will be an exceptional case where P is neither assisted nor encouraged by the agreement and D does not intend the conduct element to be committed. In addition, there are unlikely to be issues regarding the other elements of the agreed offence. Ordinarily, D will believe that should P (or another party to the joint criminal venture) commit the conduct element of the agreed offence, the offence will be committed.

---

[110] See Theft Act 1968, s 2(1)(c).

3.125   However, we can identify at least two kinds of case involving an agreed offence which would only fall within clause 2. The first kind is where the prosecution can show that D shared a common intention with P to commit an offence but cannot show that D provided P with any specific piece of assistance or encouragement. The second kind is the case where, despite agreeing with P to commit offence x and intending to assist or encourage P, D nevertheless does not intend that the conduct element should be committed. An example of this second kind is *Rook*[111] in which D was involved in a plan with P and others to murder V. At his trial, D testified that he did not intend that V should be killed. He said that he became involved in the hope of making some money. He claimed it was his belief that if he did not turn up on the day of the murder, P would refrain from committing the murder.[112]

3.126   In *Rook* the Court of Appeal held that D can be convicted of the agreed offence if he or she foresaw that it might be committed even if he or she did not intend that it would be committed. Previously, in *Chan Wing-siu*[113] the Privy Council had held that D could be convicted of a collateral offence if he or she foresaw that it might be committed even if he or she did not intend that it should be committed. In this respect in joint criminal venture cases, English law makes no distinction between the agreed offence (or offences) and collateral offences. Consequently, clause 2 (and the discussion that follows below) does not distinguish between the agreed offence (or offences) and collateral offences. Instead, clause 2(2) speaks simply of any 'criminal act [that] falls within the scope of the venture'. We have avoided the use of more intricate clauses which would have distinguished between agreed and collateral offences. Such clauses would have made the Bill too unwieldy and complex. The Bill, and clause 2 in particular, seeks to set out the law in a simple and intelligible manner.

D's state of mind in relation to the conduct element of the principal offence

THE ATTITUDE OF D TOWARDS THE COMMISSION OF THE CONDUCT ELEMENT

3.127   We recommended above that where D and P are not parties to a joint criminal venture, D must intend P to engage in the conduct element of the principal offence. Only that intent should be capable of turning what might otherwise be innocent conduct, such as selling a bat or knife, into conduct that justifies D being convicted of the principal offence committed by P.

---

[111] [1993] 2 All ER 955.

[112] Although it is possible to maintain that by initially participating in the plan D intended to assist or encourage P. See G R Sullivan, "Complicity for First degree Murder and Unlawful Killing" [2006] *Criminal Law Review* 502, 507. It is nevertheless clear that on D's testimoney, it was not D's intention that P should commit the conduct element of the offence.

[113] [1985] 1 AC 168.

3.128   We are recommending that very different principles should govern D's liability for offences committed by P pursuant to a joint criminal venture. In particular, D should not have to intend P to commit the conduct element of the principal offence (irrespective of whether the principal offence is the agreed offence or a collateral offence).[114] The reasons why, in cases where there is no joint criminal venture, D should not be convicted of P's offence unless he or she intended P to commit the conduct element do not apply where D and P are parties to a joint criminal venture. This is so even in the very unusual instance where the offence committed is the offence that D and P agreed to commit but D did not intend P to commit.[115] Although it might be said that, if D did not intend that the agreed offence should be committed, there was no 'shared criminal purpose', what is crucial is the fact that D agreed with P to commit the offence.

3.129   As we have said,[116] entering into an agreement with someone to commit an offence (or sharing a common intention with them to commit it) makes a distinct normative difference to D's position in point of liability. Such conduct on the part of D in and of itself creates obligations, commitments and expectations as to future conduct sufficient in themselves to justify imposing criminal liability on D where those obligations, commitments and expectations concern the commission of offences.

3.130   In saying this, we are not necessarily saying that joint criminal venture liability is doctrinally distinct from 'standard forms of secondary liability'[117] based on 'aiding, abetting, counselling or procuring' the commission of an offence. In arriving at our recommendations, we have not considered it necessary to express a preference for any of the competing views on the doctrinal issue.[118] Rather, we believe that the importance of any doctrinal difference is secondary to the normative difference that exists between joint criminal venture liability and other forms of secondary liability. It is this normative difference which underpins the recommendations in this report.

3.131   Professor Simester has explained the normative difference in the following way. We have in part already set it out[119] but it bears repetition:

---

[114] As noted above, it will be an exceptional case where D does not intend P to commit the conduct element of the agreed offence.

[115] See paras 3.125 and 3.126 above.

[116] See para 3.45 above.

[117] The expression is taken from Professor A P Simester, "The Mental Element in Complicity" (2006) 122 *Law Quarterly Review* 578, 592. Professor Simester is in no doubt that there is a doctrinal difference.

[118] See paras 3.47 to 3.58 above.

[119] See para 3.51 above.

Through entering into a joint enterprise, [D] changes her normative position. [D] becomes, by her deliberate choice, a participant in a group action to commit a crime. Moreover her new status has moral significance: she associates herself with the conduct of the other members of the group in a way that the mere aider and abettor, who remains an independent character throughout the episode does not. Whereas aiding and abetting doctrines are grounded in [D's] contribution to another's crime, joint enterprise is grounded in *affiliation*. [D] voluntarily subscribes to a co-operative endeavour, one that is identified by its shared criminal purpose. As such, joint enterprise doctrines impose a form of collective responsibility, predicated on membership of the unlawful concert... .

By forming a joint enterprise, [D] signs up to its goal. In doing so, she accepts responsibility for the wrongs perpetrated in realising that goal, even though they be done by someone else. Her joining with P in a common purpose means that she is no longer fully in command of how the purpose is achieved. Given that P is an autonomous agent, [D] cannot control the precise manner in which P acts. Yet her commitment to the common purpose implies an acceptance of the choices and actions that are taken by P in the course of realising that purpose.

By offering allegiance to the enterprise, [D] implicitly condones its furtherance. It is appropriate, where she does so to extend liability to the crimes that grow out of that wrong, whether or not they are individually aided or abetted.[120]

SHOULD D HAVE TO BELIEVE THAT P (OR ANOTHER PERSON) WILL COMMIT THE CONDUCT ELEMENT OF THE PRINCIPAL OFFENCE?

3.132 Having concluded that the fault element of clause 2 should be wider than that of clause 1 in order to take account of the normative difference, we now explore what that fault element should be.

---

[120] A P Simester, "The Mental Element in Complicity" (2006) 122 *Law Quarterly Review* 578, 598 to 600 (emphasis in original).

Introduction

3.133   In analysing the normative features of joint criminal venture liability, Professor Simester was not concerned with D's *attitude* towards the commission of the principal offence. Instead, he was considering whether, in order to be convicted of the principal offence, D had to know or believe that P would commit it or whether it sufficed that D believed that P might commit it. In *Chan Wing-siu*,[121] the offence that P and D agreed to commit was armed robbery. In the course of the robbery, P murdered V. The issue was whether D was guilty of V's murder. Murder is an offence that consists of a conduct element (for example an act of stabbing or shooting) and a consequence element (death of a human being). In addition, for P to be liable, he or she must intend to cause death or serious bodily harm. In delivering the opinion of the Privy Council, Sir Robin Cooke did not attempt to isolate each element of the offence with a view to considering D's state of mind in relation to each one. However, in upholding D's conviction for murder, the Privy Council established the following principle ('the *Chan Wing-siu* principle'):

> D can be convicted of an offence committed as an incident of a joint criminal venture if D foresaw that:
>
> (a)   P *might* commit the conduct element of the offence; and
>
> (b)   should P do so, P *might* do so with the state of mind required to be convicted of the offence.

Professor Simester believes that *Chan Wing-siu* was correctly decided. We agree and now set out our reasons.[122]

3.134   It is important to note that the following discussion will focus on collateral offences, not because we believe that the fault required of D should be any different from that required for agreed offences but, because collateral offences have emerged as the more controversial area.

---

[121] [1985] AC 168.

[122] The High Court of Australia has considered the issue on a number of occasions - *McAuliffe v The Queen* [1995] 183 CLR 108; *Gillard v The Queen* [2003] 219 CLR 1 and *Clayton v The Queen* [2006] HCA 58. On each occasion, the High Court has applied the *Chan Wing-siu* principle.

Understanding the Chan Wing-siu principle

3.135   Whatever may have been the position in earlier times, the *Chan Wing-siu* principle does not import an objective test for attributing liability to D for collateral offences. Thus, if the principal offence that P commits is rape, it is not enough that D ought to have foreseen that P might penetrate V. D must actually have contemplated that there was a more than negligible risk that P might do so. [123]

3.136   Further, D must foresee not merely that P might commit the conduct element of the principal offence but that, if P did commit it, he or she might do so with the fault element required to be convicted of the offence. In relation to murder, Professor Sir John Smith observed:

> The accessory to murder ... must be proved to have been reckless, not merely whether death might be caused, *but whether murder might be committed*: he must have been aware, not merely that death or grievously bodily harm might be caused, but that it might be caused intentionally by a person whom he was assisting or encouraging to commit a crime. Recklessness whether murder be committed is different from, and more serious than, recklessness whether death be caused by an accident.[124]

Judicial and academic reservations concerning the severity of the Chan Wing-siu principle

3.137   In *Powell and Daniels, English*, Lord Mustill was troubled by the fact that, under the *Chan Wing-siu* principle, D can be guilty of a collateral offence by virtue of mere foresight. Focusing on cases where D expresses to P his or her opposition to P committing a collateral offence, Lord Mustill said:

> Many would say, and I agree, that the conduct of [D] is culpable, although usually at a lower level than the culpability of [P] who actually does the deed.[125]

More recently in *Clayton v The Queen*[126], Kirby J delivered a strong dissenting judgement in the High Court of Australia. He said:

---

[123]   By contrast, section 21(2) of the Canadian Criminal Code uses an objective standard to assess liability. In language that is reminiscent of Foster, *Crown Cases* (1762 ed) p 372, s 21(2) provides that parties to a joint criminal venture are guilty of an offence if they "knew or ought to have known that the commission of the offence would be a probable consequence of carrying out the common purpose". In *Logan* (1988) [1990] 2 SCR 731 the Supreme Court of Canada concluded that, in permitting a conviction for attempted murder (an offence where subjective foresight is a constitutional requirement) on the basis of an objective test, s 21(2) was contrary to the Canadian Charter of Rights and Freedoms. In *Wise* (2002) BCCCA 80, the Court of Appeal for British Columbia held that "only subjective foresight of death could lead to liability for murder under the provisions of s 21(2)."

[124]   "Criminal Liability of Accessories: Law and Law Reform" (1997) 113 *Law Quarterly Review* 453, 464 (emphasis added). Professor John Smith did have some reservations – see para 3.138 below. However, it is noteworthy that another eminent "subjectivist" supported what we term the *Chan Wing-siu* principle. J H C Turner edited *Russell on Crime* (12th ed 1964). He wrote (p 162), "[D] should not be held liable for anything but what he either expressly commanded or *realised might be involved* in the performance of the project agreed upon." (emphasis added)

[125]   [1999] 1 AC 1, 11.

> To hold an accused liable for murder merely on the foresight of a possibility is fundamentally unjust. It may not be truly a fictitious or "constructive liability". But it countenances what is "undoubtedly a lesser form of mens rea". It is a form that is an exception to the normal requirements of criminal liability. And it introduces a serious disharmony in the law, particularly as that law affects the liability of secondary offenders to conviction for murder upon this basis.[127]

3.138 Likewise, Professor Sir John Smith thought that the *Chan Wing-siu* principle might be "too harsh". He suggested that the principle might be modified to "require intention (or even purpose) on the part of [D] that in the event which has occurred, [P] should act as he did".[128]

3.139 Professor Sullivan has suggested that consideration should be given to reforming the *Chan Wing-siu* principle by requiring that D should have foreseen the commission of the principal offence as not merely a possibility but as a probability or a high probability.[129]

Defending the Chan Wing-siu principle

3.140 First, a collateral offence will frequently be logically referable to the success of the joint criminal venture and, therefore, is of benefit to all the parties involved. Very often, the whole point of P committing the collateral offence is to enhance the likelihood of successfully committing the agreed offence, including ensuring that the participants, including D, are not apprehended or detected. In other words, P's commission of the collateral offence is done 'on behalf of' both P and D.

3.141 Secondly, D has agreed and chosen to participate with P in a venture which according to the terms of the agreement has a criminal objective - the commission of an agreed offence. As we argue below, such ventures have the potential to escalate and involve the commission of more serious offences.[130] This is, after all, something that D will be only too well aware of if he believes that there is a risk that P may, in addition to or instead of the agreed offence, commit a collateral offence. Ironically, evidence of this 'belief in the risk' can often be demonstrated by D's efforts to persuade P not to commit the particular collateral offence.

---

[126] [2006] HCA 58.

[127] Above, at [108].

[128] "Criminal Liability of Accessories: Law and Law Reform" (1997) 113 *Law Quarterly Review* 453, 465.

[129] G R Sullivan, "The Law Commission Consultation Paper on Complicity (2): Fault Elements and Joint Enterprise" [1994] *Criminal Law Review* 252, 261 to 263.

[130] See paras 3.144 to 146 below. This point is emphasised by Lord Steyn in *Powell and Daniels, English* [1999] 1 AC 1, 14.

3.142 Further, we do not believe that D, if he or she anticipates the possible commission of a range of different offences, ought to be able to pick and choose which of those offences he or she will be liable for, simply on the basis of his or her attitude towards their occurrence. It must be kept in mind that when D anticipates the commission of an offence as a possible incident of a joint criminal venture, D may well be anticipating that the offence may be committed by any party to the venture, including *him or herself*.

3.143 It is true that in *Powell and Daniels, English*, Lord Mustill said:

> Yet try as I may, I cannot accommodate ... culpability [for a collateral offence] within a concept of joint enterprise. How can a jury be directed at the same time that [D] is guilty only if he was a party to an express or tacit agreement to do the act in question, and that he is guilty if he not only disagreed with it, but made his disagreement perfectly clear to P? Are not the two assertions incompatible?[131]

However, in our view culpability for collateral offences can be accommodated within the concept of joint criminal venture. In entering into an agreement with P to commit offence x and at the same time foreseeing that P might commit offence y, D knowingly runs the risk that P will commit offence y. Although D may not agree to the commission of offence y and may hope that it will not be committed, his decision to continue to participate in the venture means that he or she is quite prepared to countenance its commission.

3.144 In November 2005 the Jill Dando Institute of Criminal Science, University College London published a report drawing mainly on 12 research studies comprising current or recently completed research projects covering a broad range of topics within the remit of gangs, guns and other weapons.[132] One section[133] of the report is entitled "Gangs and crime". It states that gang members commit over five times as many offences as non-gang members. One of the surveys that the report drew on found that 38% of those claiming to be part of a gang with a name and a territory had attacked someone, and 55% had vandalised property. According to the report:

> There is a strong social science research literature which shows that individuals in groups behave very differently than they do when alone. They take more risks, they feel pressure to conform with the majority, and they feel less personal responsibility.[134]

---

[131] [1999] 1 AC 1, 11.

[132] Marshall, B; Webb, B & Tilley N, *Rationalisation of Current Research on Guns, Gangs and Other Weapons: Phase 1* (2005).

[133] 3.4.

[134] Above. See further, Neal Kumar Katyal "Conspiracy theory" 112 *Yale Law Journal* (2003) 101.

3.145   Another section of the report focuses on weapons and gangs.[135] The report traces the literature which suggests that gang members are much more likely than others to carry weapons and guns with analysis of the data relating to those arrested showing that gang members are five times as likely as non-gang members to report owning a gun. A similar pattern is discernible in relation to knives. 39% of self-reported gang members admitted to carrying one within the previous twelve months compared to 7% of non-gang members. Most offences involving knives were thought to be carried out in the company of friends with peer pressure commonly cited as a motivating factor. Over a quarter of knife related homicides involved more than one offender. The report suggests that involvement with weapons is very much dependent on the level of gang involvement with street gangs rarely using guns to kill each other, preferring knives. These studies show that there is sound empirical support for Lord Steyn's opinion that, "Experience has shown that joint criminal [ventures] only too readily escalate into the commission of greater offences."[136] This opinion has been confirmed by American research. Professor Katyal has argued:

> What are somewhat less obvious … are psychological accounts of the dangers of group activity. Advances in psychology over the past thirty years have demonstrated that groups cultivate a special social identity. This identity often encourages risky behaviour, leads individuals to behave against their self-interest, solidifies loyalty, and facilitates harm against non-members… a study of active burglars… found that people in groups are more likely to be aroused, raising the possibility that group crimes lead to *unplanned* violence.[137]

3.146   It might be thought that employing such empirical evidence to ground D's liability in the way that we are recommending is severe on D. However, this is more than compensated for by three factors. First, there is the 'subjectivist' requirement that D must foresee that P may commit the principal offence. Secondly, D has the opportunity to claim that P's offence was too remote from the agreed offence to fall within the scope of the joint venture.[138] Thirdly, it is always open to D to withdraw from the joint venture by negating the effect of the original agreement before P commits the principal offence.[139]

---

[135] 5 – "Weapons and gangs".

[136] *Powell and Daniels, English* [1999] 1 AC 1, 14.

[137] Neal Kumar Katyal "Conspiracy theory" 112 *Yale Law Journal* (2003) 101 at 104 and 110 (our emphasis), citing Paul Cromwell and others "Group effects on decision-making by burglars" 69 *Psychological Reports* 579 at 586. Professor Cromwell found that burglars tended to "pscyh each other up".

[138] See paras 3.153 to 3.166 below.

[139] See paras 3.60 to 3.67 above.

Logical incongruity

3.147   We acknowledge that under the *Chan Wing-siu* principle D can be convicted of a collateral offence committed by P if he or she foresees that P might perpetrate its conduct element, whereas it may be that P can only be convicted of that offence if he or she intended to commit the conduct element. However, despite Lord Hutton suggesting otherwise,[140] there is no *logical* incongruity in stipulating different fault elements for principal offenders and secondary parties. The conduct of each is different and, accordingly, there is no logical reason why the fault element must be the same for each.

Substituting a test of foresight of probability

3.148   In recognition of the criticism levelled at the *Chan Wing-siu* principle, we should consider an alternative. Professor Sullivan has suggested that the test should be whether P foresaw it as probable or highly probable that P would commit the conduct element of the collateral offence.[141] At first sight, section 66(2) of the New Zealand Crimes Act 1961 lends support to Professor Sullivan. It provides that D is liable for a collateral offence if the commission of the offence "was known [by D] to be a probable consequence of the prosecution of the common purpose." However, the provision has been interpreted so that D is liable if he or she believes that there is "a real or substantial risk" that the collateral offence will be committed.[142] In other words, D need only foresee a realistic possibility that the collateral offence will be committed.

3.149   Determining the meaning of 'probable' or 'highly probable' is fraught with difficulty. Recently in *Darkan v The Queen*[143] the High Court of Australia had to consider section 8 of the Queensland Criminal Code. Section 8, like section 21(2) of the Canadian Criminal Code, contains an objective test for determining D's liability for a collateral offence committed by P. It provides that D is liable for the offence if "its commission was a probable consequence" of D and P having "a common intention to prosecute an unlawful purpose". The High Court considered no less than four possible meanings of 'probable' including 'a probability of less than 50%, but more than a substantial or real and not remote possibility' and 'a substantial or real and not remote possibility'.[144] The Court, in rejecting a submission that the trial judge had wrongly directed the jury as to the meaning of 'a probable consequence' stressed that the meaning of the phrase "is not relatively simple".[145]

---

[140] *Powell and Daniels, English* [1999] 1 AC 1. However, Lord Hutton was in no doubt (p 25) that the *Chan Wing-siu* principle was justified because of "practical considerations of weight and importance related to considerations of public policy ... which prevail over considerations of strict logic".

[141] This was the very point on which the appeal in *Chan Wing-siu* was founded.

[142] *Te Moni* [1998] 1 NZLR 641.

[143] [2006] HCA 34.

[144] Above, [27].

[145] Above, [68].

3.150   The High Court concluded that, in the context of section 8, 'probable' did not mean 'on the balance of probabilities' but did mean more than 'a real or substantial possibility or chance'. The majority of the Court, having reached that conclusion, said it is:

> … difficult to arrive at a verbal formula for what it does mean and for what the jury may be told. The expression "a probable consequence" means that the occurrence of the consequence need not be more probable than not, but must be probable as distinct from possible. It must be probable in the sense that it could well happen.[146]

We are not persuaded that the law would be improved by a test that would involve a jury being directed in such terms.

Recommendation

3.151   **We recommend that, if P and D are parties to a joint criminal venture, D satisfies the fault required in relation to the conduct element of the principal offence committed by P if:**

   (1)   D intended that P (or another party to the venture) should commit the conduct element;

   (2)   D believed that P (or another party to the venture) would commit the conduct element; or

   (3)   D believed that P (or another party to the venture) might commit the conduct element.

3.152   The reference to 'or another party to the venture' reflects the fact that at the time of entering into the joint criminal venture, D may have no settled knowledge or belief as to who will commit the conduct element. Indeed, at that stage, it is possible that D may believe that he or she is the person who will commit the conduct element.

   'Scope of the venture'

LIMITING D'S LIABILITY EVEN THOUGH D INTENDS OR BELIEVES THAT P WILL OR MIGHT COMMIT THE CONDUCT ELEMENT OF THE PRINCIPAL OFFENCE

3.153   Our recommendations would, in the majority of joint criminal ventures, provide a more focused and precise means of determining liability. However, there will be such cases where, although D intended or believed that P would or might commit the conduct element of the principal offence, the particular act that P does in committing the conduct element is factually different from the act that D intended or expected P to commit. Such cases can arise regardless of whether the principal offence is the agreed offence or a collateral offence.

3.154   An example in the context of an agreed offence is:

---

[146] Above [78] to [79].

Example 3EE

D sees P in an altercation with X in a public house. D, who hates X, urges P to hit X and gives P a stick with which to do so. However, P, by chance seeing V, an ex girlfriend flirting with another man, instead hits V with the stick.

In this example, D may dispute his or her liability on the basis that he or she did not intend or foresee V being assaulted. However, D did foresee P committing an assault and this is what P has done.

3.155   An example in the context of a collateral offence is:

Example 3FF

D and P agree to commit a burglary. D, knowing that P is armed with a gun, realises that P may use his gun to murder anyone who disturbs them in the course of the burglary. D urges P not to do so. In the event, D and P are not disturbed. However, in the course of the burglary, by chance P sees a rival gang leader, V, walking past. P takes the opportunity to shoot V dead.

Again, D is likely to feel aggrieved if he or she is convicted as a secondary party to P's murder of V. Yet, D foresaw that P might commit murder in the course of the venture and this is what P has done.

3.156   We believe that the law would be too harsh if no account could be taken of the extent to which P's act was not the act that D intended P to commit or foresaw that P might commit. However, having agreed to participate in a joint criminal venture, D ought not to escape liability for P's offence *merely* because the specifics of the act of P differed from the act that D intended or foresaw that P might commit. The law should require that the act committed by P is an act that comes within the definition of the conduct element of the principal offence but not that it has to be identical to the act that D intended or foresaw might be committed. If the act had to be identical, the law would be brought into disrepute. For example, if D and P agreed to commit criminal damage using a hammer to smash a window, it would be absurd if D avoided liability for P's offence if it emerged that P had used a spanner.

3.157   The difficulty lies in identifying a suitable test to cater for cases where P's act in committing the agreed offence or the collateral offence is not the particular act that D intended or believed would be committed. One possibility would be to formulate a statutory test based on the concept of 'remoteness'. The idea would be that D should not be liable for P's act if the circumstances in which it was committed made it too far from or too distantly connected to what D intended for such liability to be a fair reflection of the joint nature of their venture.

3.158   However, there could be problems with the interpretation of a concept such as 'remoteness'. 'Remoteness' is a concept familiar to civil lawyers as being concerned with, for example, unexpected consequences (damage suffered) flowing from a binding agreement. We are, in contrast, concerned with the fairness of whether or not certain conduct should be treated as a joint criminal venture.

3.159   So, in clause 2, we have opted for the simplest course. The question for the jury will be one of fact and degree: have the prosecution shown that the act fell within the scope of the joint criminal venture? This test should not be made more complex by additional legal tests being superimposed upon it.

3.160   In line with this test, the mere occurrence of some delay or the fact that P deviates from the act that D intended would not necessarily relieve D of liability for P's offence:

> **Example 3GG**
>
> D and P hatch a plot to harm V. D writes P a letter urging P to burn down V's house. P puts the letter away in a drawer. A year later, brooding on the contents of the letter, P is moved to commit the offence that D encouraged him to commit.

> **Example 3HH**
>
> D and P, two racists, agree that P to set fire to the local Afro-Caribbean community centre. P, finding blanket security at the centre, instead sets fire to a local public house that is frequented by people from the centre. Unbeknown to P, D's brother owns the public house.

3.161   In each example, there are strong grounds for the tribunal of fact to find that D is liable for the offence that P commits. Admittedly, in example 3HH, it was not D's intention that his own brother's public house should be targeted and in example 3GG a long period of time has elapsed. However, the decision will be for the jury based on the totality of the facts. A jury will take account of factors such as the interval between D and P's agreement and P's commission of the offence, the context in which D's agreement took place and whether, in the jury's opinion, D would nevertheless have agreed to the joint criminal venture had he or she anticipated the particular act committed by P. However, no one factor will necessarily prove conclusive.

3.162   In examples 3GG and 3HH, the offence committed by P is the agreed offence. Likewise, in the context of collateral offences, the fact that P did not commit the act to secure the success of the joint venture (even if combined with D expressing his or her opposition to P doing the act) should not necessarily lead the tribunal of fact to conclude that P's act was outside the scope of the venture. As the test is one of fact and degree, the way that cases are resolved, such as example 3FF, will inevitably be heavily dependent on their specific facts.

3.163   The same test, of fact and degree, will apply when the principal offence is murder. In Part 5 of our consultation paper *A New Homicide Act for England and Wales?*[147] in which we address complicity in the context of homicide, there was not space to address this question of 'scope'. The omission was criticised by some commentators but we always believed that the principle should apply to murder as to any other crime:

Example 3JJ

D agrees with P, a professional assassin, to provide P with a gun to murder D's wife. P is then paid a large sum of money by X to murder X's wife, V. P murders V with D's gun. P does not shoot D's wife.

In this example, under the recommendations that we made in the first report, D would be guilty of the inchoate offence of assisting or encouraging murder and could be sentenced to anything up to and including life imprisonment. It does not necessarily follow that D should be convicted of V's murder. It should be open to the tribunal of fact, following the principle now under discussion, to find that what P did was not within the scope of the joint criminal venture with D.

TRANSFERRED MALICE

3.164   The purpose of the 'scope of the venture' test is to avoid rigid criteria which would unfairly criminalise certain defendants. However, the fact that P's act can be so remote from what D intended or anticipated so as to fall outside the scope of the joint criminal venture does not affect the application of the doctrine of 'transferred malice'.[148] In examples 3GG, 3HH and 3JJ, P's potential departure from the scope of the joint venture comes through a conscious decision on P's part. By contrast, a potential departure could equally arise as a result of some mischance or accident in the furtherance of the venture:

Example 3KK

D encourages P to hit X and gives P a stick with which to do it. D takes a swing at X but X ducks and the blow strikes and injures V.

In this example, P's action in swinging at X takes place in pursuance of the joint criminal venture. Accordingly a jury should be told that the fact that P happens to miss X and hit V cannot in itself relieve either P or D of liability for an offence against V. This is not only consistent with the 'scope of the venture' test, but also accords with normal principles of transferred malice.

---

[147] (2005) Law Com No 177.

[148] For the meaning of 'transferred malice' see Appendix B, n 121.

3.165   The question of 'scope' in the Bill is isolated to clause 2 and so it will not cover acts of assistance or encouragement outside of a joint criminal venture. We have chosen to isolate the provision because, in practical terms, it is very unlikely that this type of dispute will arise outside of the context of a joint criminal venture. Having said this, we remain open to the possibility of extending the provision to include non-joint venture cases. This would, however, require an amendment to clause 1 of the Bill.

Recommendation

3.166   **We recommend that, even if D intended or believed that P would or might commit the conduct element of the principal offence, he or she should nevertheless not stand to be convicted under clause 2 of the principal offence if P's actions in committing the principal offence fell outside the scope of the joint venture.**

The fault required of D in relation to elements of the principal offence other than the conduct element

3.167   In explaining clause 1, we referred to the fact that undesirable consequences would follow if the issue of D's fault was confined exclusively to the conduct element of the principal offence. The same is true in relation to joint criminal ventures.

3.168   For D to be liable by virtue of clause 1, he or she must believe that in committing the conduct element P would be committing the principal offence. In relation to joint criminal ventures, we are recommending a similar fault requirement but with an important difference. We have explained that the normative features of joint criminal ventures justifies a less stringent fault requirement in relation to the conduct element of the principal offence. Likewise, we believe that it does so in relation to the other elements of the offence. D should not have to believe that, in committing the conduct element, P would commit the principal offence. It should suffice that D believes that in committing the conduct element, P might commit the principal offence:

Example 3LL

D and P agree to commit a burglary. D believes that, should V interrupt them, D might attack V. D is uncertain regarding the intention with which P might attack V. However, he foresees the possibility that P might attack V intending to cause serious harm to V. In the event, V does interrupt them and P attacks V intentionally causing V serious bodily harm.

P has committed the offence of causing grievous bodily harm with intent. Likewise, D would be guilty of the offence because he believed that P might commit the offence.

Recommendation

3.169 **We recommend that, if D and P are parties to a joint criminal venture, for D to be convicted of a principal offence that P commits, D must believe that P, in committing the conduct element of the offence, might be committing the offence.**

PART 4
CAUSING OTHERS TO COMMIT OFFENCES

INTRODUCTION

4.1   In this Part we set out and explain our recommendations:

(1)   for replacing the common law doctrine of innocent agency with a statutory version of the doctrine; and

(2)   for a new offence of causing a person to commit a no-fault offence which would replace the current law whereby D incurs secondary liability for 'procuring' P to commit a no-fault offence.

'Procuring' as a basis of secondary liability

4.2   In Part 3, we recommended that section 8 of the Accessories and Abettors Act 1861 should be repealed and that the conduct element of secondary liability should consist of assisting and encouraging. Section 8 currently enables D to be convicted of an offence as a secondary party if he or she 'procures' the commission of an offence. 'Procuring' implies a special kind of causal link between D's conduct and P's commission of the principal offence. Where D procures P's offence, the offence would not have taken place without D's conduct (or D's conduct together with that of another who jointly with D procures the offence).[1] That kind of causal link is not required when D merely encourages or assists P to commit the principal offence. In such cases, D can be liable even though P would have gone on to commit the offence without D's assistance or encouragement.

4.3   Although a scheme of secondary liability limited to 'assisting' and 'encouraging' would encompass certain cases that currently fall within the concept of 'procuring', it would not cover all of them.[2] In this Part, we explain how cases of 'procuring' would be accommodated within the scheme that we are recommending.

4.4   The inclusion of 'procuring' in section 8 means that under the current law D can be convicted as a secondary party in three situations despite P not having committed a principal offence:

(1)   D causes P to commit the conduct element of an offence that P cannot commit because P is under the age of criminal responsibility or is insane;

(2)   D causes a non-culpable P to commit the conduct element of an offence that requires fault on the part of P. P commits no offence because he or she does not satisfy the fault element of the offence;

---

[1]   *Attorney-General's Reference (No 1 of 1975)* [1975] QB 773, 780.

[2]   The exception would be cases where D encourages P to commit an offence and the encouragement takes the form of threatening P with violence.

(3)   P perpetrates the conduct element of an offence following threats of violence (duress) by D. P is not guilty of the offence despite satisfying the fault element of the offence because duress is a complete defence.

4.5   Under our recommendations, in cases within category (3), D would still be liable as a secondary party even though P would not have committed a principal offence.[3] In cases within categories (1) and (2), D would be liable as a principal offender by virtue of the statutory doctrine of innocent agency that we are recommending should replace the common law doctrine of innocent agency.

4.6   Under the current law, in cases falling within categories (1) and (2), D is usually convicted as a principal offender (under the common law doctrine of innocent agency) rather than as a secondary party. However, sometimes it is not possible in such cases to invoke the doctrine to convict D as a principal offender because:

(1)   the conduct element of the principal offence may be defined in such a way that, as a matter of law, D cannot perpetrate it as a principal offender. For example, suppose D, a bachelor, encourages P, a married woman, to go through a ceremony of marriage with him by falsely persuading her that her current marriage is void. Only those who are married can commit the conduct element of the offence of bigamy. It is, therefore, wrong to posit that D himself commits bigamy through the innocent agency of P.[4]

(2)   the principal offence can only be committed by a member of a particular class of persons and D is not such a person. For example, D, aged 40, falsely persuades P, aged 40, who is the sole person who has trust and care of V, aged 17, that P is at liberty to engage in sexual activity with V because the relationship of trust and care has come to an end. Only a person who abuses a position of trust can be guilty of the relevant offence and D is not such a person.[5]

4.7   In order to convict D, the courts have resorted to the concept of 'procuring'. In doing so, they have held that D can be convicted as a secondary party by virtue of having procured the commission of the conduct element of an offence. These cases[6] are exceptions to the derivative nature of secondary liability and, according to Professor Ashworth, represent "the high-water mark of causal connection among the various types of accessorial conduct".[7]

---

[3]   For our reasons, see paras 4.11 to 4.13 below.

[4]   A further example is rape. The law defines rape in such a way that a woman cannot commit the offence as a principal offender – see Sexual Offences Act 2003, s 1.

[5]   In the example, the relevant offence is abusing a position of trust and engaging in sexual activity with a child contrary to Sexual Offences Act 2003, s 16. In the example, it is assumed that P has good reason to believe what he is told by D. Therefore, P is an innocent agent of D.

[6]   *Cogan and Leak* [1976] QB 217; *Millward* [1994] *Criminal Law Review* 527; *DPP v K and B* [1997] 1 Cr App R 36.

[7]   *Principles of Criminal Law* (4th ed 2003) p 423.

A STATUTORY DOCTRINE OF INNOCENT AGENCY

The elements of the doctrine

4.8 The essence of the doctrine should continue to be what it is at common law. Under our recommendations, D would be guilty of an offence as a principal offender if he or she uses an innocent agent, P, to commit an offence. However, our recommendations would address the limitations of the current common law doctrine.

Liability not restricted by special characteristics required of principal offender

4.9 The common law doctrine of innocent agency encounters difficulty in coping with cases where the principal offence can only be committed by those who meet a particular description, for example, only men can commit rape and only married persons can commit bigamy. Accordingly, clause 3 of the Bill provides that, if an offence is one that may be committed only by a person who meets a particular description, D can be guilty of the offence even though he or she does not meet the description. Thus, although by virtue of section 1(1)(a) of the Sexual Offences Act 2003 a woman cannot be convicted of rape as a principal offender, it would be possible for a woman to be convicted of rape if she uses an innocent agent, P, to perpetrate the conduct element of rape.

Meaning of innocent agent

4.10 Under our recommendations, P would be an innocent agent if he or she perpetrated the conduct element of a principal offence but was not guilty of the offence because:

    (1)   P was under the age of 10;

    (2)   P had a defence of insanity; or

    (3)   P acted without the fault required for conviction of the principal offence.

4.11 We have considered whether the doctrine should also apply in cases where the reason why P does not commit the principal offence is that P has a complete defence, for example, duress[8] or, if the principal offence is murder, a partial defence, for example, provocation or diminished responsibility.[9] We recognise that there is a case for including such persons and that not to do so would perpetuate exceptions to the derivative theory of secondary liability. Further, we acknowledge that we have previously recommended that in such cases D should be liable as a principal offender.[10]

---

[8] Duress is a complete defence to all offences apart from murder, attempted murder and possibly some forms of treason.

[9] Provocation and diminished responsibility are partial defences to murder. If successfully pleaded, they result in a conviction for manslaughter.

[10] Criminal Law: A Criminal Code for England and Wales (1977) Law Com No 177, cl 26 (1)(c).

4.12   We believe, however, that they are exceptions in only the narrowest sense. Although a successful plea of duress excuses P from liability, P has not only perpetrated the conduct element of the principal offence but has done so with the requisite fault element. Likewise, a successful plea of provocation or diminished responsibility does not alter the fact that P has committed the conduct element of murder with the requisite fault element.

4.13   On balance, we are persuaded that such cases are conceptually distinct from those where the reason that P does not commit the principal offence is either because P lacks capacity or acts without the requisite fault element. Neither duress, on the one hand, nor provocation or diminished responsibility, on the other, renders P a wholly innocent agent. In both cases, P is aware of the nature of the act that he or she is committing and the circumstances in which he or she is committing it. This is not altered by the fact that in cases of duress, D is the source of P's claim to be excused. D should continue to be liable as a secondary party.[11]

SEMI-INNOCENT AGENTS

4.14   In Part 2, we explained that the common law had encountered difficulties in cases where two offences of different seriousness consisted of the same conduct element but had different fault elements. Following the disapproval of *Richards*[12] by the House of Lords in *Howe,*[13] it is now settled that, if D satisfies the fault element of the more serious offence, he or she can be convicted of that offence despite P only satisfying the fault element of the less serious offence.[14]

4.15   Under our recommendations, the basis of D's liability for the more serious offence would be clear. Provided that D had intended to and did cause P to perpetrate the conduct element of the more serious offence, D would be liable for the more serious offence as a principal offender. P would be an innocent agent in relation to that offence because he or she would not have satisfied its fault element.

'Using' P to commit the principal offence

4.16   D must satisfy three requirements before he or she can be held to have "used" P to commit the principal offence:

   (1)   D must intend to cause a person, whether P or another person, to commit the conduct element of the principal offence;

   (2)   D must cause P to commit the conduct element; and

   (3)   D must be at fault in relation the principal offence.

We consider briefly each of these requirements.

---

[11]   Clause 8(1) of the Bill provides that encouraging a person to do an act includes doing so by threatening that person. Accordingly, under our scheme, in cases of duress D would have 'encouraged' P.

[12]   [1974] QB 776.

[13]   [1987] AC 417.

[14]   See example 2H in Part 2, para 2.18 and Appendix B, para B.10.

INTENDING TO CAUSE A PERSON (WHETHER P OR ANOTHER PERSON) TO COMMIT THE CONDUCT ELEMENT OF THE PRINCIPAL OFFENCE

'Intending' to cause

4.17   Consider the following example:

Example 4A

D, the owner of a shotgun forgets that he has left it loaded on the kitchen table. His seven-year-old son picks it up and accidentally shoots and kills V, the postman.[15]

D did not intend to cause P to perpetrate the conduct element of manslaughter.

4.18   Professor K J M Smith has pointed out that:

> There is no inherent conceptual restriction of innocent agency to cases where the defendant has intentionally or purposefully caused or brought about the innocent agent's actions.[16]

Accordingly, it is arguable that the doctrine can and should apply if D is culpable in the way required by the principal offence, in this case, manslaughter by gross negligence. Indeed, this is the view that the Commission adopted when it published its draft Criminal Code Bill.[17]

4.19   However, we now believe that the notion of 'agency' in innocent agency implies that D intends to act through P. P cannot properly be said to be the agency through which D him or herself acts unless D intended that P should act in a particular way. Accordingly, in example 4A, under our recommendation, D would not be guilty of manslaughter by virtue of innocent agency. Rather, determining whether D was guilty of manslaughter would involve consideration of the orthodox principles of primary liability: was D's breach of duty in leaving the gun on the table a sufficiently proximate cause of V's death and, if so, was he grossly negligent in leaving the gun as he did?

'P or another person'

4.20   In most cases it will be D's intention to cause P to commit the conduct element of the offence and it will be P who commits it. However, D ought not to escape liability merely because D intended that someone other than P should commit the conduct element:

Example 4B

D sends a letter to his nine-year-old nephew, X, telling him to set fire to the local cricket club's pavilion. D tells X that if he does so, D will buy X and his eight-year-old brother, P, a present. X shows the letter to P and it is P who sets fire to the pavilion.

---

[15]   An example provided by Professor K J M Smith, *A Modern Treatise on the Law of Criminal Complicity* (1991) p 98.

[16]   Above, p 98.

Although D did not intend that P should set fire to the pavilion, D is as culpable as he would have been had X had set fire to the pavilion.

Variation in the details of the conduct element

4.21   Further, while it must be D's intention that someone commit the conduct element of the principal offence, it should be irrelevant whether the act perpetrated by P in committing the conduct element of the offence was the particular act that D intended should be perpetrated:

Example 4C

P, aged 9, is staying with his grandmother, V. D telephones P and promises to give P a present if he steals a video recorder from V. P cannot find any video recorder. However, anxious to secure the present, P takes a digital radio and gives it to D.

D's intention was that P should commit the conduct element of theft by appropriating V's property. P has done what D intended albeit the item of property taken is not what D intended. That should not prevent D being convicted of theft. It would be different if P, annoyed at not finding the recorder, had decided to set fire to V's premises. D had not intended that the conduct element of arson should be committed and, ought not to be guilty of arson.

'CAUSING' P TO PERPETRATE THE CONDUCT ELEMENT OF THE PRINCIPAL OFFENCE

4.22   In most cases it will be clear whether D has caused P to commit the conduct element. However, there will be borderline cases:

Example 4D

D comes across his son P, aged 9, assaulting another child V, aged 6. Rather than stop P attacking V, D urges P to step up the attack. V suffers multiple bruising.

On one view, D has not caused P to attack V because P was already attacking V before D intervened. However, despite not causing P initially to attack V, we believe that D ought to be liable by virtue of urging P to continue the attack. Accordingly, clause 11(3) of the Bill provides that the doing of a criminal act includes 'the continuation of an act that has already begun'.

4.23   By contrast:

Example 4E

D's son P, aged 9, tells D that he has made up his mind to attack V aged 6. D urges P to go ahead with the plan. P does so inflicting actual bodily harm on V.

---

[17]   Criminal Law: A Criminal Code for England and Wales (1977) Law Com No 177, cl 26 (1).

In the first report, we made recommendations that would enable D in this example to be held inchoately liable for encouraging P to commit assault occasioning actual bodily harm.[18] However, D cannot be convicted of the principal offence by virtue of innocent agency because he has not caused P to do the act of assaulting V.

BEING AT FAULT IN RELATION TO THE PRINCIPAL OFFENCE

Principal offences that require proof of fault

4.24 We are recommending that, if a particular state of mind must be proved for conviction of the offence that D uses P to commit, D's state of mind must be such that were he or she to engage in the conduct element, it would be with that state of mind:

> **Example 4F**
>
> D tells his 6-year-old son, P, to go to the grocer and purchase a carton of milk. D gives P the money to pay for it. Instead, P goes to the shop and takes the milk without paying.

Had P been an adult, he would have committed theft because he appropriated the milk 'dishonestly'. D is not guilty of theft because, although he intended to and has caused P to perpetrate the conduct element of theft, he did not do so 'dishonestly'.

Principal offences that do not require proof of fault

4.25 Cases where D will be liable for a no-fault offence by virtue of the statutory doctrine of innocent agency that we are recommending will be very rare. They will be cases where D causes P, a person who is under the age of criminal responsibility, to commit the conduct element of a no-fault offence.[19] If such a case were to arise, D should have to know or believe that were P to commit the conduct element, P would do so in the circumstances and with the consequences required for conviction of the principal offence:

> **Example 4G**
>
> D allows her nine-year-old son, P, to drive her car on a public road. Unknown to D, her husband had given P some beer shortly before D allowed P to drive the car. As a result, P is in excess of the prescribed limit when driving the vehicle.

Under our recommendations, D would not be guilty of driving with excess alcohol because she did not know that P was in excess of the prescribed limit.

---

[18] See para 5.105.

[19] In *DPP v H* [1997] 1 WLR 1406 the Divisional Court held that insanity is not a defence to a no-fault offence. Accordingly, if D causes P, who is insane, to commit a no-fault offence, P is guilty of the offence and D is also guilty of the offence as a secondary party. Simester and Sullivan, *Criminal Law Theory and Doctrine* (2nd ed 2003) p 178 is very critical of *DPP v H*.

Summary

4.26   Professor Ashworth has stated:

> Some offences are phrased in terms which imply personal agency (rape is said to be one) or which apply only to the holder of a certain office or licence. There is no reason why the law should be constrained by [the linguistic] barrier.[20]

We agree. It is for this reason that, although the statutory doctrine of innocent agency that we are recommending is not dissimilar to the common law doctrine, we have endeavoured to free the doctrine from the constraints that confine its scope at common law.

Recommendations[21]

4.27   **We recommend that:**

(1)   **if D uses an innocent agent (P) to commit an offence ("the principal offence"), D is guilty of the principal offence.**

(2)   **P is an innocent agent if:**

(a)   **he or she commits the conduct element of the principal offence; and**

(b)   **he or she does not commit the principal offence itself solely because:**

(i)   **he or she is under the age of 10;**

(ii)   **he or she has a defence of insanity; or**

(iii)   **he or she acts without the fault required for conviction of the principal offence.**

(3)   **D uses P to commit the principal offence if:**

(a)   **D intends to cause a person (whether or not P) to commit the conduct element of the principal offence;**

(b)   **D causes P to commit the conduct element of the principal offence; and**

(c)   **D is at fault in relation to the principal offence.**

(4)   **D is at fault in relation to the principal offence if:**

---

[20]   *Principles of Criminal Law* (4th ed 2003) p 438.

[21]   Clause 4 of the Bill and clause 8(b) of the Supplementary Bill.

(a) where conviction of the principal offence requires proof of fault, D's state of mind is such that, were he or she to commit the conduct element of the principal offence, he or she would do it with the state of mind necessary to be convicted of the offence; or

(b) where conviction of the principal offence does not require proof of fault, D knows or believes that were a person to commit the conduct element of the principal offence, that person would do so:

(i) in the circumstances (if any); and

(ii) with the consequences (if any)

proof of which is required for conviction of the principal offence.

(5) D may be guilty of the principal offence through using P to commit the offence:

(a) even though the principal offence is one that may be committed only by a person who meets a particular description; and

(b) D does not meet that description.

(6) The common law doctrine of innocent agency should be abolished.

CAUSING THE COMMISSION OF A NO-FAULT OFFENCE

4.28 In the CP,[22] the Commission suggested that, in addition to the two inchoate offences then proposed of encouraging crime and assisting crime, there might be a case for a separate offence of 'procurement'. The offence would have imposed secondary liability on D for procuring the commission of a no-fault offence. The offence would have covered the situation where D 'laces' P's non-alcoholic drink and as a result P commits the offence of driving with excess alcohol. A significant number of respondents agreed.

4.29 However, we no longer believe that there should be a separate offence of 'procuring' whereby D incurs liability as a secondary party for the principal offence that P commits. Instead, we believe that there should be a discrete offence of causing another person to commit a no-fault offence. The offence is necessary because under our scheme secondary liability would be confined to conduct that consists of encouraging or assisting. It is inappropriate to describe D's conduct in causing P to commit a no-fault offence as encouraging or assisting P to commit the offence.

---

[22] Para 4.196.

The elements of the offence

4.30 D would commit the offence if he or she caused P to commit a no-fault offence and:

(1) it was D's intention that a person, whether or not P, should commit the offence; or

(2) D knew or believed that his behaviour would cause the offence to be committed.

D does not have to cause P to commit the conduct element of the offence

4.31 Rather than requiring D to have caused P to commit the conduct element of the offence in every case, it suffices that D causes P to commit the offence. In this sense, causing the presence of the circumstances which make the commission of the conduct element a criminal offence will suffice:

Example 4H

D and P are in a pub. D knows that P will be driving home. D "laces" P's non-alcoholic drink with a large vodka. P drives home and is stopped. He is in excess of the prescribed limit because of the vodka dispensed by D. P is convicted of driving with excess alcohol.

D has not caused P to commit the conduct element of the offence (driving). However, D has caused the driving to take place in circumstances that make the driving a criminal offence. D has caused P to commit a no-fault offence.

4.32 By contrast:

Example 4J

D invites P to dinner. P drives to D's home and D knows that P will be driving back to his house. D generously refills P's glass of wine regularly. In fact, D is very anxious that P drinks plenty of alcohol because D and P are applicants for a position that requires the post holder to have a current driving licence. P drives home, is breathalysed and found in excess of the prescribed limit. P is disqualified for three years from holding or obtaining a driving licence.

In this example, P was aware of what he was drinking and acted as an autonomous and fully informed individual. Consequently, D is guilty of the principal offence committed by P because D has assisted and encouraged but has not caused P to commit that offence.

The person that D intended to commit the no-fault offence need not be P

4.33 As with the statutory doctrine of innocent agency, it does not have to be D's intention that the offence be committed by P as opposed to some other person:

> **Example 4K**
>
> D is at a party with P and X. P and X are drinking non-alcoholic drinks as they will be driving home. D is aware of this. D, who hates X, slips a large vodka into what he thinks is X's glass. In fact, the glass is P's. P leaves the party and drives home. He is stopped, breathalysed and found to be over the limit. Ultimately, P is convicted of driving with excess alcohol.

D ought to be guilty of causing P to commit a no-fault offence. D's culpability is in no way reduced by the fact that he was mistaken as to who would drink the vodka. It should suffice that D intended that a person should commit the offence.

D's attitude towards the commission of the no-fault offence

4.34   We have considered whether it should suffice if D knew or believed that his or her behaviour *might* cause a person to commit a no-fault offence. In *Blakely and Sutton v DPP*[23] the Divisional Court suggested that such a state of mind would fix D with secondary liability for procuring the commission of a no-fault offence.[24]

4.35   In the CP,[25] the Commission said that, "it would seem to be correct" that D could be liable on the basis of foreseeing a risk that the no-fault offence might be committed. Respondents expressed differing views as to how the offence might be defined.

4.36   Notwithstanding the decision in *Blakely and Sutton V DPP*, we believe that the basis of liability would be too wide if it encompassed foresight of a risk of P committing the offence. At the same time, we believe that the basis of liability would be too narrow if it was restricted to cases where D intends P to commit the offence. Admittedly, in most cases D will be acting in order to bring about the commission of the offence. However, we see no reason why D should not also be liable if he or she believed that his or her behaviour would cause P to commit the no-fault offence.

Recommendation[26]

4.37   **We recommend that:**

> (1)   **there should be an offence of causing the commission of a no-fault offence which D would commit if he or she caused another person to commit a no-fault offence and**
>
> > (a)   **it was D's intention that a person should commit the offence; or**

---

[23]   [1991] RTR 405.

[24]   It was a very unusual case in that, in 'lacing' P's drink, it was D's intention that P should *not* drive. Unfortunately, P drove off before D could tell him what she had done. In the CP, the Commission said that it thought that *Blakely and Sutton v DPP* was an accurate statement of the law. However, not only were the observations of the Divisional Court unnecessary to the decision but they are difficult to reconcile with the 'procuring' case of *A-G's Reference (No 1 of 1975)* [1975] QB 773, a decision of the Court of Appeal.

[25]   Para 4.195.

[26]   Clause 5 of the Bill and cl 6(2) of the Supplementary Bill.

        (b)   **D knew or believed that his or her behaviour would cause a person to commit it;**

(2)   a person convicted of the offence should be liable to any penalty for which he or she would be liable if convicted of the no-fault offence concerned.

PART 5
DEFENCES AND EXEMPTIONS

INTRODUCTION

5.1 In this Part we consider defences and exemptions. We are considering them in relation to two of the three forms of liability that we have previously discussed: secondary liability and liability as a principal offender by virtue of innocent agency. However, neither the defence nor the exemption that we are recommending would apply to the offence of causing P to commit a no-fault offence.

5.2 In the CP, our approach to defences and exemptions reflected the fact that not only were we proposing that secondary liability should be replaced by a scheme of inchoate liability but also that there should be two distinct inchoate offences. Broadly, we proposed that there should be no defences and exemptions available to those who *encouraged* the commission of an offence. By contrast, we proposed that some defences and exemptions should be available to those who indifferently *assisted* the commission of an offence.

5.3 In the first report,[1] we made recommendations concerning the defences which ought to be available to the inchoate offences of assisting and encouraging that we were recommending. We concluded that there should be two defences:

    (1)   acting in order to prevent the commission of offences or to prevent, or limit, harm; and

    (2)   acting reasonably in all the circumstances.[2]

However, we qualified (2) by recommending that the defence of acting reasonably in all the circumstances should not be available if D *intended to* assist or encourage P to do a criminal act.[3]

5.4 In addition, we recommended that there should be an exemption from liability where D assisted or encouraged P to commit an offence which was intended to protect a category of persons and D was not only a member of the category but also a victim of the offence.[4]

5.5 In this report, we are considering which defences and exemptions should be available to D where D's liability is secondary rather than inchoate. We have born in mind that our recommendations in relation to secondary liability, if implemented, would narrow the scope of secondary liability. Apart from offences committed by P as an incident of a joint criminal venture, D would incur secondary liability only if he or she intended P to do a criminal act. This narrowing of secondary liability leads us to believe that the following defences ought not to be available.

---

[1] Part 6.

[2] Para 6.16.

[3] Para 6.24.

[4] Para 6.44.

DEFENCES THAT WE ARE NOT RECOMMENDING

Acting reasonably in all the circumstances

5.6 In line with the view that we took in relation to inchoate liability, we are not recommending that acting reasonably in all the circumstances should be a defence to secondary liability. It should not be open to D to plead that he or she acted reasonably when his or her intention was that P should commit the conduct element of the principal offence. The general policy of the criminal law does not permit a person who intentionally sets out to commit an offence to excuse or justify him or herself by reliance on any motive the tribunal of fact happens to find sufficiently compelling.

Assistance in the course of employment

5.7 Under our recommendations, the employee (D) who assists his or her employer (P) to commit an offence would no longer be secondarily liable merely because he or she believed that P would commit an offence. Rather, the employee would be secondarily liable only if he or she acted intending that the conduct element of the principal offence be committed. If so, the employee ought to be convicted of the principal offence subject to the other requirements of secondary liability being satisfied. It should be no defence that the employee was doing what his or her employer had ordered.

Assistance in the course of business

5.8 The same considerations apply as in the case of assistance rendered by employees.

DEFENCE AND EXEMPTION THAT WE ARE RECOMMENDING

5.9 In this section, we outline the defence and the exemption that we are recommending. As with inchoate liability for assisting and encouraging crime we are recommending that there should be:

(1) a defence of acting to prevent the commission of crime or to prevent, or limit, harm; and

(2) an exemption from liability where D assists or encourages P to commit an offence which is intended to protect a category of persons and D is both a member of the category and a victim of the offence.

We are conscious that we will be repeating the arguments that we set out in the first report. However, we believe that it would be inappropriate to merely refer the reader to the first report.

Acting to prevent the commission of offences or to prevent, or limit, harm

5.10 There is uncertainty as to the circumstances in which acting for the purposes of law enforcement is a defence to secondary liability. Frustrating the commission of crime can take one of three forms:

(1)   encouraging or assisting the commission of an offence with the purpose of preventing its commission. An example is where a police informer or undercover officer does something to encourage or assist the commission of a robbery, but the purpose is to ensure that it is not committed;

(2)   encouraging or assisting the commission of an offence not in order to prevent its commission but in order to reduce its harmful effects;[5]

(3)   encouraging the commission or attempted commission of an offence in order to prevent the commission of future offences, for example an undercover officer who acts in a way designed to encourage a hitherto undetected serial rapist to attack her.

The proposals in the CP

5.11   In the CP, we proposed that there should be a defence of law enforcement to the proposed offence of assisting (but not encouraging) crime. We proposed that the defence should be available to any individual whose 'overall course of conduct' was directed towards frustrating the commission of the principal offence.[6] We invited comment on whether the defence should extend to incidental offences, for example a theft committed in order to obtain property to be used in a robbery.

Responses to the proposals in the CP

5.12   The majority of respondents who addressed the issue thought that there should be a defence of acting in order to prevent crime. Of the majority, some felt that the assister should be exonerated for the offence that he or she intended to frustrate but not for an incidental offence. Some respondents expressed misgivings about the defence being available to private citizens.

5.13   One respondent, while accepting that the defence should be wide enough to exonerate those involved in undercover "sting" operations, such as test purchases and "manna from heaven" operations,[7] thought that a criterion of 'reasonableness' should be built into the defence. Most respondents believed that D should bear the burden of proving the defence.

5.14   We believe that in principle there should be a defence of acting, whether by assisting or encouraging, in order to prevent the commission of an offence or in order to prevent or limit harm. We do so for two reasons:

---

[5]   *Clarke* (1984) 80 Cr App R 344 is an illustration. D participated in a burglary but claimed to have done so in order to prevent the other participants escaping and to ensure that the property would be recovered.

[6]   Para 4.125.

[7]   An example of a test purchase is a child under the age of 16, and under the control of the local authority trading standards department, going into a shop and buying a lottery ticket. A "manna from heaven" operation is one where police, in the course of an investigation into suspected criminal behaviour, provide an opportunity for anybody to commit the criminal behaviour that they are investigating, eg the police expose cartons of cigarettes, apparently unguarded, in the back of a van parked in the street – *Williams v DPP* (1993) 98 Cr App R 209.

(1)   it is in the public interest that acts be done in order to prevent crime or to prevent or limit the occurrence of harm. Accordingly, an act of encouragement or assistance, the overall purpose of which is to prevent crime or to prevent or limit harm, is justified because of its value to society; and

(2)   those whose overall purpose in encouraging or assisting the commission of an offence is to prevent crime or to prevent or limit harm are acting as good citizens and should not be stigmatised or punished for doing so.

Should those to whom the defence is available be restricted?

5.15   At one stage, we thought that the defence should only be available to formal and informal agents of the state - police and customs officers, local authority trading standards officers, agents working under their control and civilian informers subject to regulation and supervision by the relevant law enforcement authority. We thought that the arguments in favour of such a restriction were:

(1)   law enforcement is primarily the responsibility of the state. Private citizens and the media should be discouraged from participating in offences on their own initiative even if the motive is to prevent crime. Important considerations are the safety of the citizen, the dangers of private vendettas being pursued and private acts hindering the activities of the state's law enforcement agencies;

(2)   there should be external controls in order to ensure that D's involvement is proportionate to the overall aim of an operation to prevent crime; and

(3)   to obviate the possibility of the defence being raised by criminals who might prepare the necessary groundwork for a false defence of crime prevention prior to and during their involvement in a criminal enterprise.

5.16   At the same time, we recognised that the defence would be open to abuse even if restricted to agents of the state. Test purchases can be made when there are no reasonable grounds for suspecting or believing that a trader is flouting the law. Police informers sometimes have their own agenda and it may sometimes be unclear whether their actions have been properly supervised and controlled.

5.17   In addition, we now believe that it would be exceedingly difficult to define exhaustively the persons who would be eligible to plead the defence. It is vital that the question of who can rely on the defence does not turn on technicalities. Accordingly, we are not recommending that the defence should be limited to particular individuals or categories.

Should incidental offences be excluded from the scope of the defence?

5.18   We believe that the defence should exonerate D for encouraging or assisting *any* offence provided D's overall purpose was to prevent the commission of crime or to prevent harm and provided that D acted reasonably in the circumstances:

> **Example 5A**
>
> P is a member of a gang planning an armed robbery. D, who has infiltrated the gang, tells P where to steal a lorry which can be used in the robbery. D does so in order to maintain credibility with members of the gang. D's aim is to prevent the commission of the robbery.

Admittedly, D's assistance was not for the purpose of preventing P committing theft. However, that ought not to preclude D pleading the defence to a charge of encouraging or assisting theft. D ought to be able to say that what he or she did was in order to frustrate the commission of another offence. The critical issue is the reasonableness of D's conduct: was it reasonable in the circumstances to assist the commission of offence *x* in order to prevent the commission of offence *y*?

A requirement of acting reasonably

5.19   In the CP, we said:

> ... it should be enough that [D] *believes* that his act of assistance is necessary as part of the implementation of his purpose of preventing the commission of the principal crime.[8]

However, we now believe that in order to rely on the defence, it must have been reasonable in the circumstances for D to have acted as he or she did.

5.20   This is to ensure that D can only successfully plead the defence if what D did was proportionate to the seriousness of the offence or harm that D was trying to prevent or limit. It is not in the public interest for D to encourage or assist the commission of an offence if the offence in question is more serious than the offence that D is seeking to prevent. In this regard, the requirement of reasonableness is a restraining principle and will operate as a curb on those who might think that any conduct is justifiable in the public interest. For example, the defence should not be available if D encourages P to shoot V when V is stealing some vegetables from P's allotment, even if D believes that it is necessary to shoot V in order to prevent V stealing the vegetables.

5.21   D should bear the legal burden of proving the defence on a balance of probabilities. We do not believe that placing the legal burden on D is incompatible with the presumption of innocence contained in Article 6(2) of the European Convention on Human Rights and Fundamental Freedoms. This is because the prosecution will still have had to prove the elements of the offence and if D raises the defence he or she is likely to be the only or, at least, the primary source of information as to his or her purpose.

---

[8]   Para 4.126 (emphasis added).

Implications for conspiracy

5.22 We repeat what we said in the first report. It is beyond the scope of this report to make formal recommendations in relation to the inchoate offence of conspiracy. However, we think that it would be anomalous if there were a defence of crime prevention to encouraging or assisting the commission of an offence but not to conspiring to commit an offence. Accordingly, we suggest that consideration be given to reversing the decision of the Privy Council in *Yip Chiu-Cheung v R*[9] by way of a statutory defence of crime prevention in cases of conspiracy.

Recommendation[10]

5.23 **We recommend that it should be a defence to liability for an offence as a secondary party[11] if D proves that:**

    (1) he or she acted for the purpose of:

        (a) preventing the commission of either the offence that he or she was encouraging or assisting or another offence; or

        (b) to prevent or limit the occurrence of harm; and

    (2) it was reasonable to act as D did in the circumstances.

An exemption from liability in cases of protective offences

The common law

5.24 In *Tyrrell*,[12] an adult (P), had unlawful sexual intercourse with a child aged between 13 to 16 (D).[13] It was alleged that D had encouraged P to commit the offence. It was held that D could not be convicted of committing the offence as a secondary party (or of inciting the offence) because the offence had been enacted for the purpose of protecting a category of persons and D fell within the category. This was because the relevant statutory provision was "passed for the purpose of protecting young women and girls against themselves".[14] According to Lord Coleridge CJ, Parliament could not "have intended that the girls for whose protection [the offence] was passed should be punishable under it for the offences committed upon themselves".[15]

---

[9] [1995] 1 AC 111.

[10] Clause 7 of the Bill.

[11] The defence would not be available to a person who is liable on the basis of using an innocent agent to commit an offence.

[12] [1894] 1 QB 710.

[13] Contrary to the Criminal Law Amendment Act 1885, s 5.

[14] [1894] 1 QB 710, 712.

[15] Above.

5.25   This suggests that the underlying principle is that where the purpose of a statutory offence is to protect a category of persons, no member of that category can be convicted of committing the offence as a secondary party or of inciting its commission. The principle has been applied to the offence of incest,[16] although it is arguable that the basis of the offence was eugenic rather than protectionist.[17] The principle has also been applied where D, a prostitute, was charged with being an accessory to her husband's offence of living on immoral earnings.[18] The offence existed in part to protect prostitutes but that was not its only function. An additional reason for the offence was to prevent fortunes being made by those who organise prostitution.

The Sexual Offences Act 2003

5.26   The Sexual Offences Act 2003 is largely silent on the *Tyrrell* exemption. The Act creates specific sexual offences designed to protect children under 13, namely rape of a child under 13,[19] assault of a child under 13 by penetration[20] and sexual assault of a child under 13.[21] At the same time, it is clear that Parliament intended that these offences were capable of being committed by a child under the age of 13.[22]

Example 5B

D, a girl aged 12, encourages P, a boy aged 12, to allow her to perform oral sex on him. P permits D to do this.

---

[16]   *Whitehouse* [1977] QB 868; *Pickford* [1995] 1 Cr App R 420.

[17]   Thus, the offence applied to sexual intercourse between adult brothers and sisters and to intercourse between fathers and adult daughters. See Bailey and Blackburn, "The Punishment of Incest Act 1908: A Case Study in Law Creation" [1979] *Criminal Law Review* 708; S. Wolfram "Eugenics and the Punishment of Incest Act 1908" [1983] *Criminal Law Review* 308. The offence of incest has been repealed by the Sexual Offences Act 2003. Instead, there are familial child sex offences (ss 25-29) and offences of sex with an adult relative (ss 64-65).

[18]   Contrary to what was the Sexual Offences Act 1956, s 30.

[19]   Section 5. The offence is committed if a person intentionally penetrates the vagina, anus or mouth of another with his penis. The offence is punishable by a maximum term of imprisonment for life.

[20]   Section 6. The offence is committed if a person intentionally penetrates the vagina or anus of another with a part of his body (other than his penis) or anything else. The offence is punishable by a maximum term of imprisonment for life.

[21]   Section 7. The offence is committed if a person intentionally touches another and the touching is sexual. The offence is on conviction on indictment punishable by a maximum term of 14 years' imprisonment.

[22]   In addition, section 9 makes it an offence for a person aged 18 or over to engage in sexual activity with a child under 16. If the child is aged 13 to 15, the offence is only committed if the perpetrator does not reasonably believe that the child is 16 or over.

P, by intentionally penetrating D's mouth with his penis, commits the offence of rape of a child under 13. Presumably, D is not an accessory to *that* offence because she can rely on the *Tyrrell* exemption. However, D is guilty of the offence of sexual assault of a child under 13 because she has intentionally touched P and the touching is sexual.[23] Presumably, P is not an accessory to *that* offence because he can rely on the *Tyrrell* principle.

5.27 In example 5B, D encourages P to commit an offence against herself. By contrast:

Example 5C

D, a girl aged 12, encourages P, a boy aged 12, to allow D's friend V, a girl aged 12, to perform oral sex on P. P permits V to do this.

P is guilty of rape of a child under 13. V is not guilty of that offence by virtue of the *Tyrrell* principle but, like D in example 5B, is guilty of sexual assault of a child under 13. Again, as in example 5B, presumably P is not an accessory to that offence. Whether D is guilty of both offences as an accessory depends on whether the *Tyrrell* exemption is available to those who are not victims in the sense that they are not the person against whom the offence is committed. In *Tyrrell*, the girl was herself the victim of the offence and in all the other cases where the principle has been applied, the person within the protected category has been the victim of the principal offence. On the other hand, there is no case where the courts have expressly held that the exemption is only available to a person who is or would be the victim of the principal offence.

The proposals in the CP

5.28 In the CP, we described the *Tyrrell* exemption as being "of uncertain content, and uncertain effect".[24] In setting out our provisional proposals for an inchoate offence of assisting crime, we said provisionally that the exemption should be "stated much more widely than at present".[25] We believed that D ought not to be liable for assisting the commission of a statutory offence if "his conduct is inevitably incidental to its commission and that conduct is not made criminal by that offence".[26]

---

[23] To add to the complexity, D and P are also guilty of the offence under section 9 of the Act, namely having sexual activity with a child.

[24] Para 2.88. Professor Glanville Williams had previously expressed similar sentiments – "Victims and other exempt parties in crime" (1990) 10(3) *Legal Studies* 245.

[25] Para 4.102.

[26] Para 4.103.

5.29 The fault element that we were proposing for the offence of assisting crime was 'knowledge or belief' on the part of D that P "is doing ... or will do ... acts that do or will involve the commission of an offence by [P]...".[27] Some assisters would not only satisfy the 'knowledge or belief' test but would also have the more culpable fault element of *intending* that P should commit the offence with their assistance. We inclined to the view that the wider exemption of 'incidental involvement' should either not be available in such cases or at least should be available only in a very limited number of cases.[28] We invited comment on what those cases might be.

5.30 The fault element that we proposed for encouraging crime was intention on D's part that P should commit the principal offence.[29] We proposed that as a general rule it would be "inappropriate to extend the defence to an encourager".[30] However, we thought that there might be cases, conspicuously those of sexual offences against minors, where the victim "should be exculpated even though she has encouraged rather than assisted in the commission of the offence".[31] We invited comment on what those offences might be.

Responses to the proposals in the CP

5.31 Amongst those respondents who addressed the issue, the majority, with little or no elaboration, agreed with our proposal for a 'more widely' stated exemption. However, Professor Sir John Smith strongly disagreed, describing our proposal as 'dangerously wide':

> If a licensee sells liquor to a constable on duty, I see every reason why the constable should be guilty of [assisting] whether he incited the offence or not. His conduct is inevitably incidental to the commission of the offence, but the offence exists for the protection of the public, not the constable... . The conduct of the recipient of controlled drugs is inevitably incidental to the offence of supplying drugs to another, but if the recipient is buying a ton of the stuff he must surely be guilty of [assisting].

Conclusions

5.32 We now believe that the fact that D's assistance is or will be incidental to the commission of the principal offence should not in itself be a reason for exonerating D. The correct approach is one that is based on statutory interpretation. D should be exempt from liability only if, in enacting the principal offence, it was Parliament's intention to afford protection to a particular category of persons and D falls within that category.

---

[27] Para 4.99(1)(a).

[28] Para 4.139.

[29] Para 4.163(1)(b).

[30] Para 4.167.

[31] Above.

5.33 However, we recognise that, when enacting an offence, Parliament may have more than one objective. We do not think that the exemption should be confined to encouraging or assisting the commission of principal offences, the *only* purpose of which is the protection of a particular category of persons. It should suffice that one reason for enacting the offence was to protect a particular category of persons.

5.34 A more difficult issue is whether the exemption should be confined to cases where D would be a 'victim', were the principal offence to be committed. Parliament when enacting an offence for the protection of a category of persons does not usually distinguish between different individuals within the category. Instead, each person within the category is considered worthy of protection irrespective of his or her individual traits:

Example 5D

D, a girl aged 15 and sexually very experienced, encourages P, a sexually inexperienced and naïve young man aged 18, to engage in sexual activity with her.[32] P knows D is aged 15.

Under the current law, the fact that D is active in tempting P and is sexually very experienced is irrelevant. The offence was enacted for the protection of children under 16 and D is such a person. Under the current law, D is not guilty of inciting P to engage in sexual activity.

5.35 In example 5D, it might be thought that there are two reasons that justify the conclusion that D is a 'victim'. First, if the offence were committed, it would be committed against her. Secondly, she is a 'victim' because she is within the protected category and is deemed to be in need of protection from others and from herself, despite her sexual experience.

5.36 However, D may not be the person against whom the offence is committed:

Example 5E

D, a girl aged 15 and sexually inexperienced, encourages P a young man aged 18, to engage in sexual activity with her friend V, a 15 year old girl, who is sexually very experienced. V also encourages P to engage in sexual activity with her.

V is a 'victim' because, as in the case of D in example 5D, she is within the protected category and because she is the person against whom the offence would be committed. However, in contrast to example 5D, if D in example 5E is to be viewed as a 'victim' it is not because she is the person against whom the offence is committed but only by virtue of being a person who falls within the protected category.

5.37 In example 5E, it might be thought that, as V's need for protection is no greater than D's, if V is able to rely on the exemption, so too should D. However, by contrast:

[32] Contrary to the Sexual Offences Act 2003, s 9.

> **Example 5F**
>
> D, a sexually experienced girl aged 14, encourages her brother P, who is aged 18, to engage in sexual activity with D's friend, V, a girl aged 13 and a virgin.

If D is to be exonerated, it can only be because she is a member of the protected category. On balance, we do not believe that it would be right that she should be exempt from liability merely on that basis. D is prepared to encourage or assist the commission of an offence against a vulnerable person. We accept that victims will not always be as vulnerable as V is in example 5F. However, we believe that it would be very unsatisfactory for D's liability to depend on the extent of the victim's vulnerability, not least because the trial process would then involve scrutiny of the victim's character and previous behaviour.

Non-sexual offences

5.38 There is no justification for confining the exemption to sexual offences. Parliament has created offences other than sexual offences for the protection of a particular category of persons. Thus, the Care Standards Act 2000 includes offences designed to protect vulnerable adults residing in care homes. The Asylum and Immigration (Treatment of Claimants, etc) Act 2004 contains offences which are in part designed to protect people who are trafficked for exploitation. The Gangmasters (Licensing) Act 2004 contains offences which are in part designed to protect certain categories of workers.

Recommendation[33]

5.39 **We recommend that D should be exempted from liability for an offence, whether as a secondary party or by virtue of using an innocent agent, if:**

  (1) **the offence encouraged or assisted is one that exists wholly or in part for the protection of a particular category of persons;**

  (2) **D falls within the protected category; and**

  (3) **D is the person in respect of whom the offence encouraged or assisted was committed or would have been had it had been committed.**

---

[33] Clause 6 of the Bill.

PART 6
EXTRA-TERRITORIAL JURISDICTION

INTRODUCTION

6.1 The common law of England and Wales evolved over centuries when relatively few offences were committed across national boundaries. However, the last fifty years have witnessed the phenomenon of globalisation. Criminal organisations have adeptly exploited the opportunities that globalisation has brought. Thus, although most serious crimes are usually still local in their commission and effect, involving a perpetrator and victim in the same country, an increasing number transcend national boundaries. This development is particularly pertinent in the context of inchoate and secondary liability. It is not uncommon to encounter conspiracies formed in one country to import people, drugs, firearms, or rare animals into another country. Similarly, there are infinite ways in which encouragement or assistance may be sent to and from any place in the world.

GENERAL PRINCIPLES

6.2 The primary basis of English criminal jurisdiction is territorial. The English courts are concerned with the keeping of the Queen's peace within the jurisdiction.[1] Generally, offences committed abroad have not impacted upon the Queen's peace and hence are not the concern of English courts. Thus, English courts have jurisdiction to try a person, whether or not a British citizen, for an offence committed within the jurisdiction. However, generally they do not, statutory exceptions aside,[2] have jurisdiction to try a person, whether or not a British citizen, for an offence committed outside the jurisdiction. In addition, when construing a statute creating an offence, there is a "strong presumption" that Parliament did not intend that statute to criminalise conduct occurring outside the jurisdiction.[3]

6.3 Given that the general rule is that the courts have jurisdiction to try an offence provided that it is committed within the jurisdiction, the issue of where an offence has been committed is crucial. There are two competing theories. The first, and orthodox, theory is the 'last act' or 'terminatory' theory. The second, more recent and controversial, is the 'initiatory' or 'comity' theory.

---

[1] In order to avoid repetition, instead of referring to 'England and Wales' we will refer to 'the jurisdiction' and instead of referring to 'courts of England and Wales' we will refer to 'English courts'.

[2] Statutory exceptions include the Offences against the Person Act 1861, s 9 (commission of murder or manslaughter by a British subject on land overseas); the Anti-Terrorism, Crime and Security Act 2001, s 109 (bribery and corruption committed outside the United Kingdom); the Sexual Offences Act 2003, s 72 (commission of certain sexual offences outside the United Kingdom by British citizens or residents of the United Kingdom); Criminal Law Act 1977, s 1A (conspiracy to commit a crime abroad).

[3] *Treacy v DPP* [1971] AC 537, 551 by Lord Reid; *Air India v Wiggins* [1980] 1 WLR 815.

6.4 The terminatory theory holds that an offence which includes a consequence element is committed "when and where"[4] that consequence occurs.[5] Accordingly, if the consequence occurs within the jurisdiction then the offence has been committed within the jurisdiction, regardless of where the conduct element of the offence was performed. It is the consequence element, not the conduct element, which determines where the offence was committed and hence which state has jurisdiction to try the offender.

6.5 For many years the terminatory theory held sway. Hence, in cases of obtaining property by deception, the general rule was that English courts had jurisdiction providing the obtaining occurred within the jurisdiction:

Example 6A

P is in England. V is in Spain. P phones V and persuades V, by means of deception, to transfer money from V's Spanish bank account to P's bank account in England.

Example 6B

P is in England. V is in Spain. P phones V and persuades V, by means of deception, to post an envelope full of money to P's address in England.

In both examples, P obtains V's money by deception. In example 6A, the obtaining occurs in England because the effect of the deception is ultimately that P's bank in England increases the amount to which his account is in credit. Therefore, the offence is committed within England and, under the terminatory theory, English courts have jurisdiction to try the offence. In example 6B, the obtaining occurs in Spain. This is because under English law P obtained the money when the envelope was deposited in a Spanish post box. Therefore, the offence is committed in Spain and, under the terminatory theory, Spanish courts, not the English courts, have jurisdiction to try the offence.

6.6 However, the speech of Lord Diplock in *Treacy*[6] gave rise to an alternative theory: the 'initiatory' or 'comity' theory. In essence, this theory holds that the jurisdiction of English courts is limited only by the theory of international comity. Provided a statutory offence contains no express geographical limitation, English courts *must* decline jurisdiction *only* if neither the conduct element nor the consequence element occurred within the jurisdiction. According to Lord Diplock:

---

[4] M Hirst, *Jurisdiction and the ambit of the criminal law* (2003) p 123.

[5] *Ellis* [1899] 1 QB 230; *Harden* [1963] 1 QB 8. It was Professor Glanville Williams, "Venue and the Ambit of Criminal Law" (1965) 81 *Law Quarterly Review*, 276, 518 who described the theory as the "terminatory theory of jurisdiction".

[6] [1971] AC 537, 561 to 564.

... each sovereign state should refrain from punishing persons for their conduct within the territory of another sovereign state where that conduct has had no harmful consequences within the territory of the state which imposes the punishment... . In my view, where the definition of [an] offence contains a requirement that the described conduct of the accused should be followed by described consequences the implied exclusion is limited to cases where *neither* the conduct *nor* its harmful consequences took place in England and Wales.[7]

6.7 Consider the following examples:

Example 6B

P is in England. V is in Spain. P phones V and persuades V, by means of deception, to post an envelope full of money to P's address in England.

Example 6 C

P is in France. V is in Spain. P phones V and by deception persuades V to post an envelope full of money to P's address in France.

In relation to example 6B (repeated) we noted, above, that according to the terminatory theory the offence should be tried in the Spanish courts.[8] However, since the conduct element of the offence was performed in England, international comity allows the English courts to claim jurisdiction. In contrast, in example 6C, both the conduct and the consequence elements (the deceiving and the obtaining of the money) occur outside the jurisdiction. Accordingly, both the terminatory theory and the comity theory require English courts to decline jurisdiction to try the offence.

6.8 Lord Diplock's speech in *Treacy* is not free from difficulty, in part because he appeared to treat the issue as ascertaining the ambit of the offence as a matter of statutory interpretation rather than a matter of extra-territorial jurisdiction.[9] However, the comity theory has gradually increased in influence. In *Smith (Wallace Duncan)(No 1)*[10] the Court of Appeal recognised it as an alternative means of deciding the issue of jurisdiction. Subsequently, however, in *Manning*,[11] a differently constituted Court of Appeal refused to follow *Smith (Wallace Duncan) (No 1)*.

---

[7] Above, 564 (emphasis in original).

[8] Para 6.5 above.

[9] The Court of Appeal in *Manning* [1999] QB 980, 993 to 998 highlighted the problematic aspects of Lord Diplock's speech.

[10] [1996] 2 Cr App R 1.

[11] [1999] QB 980.

6.9 Despite this, the comity approach has recently been revived by the Court of Appeal in *Smith (Wallace Duncan)(No 4)*.[12] Faced with its own previous conflicting decisions, the Court of Appeal held that *Smith (Wallace Duncan)(No 1)* had been correctly decided. The policy that underpins the decision is that, given the nature of international financial activity, jurisdiction should not be restricted by the technical considerations that the terminatory theory spawns.

6.10 However, it is important to recognise that in *Smith (Wallace Duncan) (No 4)* the Court of Appeal was careful to limit the scope of *Smith (Wallace Duncan) (No 1)*. According to Lord Chief Justice Woolf, it was not authority for the view that an English court has jurisdiction merely because to do so would not breach international comity. Rather, an English court can assume jurisdiction only if the alleged offence has a "substantial connection with this jurisdiction".[13]

6.11 A recent academic article has described *Smith (Wallace Duncan) (No 4)* as "controversial" and based on "policy rather than principle".[14] However, it appears that until the House of Lords considers the issue, the current law is that jurisdiction can be determined by reference to either the terminatory theory or the comity theory. This is subject to the proviso that the latter theory can only be relied upon where the alleged offence has a substantial connection with this jurisdiction.

OUR RECOMMENDATIONS

6.12 We will explain and set out our recommendations separately in relation to the three distinct forms of liability that make up our scheme.

Secondary liability

P commits the principal offence in England and Wales

6.13 The starting point is that if P commits an offence within this jurisdiction, an English court has jurisdiction to try P. In our view, they should also have jurisdiction to try D irrespective of where D was when he or she did the act which provided the assistance or encouragement.

6.14 It might be said that our recommendation merely reflects a general rule of secondary liability, namely that for D to be liable, D's assistance or encouragement must be operative when P commits the offence:

Example 6D

D in New York provides P, also in New York, with a gun so that P can commit a robbery in London. P does so.

---

[12] [2004] EWCA Crim 631, [2004] QB 1418.

[13] Above, at 1435.

[14] D Ormerod and T Rees "Jurisdiction: jurisdiction of English courts – obtaining by deception" (2004) *Criminal Law Review* 951, 953.

D's act of assistance, although performed in New York, is a continuing act, in that P is still being assisted by it at the moment that P commits the robbery. Accordingly, D's act, although in one sense done in New York, was done within the jurisdiction.

6.15 Our recommendation accords with the comity theory because, if an offence is committed within the jurisdiction, there will necessarily be a substantial connection between the offence and the jurisdiction. If there is a substantial connection between the offence and this jurisdiction, it ought to be possible to try each person who is alleged to be a party to the offence.

Recommendation[15]

6.16 **We recommend that if P commits an offence within the jurisdiction, D may always be tried within the jurisdiction no matter where he or she was at the time of rendering the assistance or encouragement or entering into the agreement.**

P commits the principal offence outside England and Wales

D'S BEHAVIOUR TAKES PLACE WHOLLY OR PARTLY IN ENGLAND AND WALES

6.17 We believe that it ought to be possible for an English court to try D if:

(1)   it would have jurisdiction to try P; or

(2)   it would have had jurisdiction to try P had P satisfied a condition relating to citizenship, nationality or residence.

Where an English court has jurisdiction to try P

6.18 If an English court has jurisdiction to try P for an offence committed outside the jurisdiction, it should have jurisdiction to try D for the offence if D's assistance, encouragement or agreement consisted of acts done (wholly or partly) within the jurisdiction:

Example 6E

P is in England. V is in Spain. D in England encourages P to telephone V and by deception persuade V to post an envelope full of money to P's address in England. P does so and V posts the money.

6.19 By virtue of the postal rule, the offence of obtaining property by deception is committed in Spain. Under the terminatory theory, P cannot be tried in England. However, under the comity theory, P can be tried in England (assuming that the court holds that there is a substantial connection between the offence and England). Accordingly, under our recommendation, it would also be possible for an English court to try D for the offence.

---

[15]   Clause 2(1) of the Supplementary Bill.

6.20   By contrast:

Example 6F

D is in London, P is in Chicago and V is in Madrid. D telephones P and encourages him to send a package containing sweets with a toxic substance in to V. The intention of D and P is to cause serious harm to V. P sends the package. V eats the sweets and suffers serious organ failure but survives.

If the terminatory theory is applied, P cannot be tried in an English court. Further, it would appear that application of the comity theory leads to the same result because, absent D's act of encouragement, there is no substantial connection between P's offence and this jurisdiction. We doubt whether the comity theory, as so far developed, permits a court to take into account D's behaviour when determining whether there is a substantial connection for the purposes of determining P's liability. Therefore, in example 6F, P's offence is not triable in the jurisdiction and, under our recommendations, it would also not be possible to try D in an English court.

Where an English court would have had jurisdiction to try P had P satisfied a condition relating to 'citizenship, nationality or residence'

6.21   Sometimes an English court does have jurisdiction to try P for an offence committed outside the jurisdiction irrespective of whether the offence is triable in an English court under the terminatory or comity theory. These are cases where Parliament has expressly enacted that an offence committed abroad may be tried in an English court. Where Parliament does so, it is not unusual for it to provide that P must satisfy a condition relating to citizenship, nationality or residence. One example is section 9 of the Offences against the Person Act 1861 ('the 1861 Act') which provides that a British citizen who commits murder or manslaughter overseas may be tried in an English court regardless of whether the victim was a British citizen. Another example is section 72 of the Sexual Offences Act 2003 which provides that an English court has jurisdiction to try P for certain sexual offences committed abroad provided P is a British citizen or a resident of the United Kingdom:

Example 6G

P, a British citizen, murders V, in Madrid. P commits the murder by shooting V with a firearm which D gave to him in London.

P can be tried in an English court by virtue of section 9 of the 1861 Act. Accordingly, under the recommendation outlined above, D could also be tried in an English court. Whether or not D is a British citizen would be irrelevant. By contrast:

> **Example 6H**
>
> The same facts as in example 6G except that P is not a British citizen.

In example 6H, an English court would not have jurisdiction to try P because P is not a British citizen. However, under our recommendation, an English court would have jurisdiction to try D because it would have had jurisdiction to try P had P been a British citizen. Again, under our recommendation it would be possible to try D in an English court even if D was not a British citizen.

Recommendation[16]

6.22 **We recommend that if P commits an offence outside the jurisdiction, D may be tried within the jurisdiction if D's behaviour takes place wholly or partly within the jurisdiction and P**

(1) **could be tried within the jurisdiction; or**

(2) **could have been tried within the jurisdiction had P satisfied a condition relating to citizenship, nationality or residence.**

D's behaviour takes place wholly outside England and Wales

6.23 We are recommending that an English court should have jurisdiction to try D if D could have been tried in an English court had he or she committed the offence committed by P in the place where P committed it:

> **Example 6J**
>
> D is a British citizen living in Paris. P is an Australian citizen living in Chicago. V is an Italian citizen living in Madrid. D sends an e-mail to P encouraging P to travel to Madrid and cause grievous bodily harm to V. P does so.

Under both the terminatory and the comity theories, an English court lacks jurisdiction to try P. Further, causing grievous bodily harm with intent is not an offence that Parliament has provided can be tried within the jurisdiction when committed abroad. Since an English court would lack jurisdiction to try P, there would, under our recommendation, be no jurisdiction for an English court to try D.

6.24 By contrast:

> **Example 6K**
>
> The same facts as in example 6J except that D encourages P to murder V, which P does.

In this example, had D murdered V in Madrid, D could have been tried for murder by an English court by virtue of section 9 of the 1861 Act. Under our recommendation, it would be irrelevant that P, being an Australian citizen, cannot be tried by an English court by virtue of section 9.

---

[16] Clause 2(2) and sch 1, para 1 to the Supplementary Bill.

6.25 By contrast:

Example 6L

Same facts as in example 6K except that D is a South African citizen and P is a British citizen.

Under our recommendation, an English court would not have jurisdiction to try D because had D committed the murder an English court would not have had jurisdiction to try him. An English court would have lacked jurisdiction to try D under both the terminatory theory and the comity theory. Moreover, because D is a South African citizen, an English court would not have had jurisdiction to try him by virtue of section 9 of the 1861 Act either. The fact that an English court would have jurisdiction to try P by virtue of section 9 would be irrelevant to its ability to try D.

Recommendation[17]

6.26 **We recommend that if P commits an offence outside the jurisdiction , D may be tried within the jurisdiction if:**

> **(1)   D's behaviour takes place wholly outside the jurisdiction; and**

> **(2)   irrespective of whether P can be tried within the jurisdiction, D could have been tried within the jurisdiction had he or she committed the offence in the place where P committed it.**

Where D uses P as an innocent agent

P's 'offence' is committed in England and Wales

6.27 Our policy is the same as for secondary liability. If P commits the conduct element of the principal offence within the jurisdiction, an English court should be able to try D irrespective of D's location at the time when D caused P to commit the conduct element. Even if D is physically outside the jurisdiction, he or she is acting within the jurisdiction through the medium of P:

Example 6M

D, in Canada, telephones his seven-year-old nephew, P, in London telling him to stab V, the boy living next door to P. P does so, thereby causing V grievous bodily harm.

Under our recommendations, an English court could try D for causing grievous bodily harm with intent. Our recommendation is consistent with the comity theory.

---

[17]   Clause 2(2) and sch 1, para 2 to the Supplementary Bill.

P's 'offence' is committed outside England and Wales

D'S BEHAVIOUR TAKES PLACE WHOLLY OR PARTLY IN ENGLAND AND WALES

6.28 In cases where D's own culpable conduct occurs within the jurisdiction, we believe that, in accordance with the comity theory, an English court should have jurisdiction to try D for the offence even if both the conduct and the consequence elements of the offence occur outside the jurisdiction:

Example 6N

D, in London, telephones his seven-year-old nephew in Montreal and tells him to stab V, the boy living next door. P does so. V sustains serious harm.

Under our recommendation, D could be tried in an English court for causing grievous bodily harm with intent.

D'S BEHAVIOUR TAKES PLACE WHOLLY OUTSIDE ENGLAND AND WALES

6.29 In cases where D's behaviour takes place wholly outside the jurisdiction, our recommendation mirrors that which we made in relation to secondary liability. An English court ought to be able to try D provided that D could have been tried within the jurisdiction had he or she committed the principal offence in the place where P would have committed it had P not been an innocent agent:

Example 6P

D is a British citizen living in Paris. He telephones his seven-year-old-nephew, P, in Madrid telling him to cause grievous bodily harm to V, a boy living next door to P. P does so. V sustains grievous bodily harm.

Causing grievous bodily harm with intent is not an offence that Parliament has provided can be tried within the jurisdiction even if committed abroad. Under our recommendations, therefore, an English court would have no jurisdiction to try D.

6.30 By contrast:

Example 6Q

The same facts as in example 6P except that D encourages P to murder V, which P does.

In this example, had D killed V in Madrid, D could have been tried for murder by an English court by virtue of section 9 of the 1861 Act. Accordingly, under our recommendations, an English court would have jurisdiction to try D for murder.

Recommendation[18]

6.31 **We recommend that if D uses P, an innocent agent, to commit an 'offence':**

    (1)   **if P's 'offence' is committed within the jurisdiction, D may always be tried within the jurisdiction;**

---

[18] Clause 3 and schedule 1, paras 3 and 4 of the Supplementary Bill.

(2)   **if P's 'offence' is committed outside the jurisdiction, D may always be tried within the jurisdiction if D's behaviour takes place wholly or partly within the jurisdiction;**

(3)   **if P's 'offence' is committed outside the jurisdiction, D may be tried within the jurisdiction if D could have been tried within the jurisdiction if he had committed the principal offence in the place where P would have committed it had P not been an innocent agent.**

D causing P to commit a no-fault offence

6.32   In the light of the relatively minor nature of most no-fault offences, we do not favour a broad jurisdictional rule. Accordingly, we believe that an English court should only have jurisdiction to try D for causing a no-fault offence if P commits the no-fault offence within the jurisdiction and D's behaviour took place wholly or partly within the jurisdiction.

Recommendation[19]

6.33   **We recommend that an English court should not have jurisdiction to try D for causing P to commit a no-fault offence unless:**

(1)   **P commits the no-fault offence within the jurisdiction; and**

(2)   **D's behaviour took place (wholly or partly) within the jurisdiction.**

ROLE OF THE ATTORNEY GENERAL

6.34   Section 1A of the Criminal Law Act 1977 provides that proceedings in respect of a conspiracy to commit an offence outside the jurisdiction can only be instituted with the consent of the Attorney General. The requirement is a sensible safeguard to ensure that proceedings are only brought in appropriate cases. We believe that there should be a similar safeguard in the present context.

Recommendation[20]

6.35   **We recommend that if P's offence is committed outside the jurisdiction, no proceedings may be instituted except by, or with the consent of, the Attorney General.**

---

[19] Clause 4 of the Supplementary Bill.

[20] Clause 7 of the Supplementary Bill.

PART 7
LIST OF RECOMMENDATIONS

ASSISTING AND ENCOURAGING

7.1 We recommend that section 8 of the Accessories and Abettors Act 1861 and section 44(1) of the Magistrates' Courts Act 1980 should be repealed and replaced by a statutory provision which describes the conduct element as 'assisting or encouraging'.

7.2 We recommend that 'encouraging' a person to do an act should include doing so by emboldening, threatening or pressurising another person to do a criminal act.

7.3 We recommend that encouraging or assisting a person to do a criminal act should include doing so by failing to take reasonable steps to discharge a duty.

7.4 We recommend that a person failing to respond to a constable's request for assistance in preventing a breach of the peace should not be regarded as encouraging or assisting a person to do a criminal act.

7.5 We recommend that, in cases prosecuted under clause 1, for D to be liable for a principal offence committed by P, D must intend P to commit the conduct element of that offence.

7.6 We recommend that, although D must intend that the conduct element of the principal offence should be committed, D need not intend that it should be P who commits it.

7.7 We recommend that, if D intends P (or another person) to commit the conduct element, D need not believe that it will be committed.

7.8 We recommend that for D to be convicted of a principal offence that P commits:

(1) D must believe that P, in committing the conduct of the offence, would be committing the offence; or

(2) D's state of mind is such that, were he or she committing the conduct element of the offence, he or she would commit the offence.

JOINT CRIMINAL VENTURES

7.9 We recommend that, for D to satisfy the conduct element of clause 2, he or she must either:

(1) agree with P to commit an offence; or

(2) share a common intention with P to commit an offence.

7.10 We recommend that, if P and D are parties to a joint criminal venture, D satisfies the fault required in relation to the conduct element of the principal offence committed by P if:

(1) D intended that P (or another party to the venture) should commit the conduct element;

(2) D believed that P (or another party to the venture) would commit the conduct element; or

(3) D believed that P (or another party to the venture) might commit the conduct element.

7.11 We recommend that, even if D intended or believed that P would or might commit the conduct element of the principal offence, he or she should nevertheless not stand to be convicted under clause 2 of the principal offence if P's actions in committing the principal offence fell outside the scope of the joint venture.

7.12 We recommend that, if D and P are parties to a joint criminal venture, for D to be convicted of a principal offence that P commits, D must believe that P, in committing the conduct element of the offence, might be committing the offence.

INNOCENT AGENCY

7.13 We recommend that:

(1) if D uses an innocent agent (P) to commit an offence ("the principal offence"), D is guilty of the principal offence.

(2) P is an innocent agent if:

(a) he or she commits the conduct element of the principal offence; and

(b) he or she does not commit the principal offence itself solely because:

(i) he or she is under the age of 10;

(ii) he or she has a defence of insanity; or

(iii) he or she acts without the fault required for conviction of the principal offence.

(3) D uses P to commit the principal offence if:

(a) D intends to cause a person (whether or not P) to commit the conduct element of the principal offence;

(b) D causes P to commit the conduct element of the principal offence; and

(c) D is at fault in relation to the principal offence.

(4) D is at fault in relation to the principal offence if:

131

(a) where conviction of the principal offence requires proof of fault, D's state of mind is such that, were he or she to commit the conduct element of the principal offence, he or she would do it with the state of mind necessary to be convicted of the offence; or

(b) where conviction of the principal offence does not require proof of fault, D knows or believes that were a person to commit the conduct element of the principal offence, that person would do so:

(i) in the circumstances (if any); and

(ii) with the consequences (if any)

proof of which is required for conviction of the principal offence.

(5) D may be guilty of the principal offence through using P to commit the offence:

(a) even though the principal offence is one that may be committed only by a person who meets a particular description; and

(b) D does not meet that description.

(6) The common law doctrine of innocent agency should be abolished.

CAUSING THE COMMISSION OF A NO-FAULT OFFENCE

7.14 We recommend that:

(1) there should be an offence of causing the commission of a no-fault offence which D would commit if he or she caused another person to commit a no-fault offence and

(a) it was D's intention that a person should commit the offence; or

(b) D knew or believed that his or her behaviour would cause a person to commit it;

(2) a person convicted of the offence should be liable to any penalty for which he or she would be liable if convicted of the no-fault offence concerned.

DEFENCES AND EXEMPTIONS

7.15 We recommend that D should be able to avoid liability as a secondary party if he or she is able to demonstrate that he or she had negated the effect of his or her acts of assistance, encouragement or agreement before the principle offence was committed.

7.16 We recommend that it should be a defence to liability for an offence as a secondary party[1] if D proves that:

(1) he or she acted for the purpose of:

(a) preventing the commission of either the offence that he or she was encouraging or assisting or another offence; or

(b) to prevent or limit the occurrence of harm; and

(2) it was reasonable to act as D did in the circumstances.

7.17 We recommend that D should be exempted from liability for an offence, whether as a secondary party or by virtue of using an innocent agent, if:

(1) the offence encouraged or assisted is one that exists wholly or in part for the protection of a particular category of persons;

(2) D falls within the protected category; and

(3) D is the person in respect of whom the offence encouraged or assisted was committed or would have been had it had been committed.

EXTRA-TERRITORIAL JURISDICTION

7.18 We recommend that if P commits an offence within the jurisdiction, D may always be tried within the jurisdiction no matter where he or she was at the time of rendering the assistance or encouragement or entering into the agreement.

7.19 We recommend that if P commits an offence outside the jurisdiction, D may be tried within the jurisdiction if D's behaviour takes place wholly or partly within the jurisdiction and P

(1) could be tried within the jurisdiction; or

(2) could have been tried within the jurisdiction had P satisfied a condition relating to citizenship, nationality or residence.

7.20 We recommend that if P commits an offence outside the jurisdiction , D may be tried within the jurisdiction if:

(1) D's behaviour takes place wholly outside the jurisdiction; and

(2) irrespective of whether P can be tried within the jurisdiction, D could have been tried within the jurisdiction had he or she committed the offence in the place where P committed it.

7.21 We recommend that if D uses P, an innocent agent, to commit an 'offence':

(1) if P's 'offence' is committed within the jurisdiction, D may always be tried within the jurisdiction;

---

[1] The defence would not be available to a person who is liable on the basis of using an innocent agent to commit an offence.

(2)   if P's 'offence' is committed outside the jurisdiction, D may always be tried within the jurisdiction if D's behaviour takes place wholly or partly within the jurisdiction;

(3)   if P's 'offence' is committed outside the jurisdiction, D may be tried within the jurisdiction if D could have been tried within the jurisdiction if he had committed the principal offence in the place where P would have committed it had P not been an innocent agent.

7.22   We recommend that an English court should not have jurisdiction to try D for causing P to commit a no-fault offence unless:

(1)   P commits the no-fault offence within the jurisdiction; and

(2)   D's behaviour took place (wholly or partly) within the jurisdiction.

7.23   We recommend that if P's offence is committed outside the jurisdiction, no proceedings may be instituted except by, or with the consent of, the Attorney General.

(*Signed*)   TERENCE ETHERTON, *Chairman*
HUGH BEALE
STUART BRIDGE
JEREMY HORDER
KENNETH PARKER

STEVE HUMPHREYS, *Chief Executive*
28 February 2007

APPENDIX A
THE DRAFT PARTICIPATING IN CRIME BILLS: COMMENTARY AND FULL TEXT

PARTICIPATING IN CRIME BILL

Introduction

A.1 In this paper we explain the various provisions in our draft Participation in Crime Bill ('the Bill') and our draft Participation in Crime (Jurisdiction, Procedure and Consequential Provisions) Bill ('the Supplementary Bill'). The full texts of the Bills, also within this Appendix, follow on directly from the end of this commentary.

Secondary liability

A.2 Clauses 1 and 2 of the Bill set out the inculpatory provisions whereby a person ('D') will incur liability for an offence committed by a principal offender ('P').[1] These provisions must of course be read with the other relevant provisions in the Bill and Supplementary Bill, particularly clauses 6 and 7 of the former which set out our proposed limitations on liability.

A.3 For the purposes of clauses 1 and 2 (and the relevant provisions in Part 2) of the Bill, P commits an offence if he or she is aged 10 or above, is legally sane and commits the external elements of the offence with the fault (if any) required for liability as a principal offender.[2] Accordingly, when determining D's secondary liability for an offence, it is of no relevance that P has been (or would be) excused from liability because P has a complete defence such as duress or a partial defence (to murder) such as provocation.[3]

A.4 If P was not legally capable of committing the offence in question, because P was under the age of 10 or legally insane, D's liability falls to be determined by reference to clause 4 of the Bill (on innocent agency) rather than through the provisions on secondary liability.[4]

A.5 In cases where D's liability is determined under the secondary liability provisions, he or she is, as a general rule, liable for each and every offence committed by P. For example, if P has committed murder he or she will also have committed the lesser offence of unlawful and dangerous act manslaughter, as well as one or more non-fatal offences against the person. If the secondary liability requirements of the Bill are not satisfied for the most serious offence committed by P (eg, murder), then, as a general rule, D will nevertheless be liable for a lesser offence committed by P (eg, manslaughter) if the requirements are satisfied in relation to that offence.

---

[1] The common law doctrine of secondary liability is abolished by cl 8(a) of the Supplementary Bill. Section 8 of the Accessories and Abettors Act 1861 and s 44(1) of the Magistrates' Courts Act 1980 are repealed by cl 9(1) and (2) of the Supplementary Bill and Sch 3 thereto.

[2] Cl 10 of the Bill. See paras A.53 to A.55 below.

[3] Cl 10(2) of the Bill expressly provides that it is immaterial whether P has a defence (other than insanity).

[4] See paras A.34 to A.37 below.

Clause 1 of the Bill – intentional encouraging or assisting

A.6   Clause 1 provides that if P commits an offence, then D is liable for that offence if:

      (1)   D does an act which encouraged or assisted P to commit a 'criminal act';[5]

      (2)   D intended that P or another person should commit that criminal act;[6]

      (3)   D believed that a person doing the criminal act would commit the offence[7] (or D's own state of mind was such that had D committed the criminal act, he or she would have committed that offence).[8]

A.7   Thus, if the offence committed by P is murder, and it is established that D provided P with the necessary encouragement or assistance, D will be secondarily liable for that offence if it was his or her intention that P or another person should do (or continue to do) any act which, if successfully committed against another person, could result in that person's death and D believed that if the act were to be done (or continued to be done), it would be done by a person acting with the intention to cause serious harm or death.

A.8   By contrast, if in encouraging P it was D's intention that P should fire a live round of ammunition over V's head to frighten her, P's inept aim, resulting in V's being hit and killed, would give rise to secondary liability for manslaughter (rather than murder). It was D's intention that an unlawful (and objectively dangerous) act be done and D acted with the state of mind required for secondary liability for common assault (and therefore manslaughter).[9]

'CRIMINAL ACT'

A.9   The term 'criminal act' is defined in clause 11(2) of the Bill as being 'in relation to an offence, a reference to an act (or a failure to act) that falls within the definition of the act (or failure to act) that must be proved in order to be convicted of the offence'. Accordingly, as a general rule, 'criminal act' means the conduct element of the principal offence in question.

---

[5]   Cl 1(1)(c) of the Bill.

[6]   Cl 1(1)(a) of the Bill.

[7]   Cl 1(2) of the Bill.

[8]   Cl 1(3) of the Bill. This limb of the test covers offences of subjective fault and offences of objective fault where P's state of mind may nevertheless be relevant to his liability (see, for example, s 2A(3) of the Road Traffic Act 1988).

[9]   As with P's own liability for unlawful and dangerous act manslaughter, it is irrelevant to D's liability that he or she foresaw no possibility of anyone being killed.

A.10   Exceptionally, however, if the conduct element taken in isolation is neutral in terms of what D's conduct could encourage or assist, then the term 'criminal act' should be interpreted to mean the conduct element together with the circumstance element of P's offence. For example, if P's offence is drink-driving, and D is charged with committing the principal offence as a secondary party on the ground that he provided P with copious amounts of whisky before P set off in his car, the question whether D's conduct encouraged or assisted P to commit the offence will be assessed with reference to the conduct element of P's offence as a whole (the conduct element of driving together with the circumstance element of being 'over the limit').

A.11   It is important to note that, in the absence of a specific defence on the issue, D's secondary liability does not depend on the way in which P's offence was ultimately committed. D will be liable for 'offence x' if, acting with the fault required by clause 1(2) or (3) of the Bill,[10] his or her intention was that *any* act which could feasibly be the conduct element of that offence should be done. In other words, as a general rule, if the principal offender (P) was different from the person D believed would commit the offence, or there were differences between the way P committed 'offence x' and the way D envisaged 'offence x' being committed, or there were differences in the circumstances (such as the place and time of the offence or the identity of the victim), D is nevertheless liable for P's offence:

Example A1

D posts a letter to Q setting out how to gain entry into a locked building, with a view to encouraging Q to commit burglary, expecting that the information will be used by Q to break into a house via its back door. D would be liable for P's burglary of a hospital if P, having read D's letter, effected his entry by breaking in through a locked window.

A.12   With regard to D's own conduct, clause 1(c) of the Bill requires D to have done something which 'assisted or encouraged P to do his criminal act'. In other words, D's behaviour must not merely have the capacity to assist or encourage P, but must actually do so. However, if D's conduct has the capacity to assist or encourage P, proving that it did in fact have that effect should only be an issue if there is evidence before the court to realistically suggest that it might not have done so.

'INTENTION'

A.13   D must act with the 'intention' that a criminal act be committed.[11] In this context, 'intention' bears its common law meaning. In other words, a jury should be directed that they would be entitled, but not compelled, to find that D intended P to commit a criminal act if they find that D believed that it was 'virtually certain' that P would commit it.

---

[10]   Cl 6 if the offence is a no-fault offence.

[11]   Clause 1(1)(a) of the Bill.

Clause 2 of the Bill – participating in a joint criminal venture

A.14 Clause 2 of the Bill sets out the conditions for secondary liability for an offence committed by P in cases where D and P are parties to a joint criminal venture.[12]

A.15 In the first report we said that we had been greatly exercised by how best to express our policy on secondary liability in statutory form.[13] One approach would be to express the policy in a relatively open textured form, focusing on general principles. Under this approach, it would be for the courts, guided by our report feeding into Judicial Studies Board specimen directions to juries, to fill in the details in particular cases. The other approach would be a Bill which itself provided the details. Nowhere is the contrast between the two approaches more pronounced than in the respective clauses dealing with D's liability for participating in a joint criminal venture.

A.16 Parliamentary Council prepared alternative Bills reflecting each approach. We circulated both Bills to members of the Advisory Group who had assisted us in our review of the law of homicide.[14] Of those that commented, nearly all expressed a clear preference for the more open textured Bill. They found the other Bill too complex and too difficult to work with. Taking their views into account, we have opted for the more open textured Bill.

'JOINT CRIMINAL VENTURE'

A.17 The Bill does not define 'joint criminal venture'. However, the expression is employed to describe cases where D and P share a common intention to commit an offence. The obvious example of a shared common intention is where D and P are both party to an express agreement to commit an offence. In addition, clause 2(3) makes it clear that a joint criminal venture (in the sense of a shared common intention) may also be inferred from the conduct of D and P regardless of whether they are parties to an express agreement to commit an offence.

A.18 Accordingly, clause 2 of the Bill is wide enough to address three categories of joint venture:

(1) the type of venture which is preceded by a conspiracy to commit the offence ultimately committed by P;

(2) the less formal type of venture, where D and P tacitly agree (perhaps on the spur of the moment) that the offence ultimately committed by P should be committed; and

(3) the type of spontaneous venture where it would be difficult to infer a tacit agreement, but it would be possible to infer a shared common intention, such as where a number of youths spontaneously involve themselves in an attack on a person outside a public house.

---

[12] In practice, where what is at issue is D's liability for an agreed (as opposed to a collateral) offence, there will often be an overlap between cl 1 and cl 2 of the Bill, in which case D may be convicted of P's offence under either provision.

[13] *Inchoate Liability for Assisting and Encouraging Crime* (2006) Law Com No 300, Part 1, para 1.23.

[14] *Murder, Manslaughter and Infanticide* (2006) Law Com No 304.

A.19   There will be the exceptional case where D and P expressly agree to commit an offence and yet it is not D's intention that the offence should be committed. Clause 2(4) is in part designed to ensure that, should P commit the agreed offence, D does not escape liability merely because he or she is opposed to or indifferent as to whether the agreed offence is committed. Rather, if D had agreed with P to commit an offence, D is to be treated as sharing with P an intention that the offence should be committed. Thus, in a case such as *Rook*[15] where D and P were parties to an agreement to murder V, D will be liable under clause 2 should P commit the murder even though it was not D's intention that murder should be committed.

'SCOPE OF THE JOINT VENTURE'

A.20   If the prosecution can establish a joint criminal venture, clause 2(2) provides D is guilty of any offence committed by P if the criminal act constituting the offence 'falls within the scope of the joint venture'. The Bill does not seek to define that expression. Accordingly, in this section we consider how the courts should approach the issue.

'Agreed offence'

A.21   If D and P agree to commit an offence which P subsequently commits D can be liable for P's offence under clause 2 of the Bill. This is so even if the way in which it was committed, or the victim or the principal offender, or any combination thereof, was different from D's expectation. In other words, the inculpatory element in the scheme for joint criminal ventures disregards the differences in the factual circumstances:

Example A2

D and P agree on Saturday to cause serious harm to V in central London on Tuesday by beating him about the body with poles, but P instead causes V serious harm in Croydon on Monday by poisoning his food.

Prima facie, D would be liable for P's offence of causing V grievous bodily harm with intent to cause such harm.[16]

A.22   However, as we explained in Part 3,[17] we believe that the law would be too harsh if no account could be taken of the extent to which P's criminal act was not the act that D intended that P should commit. In the alternative version of the Bill which we have decided not to proceed with, we provided D with a 'remoteness' defence which would have permitted the jury to acquit D of P's offence if it would be unreasonable to convict D, notwithstanding D's prima facie liability:

---

[15]   [1993] 2 All ER 955.

[16]   Offences Against the Person Act 1861, s 18.

[17]   Para 3.156.

> **Example A3**
>
> D and P agree in June 2006 to commit a burglary in London, and D provides P with a jemmy. P subsequently uses the jemmy to commit a large number of burglaries in August 2010 in Newcastle.

If D were to be held liable, it would mean that D would be liable for any agreed 'offence x' (in the example, burglary) committed by P, even if committed many years later or in circumstances which D would never have contemplated or countenanced.

A.23   Rather than employ a statutory 'remoteness' test, we have opted for a test which is one of fact and degree: have the prosecution proved that P's criminal act fell within the scope of the joint criminal venture?

A.24   In example A3 above, if P committed the Newcastle burglaries pursuant to a frolic of his own uninfluenced by the earlier agreement with D, a jury might take the view that P's criminal acts were outside the scope of the joint criminal venture even though P received assistance from D (that is the provision of the jemmy four years earlier).

A.25   If, however, D's conspiracy with P did in fact embolden or otherwise encourage P to commit his Newcastle offences, a jury might conclude that P's criminal acts fell within the scope of the venture, regardless of the difference in factual circumstances. This is illustrated by the following example:

> **Example A4**
>
> D and P, who are motivated by racism, agree to cause a serious injury to an Afro-Caribbean man the following Saturday night. P decides to assault an Indian man (V) on Friday instead.

In this example, if the jury was satisfied P at the time of assaulting V was encouraged by the agreement with D, they might conclude that P's criminal act was within the scope of the venture.

A.26   By contrast:

> **Example A5**
>
> D agrees that P should teach D's employer, E, a lesson by breaking his legs and, to this end, provides P with a baseball bat. P instead decides to use the weapon to break the legs of his long-standing enemy, V.

In this example, although D has provided P with assistance, a jury might conclude that P's criminal act fell outside the scope of the venture. However, although D might not be secondarily liable for the offence committed by P against V, he might well be liable for an inchoate offence of encouraging or assisting crime,[18] or for conspiracy,[19] in relation to the offence he anticipated.

---

[18] Our proposals are set out in Part 1 of our Crime (Encouraging and Assisting) Bill.

A.27   If P's criminal act is different from the criminal act that D intended or contemplated because of some mischance or accident in the furtherance of the venture, D ought not to escape liability:

> **Example A6**
>
> D hires P to murder a particular man, M; but P, finding a person in M's study, and wrongly believing that person to be M, "accidentally" kills V instead.

The jury should be directed that the fact that P 'accidentally' killed V instead of M cannot in itself relieve D of liability.[20]

'Collateral offences'

A.28   It might be thought that whether a collateral offence committed by P will 'fall within the scope of the venture' will be a more difficult issue for the jury to decide. In Part 3,[21] we set out our reasons for endorsing *Chan Wing-siu*[22] principle. Accordingly, a collateral offence committed by P in the course the joint criminal venture will only 'fall within the scope of the venture' if D foresaw that P might commit the offence. If D did foresee that P might commit the collateral offence and P does so, prima facie, the offence will 'fall within the scope of the venture'.

A.29   Frequently, the collateral offence that P commits is one that P commits in order to facilitate the commission of the agreed offence or in order to reduce the possibility of criminal proceedings being brought in respect of the agreed offence. If so, the collateral offence is clearly related to the fulfilment of the shared common intention. Such collateral offences ought not, as general rule, present difficulty. If they are clearly related to the fulfilment of the shared common intention they can properly be seen to fall within the scope of the joint criminal venture. Clause 2(4) makes it clear that this is so even if D was opposed to or indifferent to the commission of the collateral offence. It suffices that D foresaw that the offence might be committed.

A.30   However, some collateral offences committed by P in the course of the joint criminal venture are not committed in order to facilitate the commission of the agreed offence or to reduce the possibility of criminal proceedings being brought in respect of the agreed offence. An example is the racially motivated attack by P on V during the course of the robbery in *Stuart and Schofield*.[23] The attack was not committed in order to facilitate the commission of the robbery or to reduce the chances of P and D being apprehended and convicted of the robbery.

---

[19] Criminal Law Act 1977, s 1.

[20] The general principle of transferred fault would apply.

[21] Paras 3.132 to 3.146.

[22] [1985] 1 AC 168.

[23] [1995] 1 Cr App R 441.

A.31　　Such collateral offences, the commission of which are foreseen as a possibility by D, are equally capable of falling within the scope of the joint criminal venture. However, as with agreed offences, the law would be too harsh if no account could be taken of the extent to which the act that P perpetrated in committing the collateral offence differed from the act that D foresaw that P might commit:

Example A7

D and P agree to commit a burglary. D, knowing that P is armed with a gun, realises that P may use the gun to murder the householder (H) should the latter disturb them. In the event, H does not disturb them. However, in the course of the burglary P sees a rival gang leader, V, walking past. P takes the opportunity to shoot V dead.

In this example it would be a matter for the jury, as a question of fact and degree, to decide whether the act of P, in murdering V, fell within the scope of the venture.

Clause 3 of the Bill – liability not restricted by special characteristics required of offender

A.32　　Some offences are defined in such a way that only persons who meet a particular description can commit them as a principal offender. For example, by virtue of section 1(1)(a) of the Sexual Offences Act 2003, a woman cannot commit rape as a principal offender.

A.33　　The purpose of clause 3 is to ensure that D may be convicted of an offence even though he or she could not be convicted of the offence as a principal offender. Thus, if D (a woman) encourages P (a man) to rape V, D can be convicted of rape by virtue of clause 3 or, if P is an innocent agent, by virtue of clause 4.

Innocent agency

Clause 4 of the Bill

A.34　　Clause 4 of the Bill provides that, where D has used P to commit the external elements of an offence,[24] but P is not liable (on the basis that or he or she acted without the fault required for liability[25] or that he or she lacked the capacity to be liable because he or she was under the age of 10 or was legally insane),[26] D is to be treated as having committed the offence and liable for it.[27]

---

[24] Cl 4(1) and cl 4(3) of the Bill.

[25] Cl 4(2)(b)(iii) of the Bill. This alternative is not relevant if the offence does not require fault.

[26] Cl 4(2)(b)(i) and (ii) of the Bill.

[27] The common law doctrine of innocent agency is abolished by cl 8(b) of the Supplementary Bill.

A.35 D is liable as the principal offender for an offence of subjective fault (the commission of which he or she has caused)[28] if he or she intended that the conduct element of the offence should be committed[29] and he or she acted with the subjective fault required to be liable for it as a principal offender.[30] For example:

Example A8

D compels P, a nine-year-old boy, to enter V's house to remove her jewellery. Because D was dishonest and had the intention permanently to deprive V of her jewellery, and it was D's intention that P should enter V's house, knowing that P would be entering as a trespasser, D would be liable for burglary.

Example A9

D tells P, a vulnerable teenager, that the gun he has provided contains only blank rounds, knowing that the ammunition is live, and directs P to shoot at V to frighten him, intending that V should be caused serious harm. If V is shot and killed by P, D would be liable for murder whereas P, intending only to frighten V, would be liable for unlawful and dangerous act manslaughter.[31]

Example A10

D, a woman, compels P, an insane man, to have sexual intercourse with V, a woman she knows will not consent. Because it is D's intention that P should have sexual intercourse with V, and D does not reasonably believe that V will be consenting, she will be guilty of rape if P has non-consensual intercourse with V.[32]

A.36 It should be noted that if D causes P to commit the conduct element of the offence, and D has the culpable state of mind to be liable, the fact that the conduct element was committed by P rather than the innocent person that D expected would commit it does not affect D's liability for the offence.[33] Further, the fact that the conduct element was not committed in the way that D envisaged does not affect his or her liability for the offence.

---

[28] Cl 4(3)(b) of the Bill. The Bill does not purport to define 'cause'.

[29] Cl 4(3)(a) of the Bill.

[30] Cl 4(3)(c) and cl 4(4) of the Bill. An offence of subjective fault includes an offence of objective fault for which P's state of mind may be relevant when determining his liability; see, for example, s 2A(3) of the Road Traffic Act 1988. In other respects, offences of objective fault do not fall within the scope of cl 4 of the Bill.

[31] In this example P is a "semi-innocent" agent, through the medium of whom D can be said to have been a cause of V's death.

[32] By virtue of cl 3 of the Bill, D will be liable for rape even though she would not have been able to perpetrate the offence directly. See paras A.32 and A.33 above.

[33] Cl 4(3)(a) of the Bill.

A.37   D is liable as the principal offender of an offence not requiring fault if he or she intended that the conduct element of the offence should be committed[34] and he or she knew or believed that it, if committed, would be committed with the circumstance and consequence elements (if any) necessary for liability as a principal offender.[35] It has been held, however, that insanity cannot be relied on to avoid liability for such offences.[36] If this approach is followed by the courts, an insane person (P) will be liable for the no-fault offence and D will not be liable under clause 4.[37] It follows that D will be liable for the no-fault offence under clause 4 of the Bill only in very rare cases, where P is a child under the age of 10.

Causing a no-fault offence

Clause 5 of the Bill

A.38   Clause 5 of the Bill addresses the situation where P commits a no-fault offence[38] for which he or she bears no moral responsibility because it was brought about by the actions of another individual (D), as in the following example:

Example A11

D, knowing that P will soon drive home from D's party, surreptitiously laces P's orange juice with alcohol causing him to commit the no-fault offence of driving while 'over the limit'.[39]

A.39   For D to be liable under clause 5(1) for causing P's no-fault offence, the Crown would need to prove, in addition to causation, that it was D's intention to cause a person to commit the no-fault offence[40] or that D knew or believed that his or her behaviour would cause a person to commit it.[41]

A.40   Clause 5(1)(a) requires D to cause 'another person' to commit a no-fault offence. Accordingly, D will be liable for causing P's no-fault offence if P was a person other than the person D envisaged would commit it, or if the way in which the offence was committed was different from D's expectation. So, if D laced M's non-alcoholic drink intending to cause M to commit the offence of 'drink-driving' in his Ford Fiesta, but M, believing the drink to be non-alcoholic, gave it to P, a bus driver, D would nevertheless be liable for P's offence of driving 'over the limit' in his bus.

---

[34]   Cl 4(3)(a) of the Bill. As explained above under secondary liability, the criminal act may exceptionally be the combination of conduct and circumstance elements.

[35]   Cl 4(3)(c) and 4(5) of the Bill.

[36]   *DPP v H* [1997] 1 WLR 1406, a case which also suggests that insanity cannot be a defence to offences of objective fault.

[37]   D may, however, be secondarily liable for P's offence (under cl 1 of the Bill) or liable for causing P's offence (under cl 5 of the Bill).

[38]   Defined in cl 5(2) of the Bill as an offence 'that does not require proof of fault'.

[39]   Road Traffic Act 1988, s 5(1)(a).

[40]   Cl 5(1)(a) of the Bill.

[41]   Cl 5(1)(b) of the Bill.

Other defences and general provisions

Clause 6 of the Bill – protective offences

A.41 The effect of this provision is to retain the exemption from secondary liability established in the case of *Tyrrell*.[42]

A.42 Clause 6(1) provides that D cannot be liable for an offence by virtue of the Bill's provisions on secondary liability and the provisions on innocent agency if D would be regarded as the 'victim' of P's offence and he or she falls within a category of persons that the offence in question was designed to protect:

Example A12

D1 (a 12-year-old girl) and D2 (D1's 15-year-old female friend) encourage P to have sexual intercourse with D1. P subsequently has sexual intercourse with D1 thereby committing the offence of rape of a child under the age of 13.[43]

A.43 D2, but not D1, would be secondarily liable for P's offence on the basis that D1 would be regarded as the 'victim' of P's offence.[44] Parliament intended section 5 of the Sexual Offences Act 2003 to protect children under the age of 13 from themselves, as well as from predatory adults. D1 would not be secondarily liable for P's offence even though it was her intention to encourage P to have sexual intercourse with her. By contrast, D2 would be secondarily liable for P's offence on the basis that she was not a 'victim' of the offence and it was her intention that P should have sexual intercourse with D1.[45]

A.44 Clause 6(2) ensures that the exemption from liability is available in the rare incidence where D is charged with causing P to commit a no-fault offence.

Clause 7 of the Bill – a defence of acting to prevent crime

A.45 This clause sets out a 'good purpose' defence to secondary liability,[46] the burden of proof in relation to which lies with the accused.

A.46 If the Crown establish a prima facie case that D is secondarily liable for an offence committed by P, D will nevertheless be entitled to an acquittal if he or she can prove on the balance of probabilities that the purpose was to prevent crime or prevent or limit the occurrence of harm and that the conduct was reasonable in the circumstances:

---

[42] [1894] 1 QB 710.

[43] Sexual Offences Act 2003, s 5.

[44] The "person in respect of whom [the offence] was committed" (cl 6(1)(b) of the Bill).

[45] In *R v G* [2006] EWCA Crim 821, [2006] 1 WLR 2052 the Court of Appeal held that s 5 of the 2003 Act is "an offence that does not require proof of fault", notwithstanding the reference in s 5(1)(a) to intentional penetration by P. Accordingly, the word 'intentionally' refers to the concept of volition (part of the conduct element of the offence) rather than an element of fault. Of course, for D2 to be secondarily liable for P's offence under cl 1 of the Bill, the Crown would need to prove that she believed that the principal offender would have sexual intercourse with a child under the age of 13 (cl 1(2) of the Bill). P, however, would be liable for the s 5 offence regardless of any belief *he* had about D1's age.

[46] The defence is not available in cases where D uses an innocent agent to commit an offence.

> **Example A13**
>
> D and P agreed to commit burglary, and burglary was subsequently committed by P. D's defence is that his only purpose in becoming involved was to obtain sufficient information about the offence to be able to inform the police in advance to ensure that P would be caught in the act.

If, in this example, the jury accept that D's explanation is more likely than any other explanation to be true[47] and (in that case) that it was reasonable for D to act in that way,[48] D will not be guilty of burglary.[49]

A.47 The defence is not, however, limited to 'joint criminal venture' secondary liability. If it was D's intention to encourage or assist a person to commit the relevant criminal act, it may well be difficult for him or her to discharge the burden of proving that the requirements of the defence are made out, but D is not precluded from relying on the defence in response to an allegation of secondary liability. The defence might, for example, be made out in the following example:

> **Example A14**
>
> Having found out that P, a person motivated by his hostility towards a racial group, is considering whether to steal a wallet from or, alternatively, to cause a serious injury to a person belonging to that group, D encourages P to commit the theft. P follows D's advice and steals from a person belonging to that group. D gives evidence in his defence that he encouraged P to steal in order to prevent the more serious crime being committed.

If the jury accept that D acted solely to prevent a serious attack by P on another person, and regard the act of encouragement as a reasonable course of conduct in the circumstances, D will not be guilty of P's offence.

Clause 8 of the Bill – encouraging or assisting

A.48 The Bill does not contain a definition of encouraging or assisting. We expect the words to be interpreted widely in accordance with their ordinary meaning.

A.49 However, for the avoidance of doubt, clause 8 of the Bill provides that conduct by D which encourages or assists a person to do an act includes:

(1) conduct which puts pressure on someone (for example where D threatens P);[50] and

---

[47] Cl 7(1)(a) of the Bill.

[48] Cl 7(1)(b) of the Bill.

[49] The legal burden is on D to prove the benevolent purpose *and* that his or her conduct was reasonable in the circumstances.

[50] Cl 8(1) of the Bill.

(2) conduct which reduces the possibility of criminal proceedings being brought in respect of the act (such as the provision of advice to P on how to avoid detection or the provision of a gun for P to use against a police officer should he be found committing the offence).[51]

A.50 In addition, clause 8(2)(b) provides that a reference to a person's doing something which encourages or assists a person to do an act may be an omission comprising a failure to take reasonable steps to discharge a relevant duty, for example where D (a security guard) fails to turn on a burglar alarm in order to assist another person's unauthorised entry as a burglar.

A.51 Clause 8(3) sets out a limitation on the scope of liability for omissions, expressly providing that one particular type of omission – the failure to respond to a constable's request for assistance – is not encompassed by clause 8(2)(b).[52]

Clause 9 of the Bill – indirect encouragement or assistance

A.52 Clause 9 of the Bill provides that a particular type of indirect encouraging or assisting by D can render him or her liable under the Bill. This provision ensures that a person such as a gang leader (D1) can be held secondarily liable for the criminal conduct of another person (D2) in carrying out D1's instructions, even though D1 himself has no further involvement in giving effect to those instructions:

Example A15

D1 instructs his minion (D2) to hire P to murder V. If D2 encourages P to commit the offence, and P murders V, then D1 as well as D2 can be secondarily liable for the murder.

Clause 10 of the Bill – committing an offence

A.53 Under clause 1(1) and clause 2(1), D's liability is contingent on P having 'committed an offence'. The purpose of clause 10 is to explain, for the purposes of clauses 1 and 2, what is meant by committing an offence. This, in turn, is to ensure that there is a clear line between D's liability under clauses 1 and 2 on the one hand, and clause 4 (innocent agency) on the other hand.

---

[51] Cl 8(2)(a) of the Bill.

[52] D's failure to provide a police officer with assistance when called upon to prevent a breach of the peace is itself a common law offence, but cl 8(3) of the Bill ensures that D will not be secondarily liable for any offence committed by P as a result of assistance provided by his passive failure to help the police when called upon to help.

A.54   Clause 10(1) provides that P commits an offence if he or she acts with the fault required for conviction of the offence, is or over the age of 10 and does not have a defence of insanity. Clause 10(2) makes it clear that if P satisfies clause 10(1), it is immaterial that P may have a complete or partial defence. Thus, if D encourages P to intentionally kill V and P does so, *for the purposes of determining D's liability*, P has committed murder even if P is convicted of manslaughter by virtue of successfully pleading provocation or diminished responsibility. Although both provocation and diminished responsibility reduce murder to manslaughter, neither negates the fault element of murder. If P is convicted of manslaughter by virtue of provocation or diminished responsibility, he or she has nevertheless acted 'with the fault required for conviction of [murder]'.[53] Likewise, if P successfully pleads duress to, for example, a charge of theft. In this instance, P is acquitted. However, like provocation and diminished responsibility, duress does not negate the fault element of the offence.

A.55   The converse of clause 10 is clause 4. As noted above, this provides that if P does not act with the fault required to be convicted of the principal offence or is under the age of 10 or has a defence of insanity, P is deemed to be an innocent agent of D.[54] Accordingly, in such cases D will be liable under clause 4, provided he or she intentionally counsels P to commit the conduct element of the principal offence and did so with the requisite state of mind.[55]

Clause 11 of the Bill – acts, criminal acts and no-fault offences

A.56   Clause 11(1) of the Bill provides that a reference to an act includes a reference to a course of conduct. This applies to D's own conduct[56] as well as any criminal act which D intends or believes will be committed by another person (for example, a course of conduct amounting to harassment).[57]

A.57   Clause 11(2) defines the term 'criminal act', as explained above.[58]

A.58   Clause 11(3)(a) provides that a reference to the doing of a criminal act includes a reference to the continuation of an act which has already begun:

> **Example A16**
>
> D enters a bedroom to find P engaged in sexual intercourse with V. D knows that V is not consenting, and that P is aware of this, but nevertheless positions himself in front of P to watch, intending to encourage P by his being there. P continues to rape V, encouraged by D's presence.

A.59   Clause 11(3)(b) provides that a reference to the doing of a criminal act includes a reference to an attempt to do such an act. For example:

[53]   Cl 10(1)(a) of the Bill.

[54]   Cl 4(2)(b) of the Bill.

[55]   Cl 4(3) of the Bill.

[56]   D can be liable under the Bill if he does a number of acts, none of which would be regarded as having the capacity to encourage or assist the doing of a criminal act, if the cumulative effect of D's course of conduct encouraged or assisted P.

[57]   Protection from Harassment Act 1997, s 1.

[58]   See paras A.9 to A.12 above.

> **Example A17**
>
> D and P agree to murder V, the plan being that D will provide the gun (for a sum of money) and P will use it to perpetrate the offence. D believes that P will indeed attempt to murder V, but that he has no chance of succeeding. P murders V. Both D and P are liable for murder.[59]

Clauses 12 to 14 of the Bill

A.60 These provisions are self-explanatory.

PARTICIPATING IN CRIME (JURISDICTION, PROCEDURE AND CONCEQUENCIAL PROVISIONS) BILL

A.61 This Bill[60] complements the Bill by setting out the rules on jurisdiction, procedure and sentencing.

Clause 1 of the Supplementary Bill

A.62 This provision is self-explanatory.

Clause 2 of the Supplementary Bill – jurisdiction (secondary liability)

A.63 This clause and Schedule 1 to the Supplementary Bill set out the rules on jurisdiction if the allegation is that D is secondarily liable for an offence committed by P.[61]

A.64 Clause 2(1) of the Supplementary Bill sets out the basic rule that D can be convicted of P's offence, by virtue of clauses 1 and 2 of the Bill, if P's offence is committed anywhere in England or Wales, regardless of where D was at any relevant time. This provision therefore encompasses the standard 'domestic' situation, where both D and P acted within the jurisdiction of England and Wales, but it also extends to the situation where D provided his or her encouragement or assistance from elsewhere:

> **Example A18**
>
> D in Berlin sends an e-mail to P in London encouraging P to commit burglary. D may be tried in England or Wales for the burglary committed by P in London.

---

[59] If the offence in respect of which D is charged is itself the offence of attempt, contrary to s 1 of the Criminal Attempts Act 1981, then cl 11(3)(b) of the Bill is inapplicable. This explains the words in parentheses. Thus, if P fails to murder V, but commits the offence of attempted murder, D can be secondarily liable for that offence without reference to cl 11(3)(b).

[60] Hereinafter, the "Supplementary Bill".

[61] Because of the multifarious ways in which encouragement or assistance may be provided, and the fact that assistance or encouragement may be sent from any part of the world to any other part of the world, the question of jurisdiction is of particular importance in the context of the Bill.

A.65   Clause 2(2) of the Supplementary Bill provides that in any other situation, where P's offence is committed outside England and Wales and D is alleged to be secondarily liable for it, D may be convicted of the offence only if the facts fall within paragraph 1 or 2 of Schedule 1 to the Supplementary Bill. Where Schedule 1 is relied on, however, the consent of the Attorney General is required.[62]

Paragraph 1 of Schedule 1

A.66   This paragraph provides the courts in England and Wales with jurisdiction in the situation where D's relevant conduct occurred (at least partly) within England or Wales and P's offence was committed elsewhere, so long as P's offence is one for which a principal offender (satisfying a relevant citizenship, nationality or residence requirement, if any) could be tried under the law of England and Wales regardless of the fact that the offence was committed elsewhere:

Example A19

D in London sends a parcel of poison to a French citizen (P) in Paris encouraging him to use it to murder V in Brussels. D can be convicted in England or Wales of the murder committed by P in Brussels, on the ground it would have been possible to convict P in England or Wales if he had satisfied the requirement of being a "subject of her Majesty".[63]

Example A20

D in London sends a letter to an Indonesian citizen (P) in Jakarta encouraging him to commit an act of piracy on the high seas. P commits an act of piracy on the high seas, and could, in theory, be convicted in England or Wales of that offence.[64] Accordingly, D may be convicted of P's offence in England or Wales.

Paragraph 2 of Schedule 1

A.67   This paragraph provides the courts with jurisdiction in the situation where P committed an offence outside England and Wales and D too was outside England and Wales at the time of all of his or her own relevant conduct, so long as D could have been tried under the law of England and Wales for the offence if he or she had been a principal offender:

---

[62]   Cl 7 of the Supplementary Bill.

[63]   Offences Against the Person Act 1861, s 9.

[64]   Piracy on the high seas is a crime against the law of nations, for which P may be tried in any sovereign state.

> **Example A21**
>
> D (a British citizen) holds V down in a Prague night-club while P1 and P2 (neither of whom are British citizens) kick him to death. D can be convicted in England or Wales of the murder because, as a British citizen, it would have been possible to convict him in England or Wales if he had been one of the principal offenders.[65]

> **Example A22**
>
> D (a British citizen) in the Philippines encourages P (who is not a British citizen) to rape a 10-year-old girl in Manila. D can be convicted in England or Wales of the child-rape because, as a British citizen, it would have been possible to convict D of the offence in England or Wales if he, rather than P, had been the principal offender.[66]

Clause 3 of the Supplementary Bill – jurisdiction (innocent agency)

A.68   Clause 3 and Schedule 1 to the Supplementary Bill set out the rules on jurisdiction if the allegation is that D is liable for an offence under clause 4 of the Bill, that is, that committed it through the medium of an innocent agent.

A.69   Clause 3(1) provides in effect that if the external elements of the offence in question are committed by P in England or Wales, D may be convicted of it irrespective of his or her own location at any relevant time. This provision therefore encompasses the standard 'domestic' situation where it can be shown that P committed the conduct element in England or Wales and D's own relevant conduct also occurred in England or Wales. The provision also extends, however, to the situation where it can be shown that D caused P's conduct (in England or Wales) from some other place:

> **Example A23**
>
> D, in Paris, telephones P, his seven-year-old son in London, directing him to break into a neighbouring house to remove V's jewellery and thereafter to post it to him. D could be convicted of the burglary he committed in London through his innocent agent (P).

A.70   Clause 3(2) provides that, if the conduct element of the offence is committed by P outside England and Wales, D may be convicted of that offence under clause 4 of the Bill only if the facts fall within paragraph 3 or 4 of Schedule 1 to the Supplementary Bill. Where Schedule 1 is relied on, however, the consent of the Attorney General is required.[67]

---

[65] Offences Against the Person Act 1861, s 9.

[66] Sexual Offences Act 2003, s 72 and Sch 2.

[67] Cl 7 of the Supplementary Bill.

Paragraph 3 of Schedule 1

A.71 Paragraph 3 provides the courts with jurisdiction in the situation where D's own conduct occurred, at least partly, within England or Wales, even though the conduct of the innocent agent (P), in committing the conduct element of the offence, occurred elsewhere:

> **Example A24**
>
> D in London sends an e-mail to his assistant (P) in Italy instructing him to dispose of certain property in Rome which he says belongs to him (D), but which in fact belongs to his ex-wife (V). If P disposes of V's property, innocently believing that he is acting in accordance with D's instructions to dispose of D's own property, D could be convicted in England or Wales of the offence or offences (for example, theft or criminal damage) he committed through P in Italy.

Paragraph 4 of Schedule 1

A.72 This paragraph provides the courts with jurisdiction in the situation where none of the relevant conduct occurred in England or Wales, but the offence D caused P to commit (in another jurisdiction) is one for which D could be tried under the law of England and Wales if he or she had directly perpetrated it in that other jurisdiction:

> **Example A25**
>
> D (a British Citizen) hands P a gun in Paris. D knows that the gun is loaded with live ammunition but tells P that it is loaded with blanks and that he should fire it at V to cause her distress, D's intention being that V should be killed. P fires the gun and kills V (in Paris).

D can be convicted in England or Wales of murder on the basis that a British citizen who perpetrates murder outside England and Wales may nevertheless be convicted of that offence in England or Wales.[68]

Clause 4 of the Supplementary Bill – jurisdiction (causing a no-fault crime)

A.73 Clause 4 sets out the rule on jurisdiction if the allegation is that D caused P to commit a no-fault offence contrary to clause 5 of the Bill. It provides that D may be convicted of the offence only if it was committed by P in England or Wales and D's own relevant conduct took place wholly or partly in England or Wales.

Clause 5 of the Supplementary Bill – mode of participation

A.74 This clause preserves one of the most important practical aspects of the doctrine of secondary liability. The accused may be convicted of an offence if it cannot be proved whether he was guilty as a principal offender or guilty as an accessory (by the application of clauses 1 and 2 of the Bill) if it can be proved that he must have been one or the other.

---

[68] Offences Against the Person Act 1861, s 9.

Clause 6 of the Supplementary Bill – procedure (causing a no-fault crime)

A.75   Clause 6(1) provides that if D is charged with causing P to commit a no-fault offence, the mode of trial of D is to be determined as if D had been charged with committing the no-fault offence.

A.76   Clause 6(2) provides that if D is convicted of causing P to commit a no-fault offence, D is liable to any penalty for which he or she would have been liable if convicted of the no-fault offence.

Clause 7 of the Supplementary Bill – Attorney General's consent

A.77   Clause 7 provides that where P's offence is committed outside England and Wales or, in cases where P is an innocent agent, would have been committed outside England and Wales, proceedings under clauses 1, 2 or 4 can only be instituted by, or with the consent of, the Attorney General.

Clause 8 of the Supplementary Bill – abolition of common law rules

A.78   Clause 8(a) abolishes the common law doctrine of secondary liability while clause 8(b) abolishes the common law doctrine of innocent agency.

Clause 9 of the Supplementary Bill – amendments and repeals

A.79   Clause 9 of the Supplementary Bill and Schedule 3 thereto repeal a number of statutory provisions, including section 8 of the Accessories and Abettors Act 1861 and section 44(1) of the Magistrates' Courts Act 1980.[69] However, special provisions on secondary liability – such as section 7(1) of the Perjury Act 1911[70] and section 21(4) of the Gas Act 1965[71] – are excluded from the Schedule.[72]

A.80   Clause 9[73] also provides that the provisions listed in Part 1 of Schedule 2 to the Supplementary Bill must be interpreted with reference to Part 1 of the Bill (that is, the provisions on secondary liability, innocent agency and causing a no-fault offence).

---

[69]   In fact the whole of the 1861 Act is repealed because s 8 is the only substantive provision in force. The only other subsisting provision (ie, s 10) simply provides that the Act (ie, s 8) does not extend to Scotland. Schedule 12 to the Criminal Law Act 1977, which amends s 8 of the 1861 Act, is included in Sch 3 on the ground that it will be rendered otiose by the repeal of s 8. Section 55(2) of the International Criminal Court Act 2001, which makes reference to s 8 of the 1861 Act to explain s 55(1)(a), can also be repealed because s 55(1)(a) is now explained by Part 1 of Sch 2 to the Supplementary Bill (para 37).

[70]   "Every person who aids, abets, counsels, procures or suborns another person to commit an offence against [the Perjury Act 1911] shall be liable … as if he were a principal offender."

[71]   "[A]ny person who aids, abets, counsels or procures the commission of an offence under [Part 2 of the Gas Act 1965] shall be guilty of that offence …"

[72]   Our view is that the Government departments responsible for these various provisions should be allowed sufficient time to determine, following consultation with other relevant bodies, whether they should be retained (to operate in tandem with the provisions of the Bill) or repealed.

[73]   Cl 9(3) of the Supplementary Bill.

A.81   Part 1 of Schedule 2 lists the existing statutory provisions which make reference to the types of conduct punishable under the old common law doctrine of secondary liability by virtue of section 8 of the Accessories and Abettors Act 1861 or section 44(1) of the Magistrates' Courts Act 1980.[74]

A.82   Not all the provisions which make reference to the language of common law secondary liability are included in Part 1 of the Schedule, however, on the ground that some such provisions fall outside our remit to reform the law of England and Wales. Thus, provisions which relate solely to the law outside England and Wales, such as section 277A of the Merchant Shipping Act 1995, and provisions relating to the law governing members of the armed forces, such as section 41(1) of the Naval Discipline Act 1957, are omitted.[75]

A.83   Clause 9(4) explains that Part 2 of Schedule 2 contains other minor and consequential amendments. For example, the reference in section 21(4) of the Gas Act 1965[76] to section 8 of the Accessories and Abettors Act 1861 and section 44(1) of the Magistrates' Courts Act 1980 is amended so that it becomes a reference to Part 1 of the Bill.

Clauses 11 to 13 of the Supplementary Bill – final provisions

A.84   These provisions are self-explanatory.

---

[74]   That is, conduct falling within the meaning of "aid, abet, counsel or procure", whether or not those particular words are used.

[75]   It will be for the Ministry of Defence to determine whether or not provisions relating to the armed forces should be brought into Part 1 of Sch 2. The power to include additional provisions (and also to remove existing provisions) within Part 1 of Sch 2 is provided by cl 9(5)(a) of the Supplementary Bill.

[76]   Para 47 of Sch 2.

Participating in Crime Bill

CONTENTS

13

PART 3

GENERAL

Participating in Crime Bill
Part 1 — Liability for participating in crime
Chapter 1 — Liability for offences committed or acts done by others

1

A

BILL

TO

Codify with amendments the law of England and Wales on the criminal liability of persons for offences committed, and acts done, by others; and to create an offence of causing a no-fault offence.

B E IT ENACTED by the Queen's most Excellent Majesty, by and with the advice and consent of the Lords Spiritual and Temporal, and Commons, in this present Parliament assembled, and by the authority of the same, as follows:—

PART 1

LIABILITY FOR PARTICIPATING IN CRIME

CHAPTER 1

LIABILITY FOR OFFENCES COMMITTED OR ACTS DONE BY OTHERS

Ways in which a person may become liable

5

1   Assisting or encouraging an offence

(1)   Where a person (P) has committed an offence, another person (D) is also guilty of the offence if—

    (a)   D did an act with the intention that one or more of a number of other acts would be done by another person,

10

    (b)   P's criminal act was one of those acts,

    (c)   D's behaviour assisted or encouraged P to do his criminal act, and

    (d)   subsection (2) or (3) is satisfied.

(2)   This subsection is satisfied if D believed that a person doing the act would commit the offence.

15

(3)   This subsection is satisfied if D's state of mind was such that had he done the act he would have committed the offence.

13

2

Participating in Crime Bill
Part 1 — Liability for participating in crime
Chapter 1 — Liability for offences committed or acts done by others

2   Participating in a joint criminal venture

(1)   This section applies where two or more persons participate in a joint criminal venture.

(2)   If one of them (P) commits an offence, another participant (D) is also guilty of the offence if P's criminal act falls within the scope of the venture.   5

(3)   The existence or scope of a joint criminal venture may be inferred from the conduct of the participants (whether or not there is an express agreement).

(4)   D does not escape liability under this section for an offence committed by P at a time when D is a participant in the venture merely because D is at that time—

    (a)   absent,   10

    (b)   against the venture's being carried out, or

    (c)   indifferent as to whether it is carried out.

Extension of liability under this Chapter

3   Liability not restricted by special characteristics required of offender

D may be guilty under this Chapter of an offence even though—   15

    (a)   the offence is one that may be committed only by a person who meets a particular description, and

    (b)   D does not meet that description.

4   Using an innocent agent

(1)   If a person (D) uses an innocent agent (P) to commit an offence, D is guilty of   20
that offence.

(2)   P is an innocent agent in relation to an offence if—

    (a)   he does a criminal act, and

    (b)   he does not commit the offence itself for one of the following reasons—

        (i)   he is under the age of 10,

        (ii)   he has a defence of insanity, or   25

        (iii)   he acts without the fault required for conviction,

    and there is no other reason why he does not commit it.

(3)   D uses P to commit an offence if—

    (a)   D intends to cause a person (whether or not P) to do a criminal act in relation to the offence,   30

    (b)   D causes P to do the criminal act, and

    (c)   subsection (4) or (5) is satisfied.

(4)   If a particular state of mind requires to be proved for conviction of the offence that D uses P to commit, D's state of mind must be such that, were he to do the act that he intends to cause to be done, he would do it with the state of mind   35
required for conviction of the offence.

(5)   If the offence which D uses P to commit is a no-fault offence, D must know or believe that, were a person to do the act that D intends to cause to be done, that person would do it—

    (a)   in the circumstances (if any), and   40

Participating in Crime Bill
Part 1 — Liability for participating in crime
Chapter 1 — Liability for offences committed or acts done by others

3

      (b)   with the consequences (if any),

proof of which is required for conviction of the offence.

CHAPTER 2

CAUSING A NO-FAULT OFFENCE

5   Offence of causing a no-fault offence

(1)   A person commits an offence if he causes another person to commit a no-fault offence, and—
      (a)   it is his intention that a person should commit the offence, or
      (b)   he knows or believes that his behaviour will cause a person to commit it.

(2)   "No-fault offence" means an offence that does not require proof of fault.

PART 2

LIMITATIONS ON LIABILITY IMPOSED BY PART 1

General limitation on liability

6   Protective offences: victims not liable

(1)   D is not liable under Chapter 1 of Part 1 for a protective offence if—
      (a)   he falls within the protected category, and
      (b)   he is the person in respect of whom it was committed.

(2)   D does not commit an offence under section 5 if—
      (a)   the no-fault offence is a protective offence,
      (b)   he falls within the protected category, and
      (c)   he is the person in respect of whom it was committed.

(3)   "Protective offence" means an offence that exists (wholly or in part) for the protection of a particular category of persons ("the protected category").

Defences

7   Defence of acting to prevent commission of offence etc.

(1)   In proceedings for an offence to which this section applies, a person is not guilty of the offence if he proves on the balance of probabilities that—
      (a)   he acted for the purpose of—
          (i)   preventing the commission of that offence or another offence, or
          (ii)   preventing, or limiting, the occurrence of harm, and
      (b)   it was reasonable for him to act as he did.

(2)   This section applies to an offence of which a person is alleged to be guilty as a result of section 1 or 2.

PART 3

GENERAL

Interpretation

8   Encouraging and assisting

(1) A reference in this Act to encouraging a person to do an act includes a reference   5
to threatening or otherwise putting pressure on him to do it.

(2) A reference in this Act to encouraging or assisting a person to do an act
includes a reference to—

(a) taking steps to reduce the possibility of criminal proceedings being
brought in respect of the act's being done,   10

(b) failing to take reasonable steps to discharge a duty.

(3) But a person is not to be regarded as encouraging or assisting another person
to do an act merely because he fails to respond to a constable's request for
assistance in preventing a breach of the peace.

9   Indirectly encouraging or assisting   15

If a person (D1) arranges for a person (D2) to do something that will encourage
or assist another person to do an act, and D2 does any such thing, D1 is also to
be treated for the purposes of this Act as having done it.

10   Committing an offence

(1) For the purposes of sections 1 and 2 and of Part 2 (so far as it relates to those   20
sections), a reference to a person (P) who commits an offence is to a person
who—

(a) acts with the fault required for conviction of the offence,

(b) is of or over the age of 10, and

(c) does not have a defence of insanity.   25

(2) For those purposes, it is immaterial whether P has any other defence.

11   Acts, criminal acts and no-fault offences

(1) A reference in this Act to an act includes a reference to a course of conduct and
a reference to the doing of an act is to be read accordingly.

(2) A reference in this Act to a criminal act is, in relation to an offence, a reference   30
to an act (or a failure to act) that falls within the definition of the act (or failure
to act) that must be proved in order for a person to be convicted of the offence.

(3) A reference in this Act to the doing of a criminal act includes a reference to—

(a) the continuation of an act that has already begun,

(b) an attempt to do an act (except in relation to an offence of attempting to   35
commit another offence).

(4) A reference in this Act to a no-fault offence is to read in accordance with section
5(2).

Final provisions

12   Commencement

This Act, except this section and sections 13 and 14, comes into force in accordance with provision made by the Secretary of State by order made by statutory instrument.

5

13   Extent

This Act extends to England and Wales only.

14   Short title

This Act may be cited as the Participating in Crime Act 2006.

Participating in Crime (Jurisdiction, Procedure and Consequential Provisions) Bill

CONTENTS

A

BILL

TO

Make provision about jurisdiction over, and procedure in relation to, offences committed under or by virtue of the Participating in Crime Act 2006; and to make consequential amendments, repeals and savings in connection with that Act.

B E IT ENACTED by the Queen's most Excellent Majesty, by and with the advice and consent of the Lords Spiritual and Temporal, and Commons, in this present Parliament assembled, and by the authority of the same, as follows: —

PART 1

INTRODUCTORY

1   Meaning and application of "the codifying Act"

(1)   In this Act "the codifying Act" means the Participating in Crime Act 2006.

(2)   Any expression used in this Act in connection with a provision of the codifying   5
Act has the same meaning as it has in that provision.

PART 2

JURISDICTION AND PROCEDURE

Jurisdiction

2   Liability under sections 1 and 2 of the codifying Act   10

(1)   If P's offence is committed in England or Wales, D may be guilty under section
1 or 2 of the codifying Act of the same offence no matter where he was at any
relevant time.

(2)   If P's offence is committed outside England and Wales, D is not guilty under
either of those sections of the same offence unless paragraph 1 or 2 of Schedule   15
1 applies.

12

3   Liability under section 4 of the codifying Act

(1)   If the offence that P would have committed ("the principal offence") would have been committed in England or Wales, D may be guilty under section 4 of the codifying Act of that offence no matter where he was at any relevant time.

(2)   If the principal offence would have been committed outside England and Wales, D is not guilty under that section of that offence unless paragraph 3 or 4 of Schedule 1 applies.

4   Offences under section 5 of the codifying Act

A person does not commit an offence under section 5 of the codifying Act unless —

(a)   P commits the no-fault offence in England or Wales; and

(b)   any relevant behaviour of D's takes place wholly or partly in England or Wales.

Proceedings etc. for offences under the codifying Act

5   Persons who may be perpetrators or encouragers etc.

(1)   A person may be convicted of an offence if, although it is not proved whether —

(a)   he is guilty of the offence on the basis that he committed it and has no defence, or

(b)   he is guilty under section 1 or 2 of the codifying Act of the offence,

it is proved that he must be one or the other.

(2)   For the purposes of subsection (1)(a), a person who used an innocent agent to commit an offence is guilty of that offence on the basis that he committed it.

6   Procedure and punishment for offences under section 5 of the codifying Act

(1)   The mode of trial of a person charged with an offence under section 5 of the codifying Act is to be determined as if he had been charged with the no-fault offence concerned.

(2)   A person convicted of an offence under section 5 of the codifying Act is liable to any penalty for which he would be liable if he were convicted in the same proceedings of the no-fault offence concerned.

Restriction on institution of proceedings

7   Role of the Attorney General

No proceedings for an offence triable by reason of any provision of Schedule 1 may be instituted except by, or with the consent of, the Attorney General.

5

10

15

20

25

30

35

Participating in Crime (Jurisdiction, Procedure and Consequential Provisions) Bill
Part 3 — Consequential provisions

3

PART 3

CONSEQUENTIAL PROVISIONS

8   Abolition of common law replaced by the codifying Act

The following (which are replaced by provisions of the codifying Act) are abolished —

5

    (a)   the rules of the common law relating to the circumstances in which a person is liable for an offence because he has aided, abetted, counselled or procured its commission; and

    (b)   the rules of the common law relating to the circumstances in which a person commits an offence through an innocent agent.

10

9   Consequential amendments and repeals

    (1)   Section 8 of the Accessories and Abettors Act 1861 (c. 94) (aiders, abettors etc. to be tried, indicted and punished as principal offenders) ceases to have effect.

    (2)   Section 44(1) of the Magistrates' Courts Act 1980 (c. 43) (aiders and abettors) ceases to have effect.

15

    (3)   In the provisions listed in Part 1 of Schedule 2 —

    (a)   any reference however expressed to conduct punishable by virtue of section 8 of the 1861 Act has effect, in England and Wales, as a reference to conduct punishable under Part 1 of the codifying Act;

    (b)   any reference however expressed to conduct punishable by virtue of section 44(1) of the 1980 Act has effect as a reference to conduct punishable under Part 1 of the codifying Act.

20

    (4)   Part 2 of Schedule 2 contains other minor and consequential amendments.

    (5)   The Secretary of State may by order —

    (a)   amend Part 1 of Schedule 2 by adding or removing a provision;

25

    (b)   amend any provision in such way as he thinks fit in consequence of the provisions of this Act.

    (6)   An order under subsection (5) shall be made by statutory instrument; and no such order shall be made unless a draft of it has been laid before Parliament and approved by a resolution of each House of Parliament.

30

    (7)   Schedule 3 contains repeals.

10   Saving for offences committed before commencement

    (1)   Nothing in this Act affects the operation of —

    (a)   any rule of the common law, or

    (b)   any provision of an Act or of subordinate legislation,

35

in relation to offences committed wholly or partly before the commencement of this Act.

    (2)   An offence is partly committed before the commencement of this Act if —

    (a)   a relevant event occurs before commencement; and

    (b)   another relevant event occurs on or after commencement.

40

(3)   "Relevant event", in relation to an offence, means any act or other event (including any consequence of an act) proof of which is required for conviction of the offence.

PART 4

FINAL PROVISIONS

5

11   Commencement

Parts 2 and 3 of this Act come into force in accordance with provision made by the Secretary of State by order made by statutory instrument.

12   Extent

(1)   Subject to subsection (2), this Act extends to England and Wales only.   *10*

(2)   Part 1 and this Part, and the provisions mentioned in subsection (3) (so far as they relate to an enactment which so extends), also extend to Scotland and Northern Ireland.

(3)   The provisions are—
    (a)   section 9(3) and (4) and Schedule 2, and   *15*
    (b)   any provision contained in an order made by virtue of section 9(5)(b).

13   Short title

This Act may be cited as the Participating in Crime (Jurisdiction, Procedure and Consequential Provisions) Act 2006.

Participating in Crime (Jurisdiction, Procedure and Consequential Provisions) Bill
Schedule 1 — Extra-territoriality

5

SCHEDULES

SCHEDULE 1   Sections 2(2) and 3(2)

EXTRA-TERRITORIALITY

PART 1

LIABILITY FOR OFFENCES COMMITTED BY OTHERS   *5*

1   (1) This paragraph applies if—

    (a)   any relevant behaviour of D's takes place wholly or partly in England or Wales; and

    (b)   either—

        (i)   P's offence is triable under the law of England and Wales; or   *10*

        (ii)   if there are relevant conditions which P does not satisfy, it would be so triable if P satisfied the conditions.

    (2) "Relevant condition" means a condition that—

    (a)   determines (wholly or in part) whether an offence committed outside Enagland and Wales is nonetheless triable under the law of   *15* England and Wales, and

    (b)   relates to the citizenship, nationality or residence of the person who commits it.

2   (1) This paragraph applies if—

    (a)   any relevant behaviour of D's takes place wholly outside England   *20* and Wales; and

    (b)   D could have been tried under the law of England and Wales if he had committed P's offence in the place where P committed it.

    (2) It does not matter whether P could be tried under the law of England and Wales.   *25*

PART 2

INNOCENT AGENTS

3   This paragraph applies if any relevant behaviour of D's takes place wholly or partly in England or Wales.

4   This paragraph applies if—   *30*

    (a)   any relevant behaviour of D's takes place wholly outside England and Wales; and

    (b)   D could have been tried under the law of England and Wales if he had committed the principal offence in the place where P would have committed it.   *35*

6   *Participating in Crime (Jurisdiction, Procedure and Consequential Provisions) Bill*
Schedule 2 — Minor and consequential amendments
Part 1 — References to aiding, abetting, counselling or procuring

SCHEDULE 2   Section 9(3) and (4)

MINOR AND CONSEQUENTIAL AMENDMENTS

PART 1

REFERENCES TO AIDING, ABETTING, COUNSELLING OR PROCURING

1   Section 2 of the Poaching Prevention Act 1862 (c. 114) (powers of constable   5
        to stop and search).

2   Section 46(1)(b) of the Children and Young Persons Act 1933 (c. 12)
        (assignment of certain matters to youth courts).

3   Section 2(1) of the Incitement to Disaffection Act 1934 (c. 56) (possession or
        control of documents liable to incite disaffection).   10

4   Section 3(4) of the Visiting Forces Act 1952 (c. 67) (restriction, as respects
        certain offences, of trial by United Kingdom courts of offenders connected
        with visiting force).

5   Section 18 of the Children and Young Persons Act 1963 (c. 37) (jurisdiction
        of magistrates' courts in certain cases involving children and young   15
        persons).

6   Section 18(2) of the Theatres Act 1968 (c. 54) (interpretation).

7   Section 1B(2) of the Biological Weapons Act 1974 (c. 6) (Customs and Excise
        prosecutions).

8   Paragraph 5(2) of the Schedule to the Prices Act 1974 (c. 24) (enforcement).   20

9   Section 17(1) of the Industry Act 1975 (c. 68) (no criminal proceedings to lie
        in respect of contravention of a prohibition order).

10   Subsections (2)(b) and (3)(b) of section 1 of the Internationally Protected
        Persons Act 1978 (secondary liability for, and threats to commit, offences
        against internationally protected persons).   25

11   Section 16(3) of the Customs and Excise Management Act 1979 (c. 2) (power
        of arrest).

12   In the Magistrates' Courts Act 1980 (c. 43) —
        (a)   section 44(2) (offences triable either way);
        (b)   section 103(2)(d) (written statement of child admissible in committal   30
               proceedings for certain offences);
        (c)   paragraph 33 of Schedule 1 (offences triable either way by virtue of
               section 17);
        (d)   paragraph 2 of Schedule 2 (offences for which the value involved is
               relevant to the mode of trial).   35

13   Section 1(4)(b) of the Criminal Attempts Act 1981 (c. 47) (attempting to
        commit an offence).

14   In the Betting and Gaming Duties Act 1981 (c. 63) —
        (a)   section 9(5) (prohibitions for protection of revenue);
        (b)   section 9A(4) (prohibitions for protection of revenue: overseas   40
               brokers).

Participating in Crime (Jurisdiction, Procedure and Consequential Provisions) Bill 7
Schedule 2 – Minor and consequential amendments
Part 1 – References to aiding, abetting, counselling or procuring

15   Section 64(5) of the Civil Aviation Act 1982 (c. 16) (restriction of unlicensed carriage by air for reward).

16   Section 1(2) of the Forfeiture Act 1982 (c. 34) (meaning of the "forfeiture" rule).

17   Section 2(2)(b) of the Aviation Security Act 1982 (c. 36) (destroying,   *5*
         damaging or endangering safety of aircraft).

18   Section 32(1)(b)(iv) of the Criminal Justice Act 1982 (c. 48) (early release of prisoners).

19   Section 80(3)(c) of the Police and Criminal Evidence Act 1984 (c. 60) (compellability of accused's spouse or civil partner).   *10*

20   Section 141(c) of the Companies Act 1985 (wilful concealment misrepresentation by officer of a company in relation to reduction of its share capital).

21   Section 49(4) of the Airports Act 1986 (c. 31) (no criminal proceedings to lie in respect of contravention of compliance order).   *15*

22   Section 30(4) of the Gas Act 1986 (c. 44) (no criminal proceedings to lie in respect of contravention of final or provisional order).

23   Section 12(6)(a) of the Outer Space Act 1986 (c. 38) (offences).

24   Section 20(4) of the Public Order Act 1986 (c. 64) (public performance of play).   *20*

25   In the Road Traffic Offenders Act 1988 (c. 53) –
         (a)   section 28(2) (penalty points to be attributed to an offence);
         (b)   section 34(5) (disqualification for certain offences);
         (c)   section 35(5A) (disqualification for repeated offences).

26   Paragraph 2(b) of Schedule 1 to the Football Spectators Act 1989 (c. 37)   *25*
         (offences).

27   In the Aviation and Maritime Security Act 1990 (c. 31) –
         (a)   section 11(3)(b) (destroying ships or fixed platforms or endangering their safety);
         (b)   section 15(2)(c) (master's power of delivery).   *30*

28   Section 53(7) of the Criminal Justice Act 1991 (c. 53) (cases involving children in which notice of transfer may be given).

29   Section 2(1)(h) of the Sexual Offences (Amendment) Act 1992 (c. 34) (offences to which Act applies).

30   Section 30A(2) of the Chemical Weapons Act 1996 (c. 6) (Customs and Excise   *35*
         prosecutions).

31   Section 14(2)(d) of the Northern Ireland (Sentences) Act 1998 (c. 35) (inadmissibility).

32   Section 62(2) of the Youth Justice and Criminal Evidence Act 1999 (c. 23) (meaning of "sexual offence" and other references to offences).   *40*

33   In the Powers of Criminal Courts (Sentencing) Act 2000 (c. 6) –

8   *Participating in Crime (Jurisdiction, Procedure and Consequential Provisions) Bill*
Schedule 2 — Minor and consequential amendments
Part 1 — References to aiding, abetting, counselling or procuring

    (a)   section 143(6) (powers to deprive offender of property used etc. for purposes of crime); and

    (b)   section 147(2) (driving disqualification where vehicle used for purposes of crime).

34   Section 18(12)(i) of the Regulation of Investigatory Powers Act 2000 (c. 23) (exceptions to exclusionary rule in section 17 of that Act).

35   Paragraph 3(t)(i) of Schedule 4 to the Criminal Justice and Court Services Act 2000 (c. 43) (meaning of "offence against a child").

36   Section 34(1) of the Criminal Justice and Police Act 2001 (c. 16) (meaning of "drug trafficking offence").

37   Section 55(1)(a) of the International Criminal Court Act 2001 (c. 17) (meaning of "ancillary offence").

38   Section 53(2) of the Anti-terrorism, Crime and Security Act 2001 (c. 24) (Customs and Excise prosecutions).

39   In the Proceeds of Crime Act 2002 (c. 29) —

    (a)   section 340(11)(c) (interpretation of Part 7: money laundering);

    (b)   section 415(2)(b) (money laundering offences for purposes of Part 8: investigations);

    (c)   section 447(9)(c) (interpretation of Part 11: national and international co-operation);

    (d)   section 451(6)(d) (Customs and Excise prosecutions);

    (e)   paragraph 10(2) of Schedule 2 (lifestyle offences: England and Wales).

40   Section 142(7)(b) of the Extradition Act 2003 (c. 41) (extradition from category 1 territory to the United Kingdom).

41   In the Sexual Offences Act 2003 (c. 42) —

    (a)   section 62(2) (committing an offence with intent to commit a sexual offence);

    (b)   section 73(1) and (3) (exceptions to aiding, abetting and counselling);

    (c)   paragraph 3(b) of Schedule 2 (sexual offences to which section 72 applies);

    (d)   paragraph 94(b) of Schedule 3 (sexual offences for purposes of Part 2);

    (e)   paragraph 173(b) of Schedule 5 (other offences for purposes of Part 2).

42   In the Criminal Justice Act 2003 (c. 44) —

    (a)   paragraph 40 of Schedule 4 (qualifying offences for purposes of section 62);

    (b)   paragraph 51 of Schedule 5 (qualifying offences for purposes of Part 10);

    (c)   paragraph 64(a) of Schedule 15 (specified violent offences for purposes of Part 10);

    (d)   paragraph 153(a) of Schedule 15 (specified sexual offences for purposes of Chapter 5 of Part 12).

43   Section 14(1)(d) of the Gangmasters (Licensing) Act 2004 (c. 11) (additional powers of arrest).

Participating in Crime (Jurisdiction, Procedure and Consequential Provisions) Bill   9
Schedule 2 — Minor and consequential amendments
Part 1 — References to aiding, abetting, counselling or procuring

44   Section 17 of the Terrorism Act 2006 (offences committed abroad).

PART 2

OTHER MINOR AND CONSEQUENTIAL AMENDMENTS

Mines and Quarries Act 1954 (c. 70)

45   In section 153 of the Mines and Quarries Act 1954 (accessories), for
paragraph (a) substitute—
      "(a)   as respects England and Wales, of Part 1 of the Participating
          in Crime Act 2006;".

Suicide Act 1961 (c. 60)

46 (1) The Suicide Act 1961 is amended as follows.

     (2) In section 2 (criminal liability for complicity in another's suicide), in
subsection (1), for "aiding, abetting, counselling or procuring" substitute
"encouraging or assisting".

     (3) In subsection (2) of that section, for "aided, abetted, counselled or procured"
substitute "encouraged or assisted".

     (4) In Part 1 of Schedule 1 (amendments limited to England and Wales), in the
entry relating to Schedule 1 to the Children and Young Persons Act 1933, in
the second column, for "aiding, abetting, counselling or procuring"
substitute "encouraging or assisting".

     (5) In Part 2 of that Schedule (amendments not so limited), in the entry relating
to section 7 of the Visiting Forces Act 1952, in the second column, for "to
aiding, abetting, counselling or procuring suicide" substitute ", in England
and Wales, to encouraging or assisting suicide and, in Northern Ireland, to
aiding, abetting, counselling or procuring suicide".

Gas Act 1965 (c. 36)

47   In section 21(4) of the Gas Act 1965 (accessories), for the words from ", as
respects" to "1980" substitute "of Part 1 of the Participating in Crime Act
2006".

Slaughterhouses Act 1974 (c. 3)

48   In section 38 of the Slaughterhouses Act 1974 (regulations for securing
humane conditions of slaughter), in subsection (6), for "section 44 of the
Magistrates' Courts Act 1980" substitute "Part 1 of the Participating in Crime
Act 2006".

Internationally Protected Persons Act 1978 (c. 17)

49   In section 2(3) of the Internationally Protected Persons Act 1978 (section 1 of
that Act not to prejudice operation of other rules), for "section 8 of the
Accessories and Abettors Act 1861" substitute "Part 1 of the Participating in
Crime Act 2006".

10   *Participating in Crime (Jurisdiction, Procedure and Consequential Provisions) Bill*
                              Schedule 2 — Minor and consequential amendments
                              Part 2 — Other minor and consequential amendments

Aviation Security Act 1982 (c. 36)

50   In section 6 of the Aviation Security Act 1982 (ancillary offences), in
          subsection (4), for paragraph (a) substitute—
                  "(a)   in England and Wales, of Part 1 of the Participating in Crime
                         Act 2006;   5
                  (ab)   in Northern Ireland, of section 8 of the Accessories and
                         Abettors Act 1861; or".

Outer Space Act 1986 (c. 38)

51   In section 12 of the Outer Space Act 1986 (offences), for subsection (6)(a)
          substitute—   10
                  "(a)   aiding, abetting, counselling or procuring the commission of
                         an offence under this Act in the United Kingdom;
                  (ab)   an offence of conspiracy or incitement in relation to the
                         commission of an offence under this Act in the United
                         Kingdom;, or".   15

Coroners Act 1988 (c. 13)

52   (1) The Coroners Act 1988 is amended as follows.

     (2) In section 16 (adjournment of inquest in event of criminal proceedings), in
          subsection (1)(a)(iii), for "aiding, abetting, counselling or procuring"
          substitute "encouraging or assisting".   20

     (3) In section 17 (provisions supplementary to section 16) in subsections (1)(c)
          and (2)(c) for "aiding, abetting, counselling or procuring" substitute
          "encouraging or assisting".

Aviation and Maritime Security Act 1990 (c. 31)

53   In section 14 of the Aviation and Maritime Security Act 1990 (ancillary   25
          offences), in subsection (6), for paragraph (a) substitute—
                  "(a)   in England and Wales, of Part 1 of the Participating in Crime
                         Act 2006,
                  (ab)   in Northern Ireland, of section 8 of the Accessories and
                         Abettors Act 1861, or".   30

Law Reform (Year and a Day Rule) Act 1996 (c. 19)

54   (1) Section 2 of the Law Reform (Year and a Day Rule) Act 1996 (restriction on
          proceedings for fatal offence) is amended as follows.

     (2) In subsection (3)(b), for "aiding, abetting, counselling or procuring"
          substitute "encouraging or assisting".   35

     (3) In subsection (5), after paragraph (a) insert—
                  "(aa) the reference in subsection (3)(b) to encouraging or assisting
                         a person's suicide is to aiding, abetting, counselling or
                         procuring a person's suicide, and".

Participating in Crime (Jurisdiction, Procedure and Consequential Provisions) Bill 11
Schedule 2 — Minor and consequential amendments
Part 2 — Other minor and consequential amendments

International Criminal Court Act 2001 (c. 17)

55   In section 55 of the International Criminal Court Act 2001 (meaning of ancillary offence), omit subsection (2).

Female Genital Mutilation Act 2003 (c. 31)

56   (1) The Female Genital Mutilation Act 2003 is amended as follows.   5

   (2) In section 3(1) (offence of assisting a non-UK person to mutilate overseas a girl's genitalia), for "aids, abets, counsels or procures" substitute "encourages or assists".

   (3) In section 4 (extension of sections 1 to 3 to extraterritorial acts), after subsection (2), add—   10

      "(3)   In any proceedings in Northern Ireland for an offence under section 3(1) a person shall be taken to have encouraged or assisted another to do a relevant act of female genital mutilation if he aided, abetted, counselled or procured that person to do that act."

SCHEDULE 3   Section 9(7)   15

REPEALS

Short title and chapter	Extent of repeal	
Accessories and Abettors Act 1861 (c. 94)	The whole Act.	
Criminal Law Act 1977 (c. 45)	In Schedule 12, the entry relating to the Accessories and Abettors Act 1861.	20
Magistrates' Courts Act 1980 (c. 43)	Section 44(1).	
International Criminal Court Act 2001	Section 55(2).	25

APPENDIX B
THE CURRENT LAW

INTRODUCTION

B.1 In this Appendix, as with Part 2, we set out and explore the current law in relation to secondary liability. In this appendix however, we do so in considerably more detail.

SECONDARY LIABILITY - A COMMON LAW DOCTRINE OF GENERAL APPLICATION

B.2 The primary source of the modern law of complicity is section 8 of the Accessories and Abettors Act 1861. As amended, it provides that anyone who 'shall aid, abet, counsel or procure the commission of any indictable offence ... shall be liable to be tried, indicted and punished as a principal offender'.[1] However, the principle that section 8 embodies is a common law principle, namely that aiding, abetting, counselling or procuring another person to commit an offence is not, and never has been, a distinct offence. Rather, a person who, with the requisite state of mind, aids, abets, counsels or procures the commission of an offence is guilty of the principal offence that he or she has aided, abetted, counselled or procured (provided that the offence is subsequently committed). Accordingly, D is liable to the same stigma and penalties as P.

B.3 In *Powell and Daniels, English*,[2] Lord Steyn referred to a particular feature of secondary liability:

> But there is no special rule governing the criminal liability of accessories in cases of murder. The principle governing the criminal liability of accessories applies across the spectrum of most criminal offences.[3]

Lord Steyn was highlighting a crucial distinction between primary and secondary liability. Offences are generally defined with reference to P. The definition of an offence will stipulate what it is that P must do, in what circumstances, with what consequences and with what state of mind. The rules that govern P's liability for a particular offence are unique to that offence.

B.4 By contrast, secondary liability is a common law doctrine the rules of which are generally the same irrespective of the context in which D provides encouragement or assistance and regardless of the seriousness of the principal offence. Accordingly, the rules governing D1's liability for robbery are the same as those governing D2's liability for theft.

---

[1] The corresponding provision for summary offences is Magistrates' Courts Act 1980, s 44.

[2] [1999] 1 AC 1.

[3] Above, 12.

B.5   It would be possible to dispense with a general doctrine of secondary liability but only if each offence had its own rules for determining not only P's but also D's liability. We believe that such an approach would be not only impracticable but would also result in the law of secondary liability being out of line with related areas of the criminal law. In particular, Parliament, on each occasion when it has reformed the inchoate offences of conspiracy and attempt[4] has done so by enacting a general inchoate offence the principles of which apply to all substantive offences.[5] Thus, if P is charged with attempted murder, the principles that determine whether or not he or she is guilty are no different from those that would govern D's liability if he or she were charged with attempted theft.[6]

B.6   Section 8 preserves another fundamental feature of the common law. In *Swindall and Osborne*,[7] D and P encouraged each other to race their respective carts along a road. One of the carts struck V who died. D and P were each charged with manslaughter. At their trial, it was submitted that neither could be convicted of manslaughter because the prosecution was unable to prove whose cart had struck V. Chief Baron Pollock rejected the submission. As a result, the case is authority for the proposition that the mere fact that the prosecution cannot prove whether a person participated in an offence as a principal offender or as a secondary party does not preclude that person being convicted of the offence.

B.7   Accordingly, although there is a conceptual distinction between the conduct of a principal offender and that of a secondary party, a participant in an offence can be convicted of it even if the prosecution is unable to prove his or her precise role.[8] It suffices that participation itself, whether as a principal offender or as a secondary party, can be proven.[9]

THE PARAMETERS OF THE DOCTRINE OF SECONDARY LIABILITY

The derivative theory of secondary liability

B.8   According to the derivative theory of secondary liability, D's liability for 'aiding, abetting, counselling or procuring' P to commit an offence derives from and is dependent upon the liability of P. Three consequences follow.

---

[4]   Criminal Law Act 1977, s 1 (conspiracy) and Criminal Attempts Act 1981, s 1 (attempt).

[5]   Subject to the qualification that the Criminal Attempts Act 1981 does not apply to 'summary only' offences.

[6]   For further discussion see R A Duff, *Criminal Attempts* (1996) pp 141 to 143.

[7]   (1846) 2 C & K 230, 175 ER 95.

[8]   The Australian courts have moved away from maintaining the conceptual distinction. In *Osland v R* (1998) 73 ALJR 173 it was said that all those involved in a joint criminal venture are principal offenders regardless of the nature of their participation.

[9]   *Swindall and Osborne* (1846) 2 C & K 230, 175 ER 95; *Du Cros v Lambourne* [1907] 1 KB 40; *Mohan v R* [1967] 2 AC 187. In *Giannetto* [1997] 1 Cr App R 1 the Court of Appeal applied the Canadian case of *Thatcher v R* (1987) 39 D.L.R. (4th) 275 in holding that D could properly be convicted even if some of the jury thought that he or she was a principal offender and some thought that he or she was a secondary party.

B.9 First, in order for D to be held liable, P must have committed a principal offence. Thus, if D prepares and hands a syringe containing heroin to P who self-injects and dies as a result, D is not criminally liable for P's death *as a secondary party* because P did not commit an offence by self-injecting.[10]

B.10 Secondly, D should be convicted of the offence that P commits even if D's state of mind justifies conviction for a more serious offence:

Example B1

D wants V to die. D hands a gun to P saying that it contains blank ammunition when D knows that it contains live bullets. D then encourages P to shoot at V, ostensibly in order to frighten V. P, who knows that V suffers from a serious heart condition, shoots at and kills V with the live ammunition.[11]

Although D's state of mind justifies a conviction for murder, application of the derivative theory of secondary liability should result, instead, in D being convicted of the offence that P has committed, namely manslaughter.[12]

B.11 Thirdly, D should incur secondary liability only if his or her conduct has made a contribution to P committing the principal offence. However, the contribution does not have to be significant[13] and it does not have to be the cause of P committing the principal offence.[14]

---

[10] *Dias* [2001] EWCA Crim 2986; [2002] 2 Cr App R 5. In addition, D ought not to be liable as a principal offender for P's death unless the jury find that the voluntary and informed act of self-injection by P has not broken the chain of causation between D's unlawful act of supply and P's death. However, in recent decisions where D has assisted P to self-inject, the Court of Appeal has held that D can be convicted of manslaughter as a principal offender - *Rogers (Stephen)* [2003] EWCA Crim 945; [2003] 1 WLR 1374; *Finlay* [2003] EWCA Crim 3868, [2003] WL 23145128; *Kennedy (Simon)* [2005] EWCA Crim 685, [2005] 1 WLR 2159. In this way it has attempted to circumvent what are perceived to be the unsatisfactory consequences of applying orthodox principles. If these decisions were to be applied more widely, the distinction between liability as a principal offender and liability as a secondary party would start to break down.

[11] P is not guilty of murder because it was not P's intention to kill or cause really serious harm. However, P is guilty of manslaughter by virtue of having done an unlawful and dangerous act that caused V's death. The act was dangerous, even on P's belief that he was firing blanks, because P was aware of V's heart condition – *Dawson* (1985) 81 Cr App R 150; *Watson* [1989] 1 WLR 684.

[12] However, as will become apparent, English law in this respect has retreated from the derivative theory of secondary liability. By contrast, if P commits a more serious offence than the offence that D intended or believed that P would commit, convicting D of the less serious offence is not inconsistent with the derivative theory of secondary liability.

[13] In *Giannetto* (1997) 1 Cr App R 1 the Court of Appeal noted, without disapproval, the trial judge's direction that D could be liable as an accessory to murder if P suggested the crime and D, patting P on the back and nodding, said "Oh goody". Delivering the judgment of the Court of Appeal, Lord Justice Kennedy- said (p 13) that any involvement from "mere encouragement upwards" suffices.

[14] See paras B.49 to B.65 below.

B.12 In earlier times the derivative theory of secondary liability was taken to extremes. Before D could be liable, a principal offence had to have been committed and P had to have been convicted and sentenced for it. D could not be convicted if, although there was no doubt that a principal offence had been committed, P was never apprehended, died before being convicted and sentenced or was pardoned.[15]

B.13 However, the extreme version of the derivative theory of secondary liability has long disappeared. Nowadays, D can be convicted even if P is not apprehended[16] or has previously been tried and acquitted.[17] These may not be significant exceptions to the derivative theory because they do not imply that a principal offence has not been committed, but only that it has not been proven to have been committed by P. However, the retreat from the derivative theory has gone further, even challenging the three central consequences listed above. As a result, a description of D's liability as still being dependent upon the commission of a principal offence requires refinement if it is to reflect accurately the way the law has developed.

Liability in the absence of any principal offence

B.14 There are a number of circumstances in which P, despite satisfying the external elements of an offence, does not commit the offence:[18]

(1) P, although satisfying the fault element of the offence, has a complete defence, for example duress[19] or self-defence. Alternatively, if the principal offence is murder, D has a partial defence, for example provocation or diminished responsibility;

(2) P cannot incur criminal responsibility either because he or she is aged under 10 years[20] or is legally insane; or

(3) P lacks the requisite fault element to be convicted of the principal offence.

---

[15] This led to the distinction, nowadays of no consequence, between principals in the second degree (those present at the commission of the principal offence) and accessories before the fact (those not present). The former could be convicted even if the principal offender was not.

[16] As in *DPP v K & B* [1997] 1 Cr App R 36. Further, in *Anthony* [1965] 2 QB 189 it was held that D may be tried and convicted even if identification of P is impossible.

[17] Evidence that P was acquitted is not even admissible at D's trial – *Hui-Chi-Ming* v R [1992] 1 AC 34. If D and P are tried together, the acquittal of P does not in itself preclude D being convicted provided the evidence is not the same against both – *Hughes* (1860) Bell CC 242; *Surujpaul v R* [1958] 1 WLR 1050; *Humphreys* [1965] 3 All ER 689 (Crown Court).

[18] By external elements, we mean those elements of an offence that come within the term 'actus reus', namely conduct, circumstance and consequence.

[19] Apart from murder, attempted murder and, possibly, some forms of treason, duress is available as a complete defence if a person commits what would otherwise be an offence as a result of being threatened with death or serious injury if a reasonable person might have responded to the threat as D did. However, although a complete defence, duress does not negate the fault element of the offence.

[20] The minimum age of criminal responsibility - Children and Young Persons Act 1933, s 50 (as amended by the Children and Young Persons Act 1963, s 16(1)).

B.15   In those cases, if the derivative theory of secondary liability were to be rigorously applied, D would not be criminally liable for an offence that he or she had sought to assist or encourage. This would give rise to some very unsatisfactory results:

Example B2

D encourages P to commit theft and says that if P does not do so, D will cut off the fingers of P's child. P commits the theft.

Example B3

D gives P, aged 6, a loaded gun knowing that P intends to use it to cause serious harm to V. P shoots at V causing serious harm.

Example B4

D encourages P to 'collect' an item from V's house and bring it to D's house. D, lying, tells P that V has consented to this.[21] P fetches the item.

In each example, the derivative theory of secondary liability prevents D being convicted of the principal offence. It is true that in examples B2 and B4, D is criminally liable by virtue of committing the common law offences of incitement to commit theft and incitement to commit burglary respectively. However, that is not the same as being convicted of theft or burglary.[22]

B.16   In such cases, the common law has resorted to two mechanisms in order to hold D criminally liable for the principal offence. The first of these is the doctrine of innocent agency by virtue of which D is convicted as a *principal offender* rather than as a secondary party. The second is to hold D liable as a *secondary party* on the basis that, although no principal offence has been committed, D has 'procured' the commission of the *conduct element* of the offence. On one occasion, the Court of Criminal Appeal upheld D's conviction on both bases.[23]

---

[21]   The external elements of the offence of burglary are satisfied. D has entered V's property and taken an item without V's consent – Theft Act 1968, s 9. However, P has not satisfied the fault element of the offence because P was unaware that D had not acted on V's authority. P believed that V was consenting and was therefore not 'intending' to commit theft – Theft Act 1968, s 9(1).

[22]   In example B3, D's conduct consists of assistance and not encouragement and, therefore, D cannot be convicted of incitement to cause grievous bodily harm. There is no equivalent common law inchoate offence to capture cases where D's conduct consists only of assistance. The recommendations in the first report would fill this gap in the law.

[23]   *Cogan and Leak* [1976] QB 217.

179

B.17   The underlying idea is simple. The doctrine serves "to convert, in effect, an apparent 'accessory' into a [perpetrator]".[24] If D uses an innocent agent in order to commit an offence, D is considered to have perpetrated the offence as a principal offender:

Example B5

D asks P to deliver a package to V. Unbeknown to P, the package contains a bomb. P delivers the package and, as D had hoped, when V opens it the bomb explodes killing V.

D is guilty of murder as a principal offender.

B.18   The doctrine of innocent agency cannot apply if the agent is guilty of the principal offence, even if the agent is morally innocent. It is for this reason that the doctrine does not apply to no-fault offences.[25] If, unknown to P, D 'laces' P's drink so that P commits the no-fault offence of driving with excess alcohol,[26] D is guilty of the offence not as a principal offender but as an accessory on the basis that he or she 'procured' P to commit the offence.

B.19   The apparent simplicity of the doctrine of innocent agency conceals some difficult issues. First, it is not clear whether D must intend to cause the innocent agent to commit the principal offence.[27] Secondly, it should not be possible to employ the doctrine if the principal offence is one that can only be perpetrated by those who meet a particular description and D does not meet that description:

Example B6

D, a bachelor, untruthfully but on reasonable grounds, persuades P that P's estranged wife died three years ago. D encourages P to 'marry' V. In consequence P does so.[28]

---

[24] K J M Smith, *A Modern Treatise on the Law of Criminal Complicity* (1991) p 94.

[25] A no-fault offence is one that P can commit without being at fault in relation to the circumstance element of the offence.

[26] Contrary to the Road Traffic Act 1988, s 5(1)(a). The offence is a no-fault offence because P can commit the offence even though he or she does not know, and could not have known, that the circumstance element of the offence – having a level of alcohol in the body in excess of the prescribed limit – is satisfied.

[27] The old case of *Tyler and Price* (1838) 8 C. & P. 616, 172 ER 643 lends some support for the view that something less than intention suffices.

[28] An example provided by Professor K J M Smith, *A Modern Treatise on the Law of Criminal Complicity* (1991) p 106.

P has not committed the offence of bigamy[29] because he reasonably believed that his estranged wife was dead.[30] Equally, it ought not to be possible to convict D of bigamy on the basis of innocent agency because as a matter of law only those who are married can commit bigamy as a principal offender. That said, the Court of Appeal has applied the doctrine when upholding the conviction of a husband for raping his wife notwithstanding that, as the law then stood, a husband could not as a matter of law rape his wife if they were cohabiting.[31]

B.20 Thirdly, in the view of some commentators,[32] some offences appear to require that their conduct element be personally performed:

Example B7

D encourages P to have sexual intercourse with his daughter V, aged 16. D has previously told V that he will cause her serious bodily harm if she does not let P have sexual intercourse with her. Terrified, V allows P to have intercourse with her. P is unaware of the threats and reasonably believes that V is freely consenting.

P is not guilty of rape if he believed on reasonable grounds that V was consenting to intercourse.[33] In *Cogan and Leak*,[34] the Court of Criminal Appeal held that in similar circumstances D could be convicted of rape as a principal offender by virtue of the doctrine of innocent agency.[35] Yet, on one view, to hold D guilty of rape as a principal to the offence is a "violent wrench of the English language"[36] because it was P, not D, who had sexual intercourse with V.[37]

---

[29] Contrary to the Offences against the Person Act 1861, s 57.

[30] *Tolson* (1889) 23 QBD 168.

[31] *Cogan and Leak* [1976] QB 217.

[32] E.g. Glanville Williams, *Textbook of Criminal Law* (2nd ed 1983) p 371.

[33] Sexual Offences Act 2003, s 1(1)(c).

[34] [1976] QB 217.

[35] The Court of Criminal Appeal held that there was an alternative basis for convicting D of rape, namely that D had 'procured' P to commit the conduct element of the offence of rape.

[36] Glanville Williams, *Textbook of Criminal Law* (2nd ed 1983) p 371.

[37] In *DPP v K & B* [1997] 1 Cr App R 36 counsel for the prosecution submitted that a woman could be convicted of rape as a principal offender by virtue of the doctrine of innocent agency. The court did not have to decide whether the submission was correct. In *People v Hernandez* (1971) 18 Cal. App (3d) 651 the Supreme Court of California held that D, *a woman*, who had *compelled* her husband to have sexual intercourse with a non-consenting woman had been properly convicted as a principal to rape. The Supreme Court of Virginia arrived at the contrary conclusion in *Dusenbery v Commonwealth* (1980) 220 Va. 770.

'PROCURING' THE COMMISSION OF THE CONDUCT ELEMENT OF THE PRINCIPAL OFFENCE

B.21 The second means by which the courts have striven to render D criminally liable despite the absence of a principal offence has been by resorting to the concept of 'procuring'. As a basis of secondary liability, 'procuring' is an anomaly. Whereas D can 'aid, abet or counsel' P to commit an offence without causing P to commit the offence, 'procuring' implies a special kind of causal link between D's conduct and P's commission of the principal offence.[38] Normally, a person who causes a proscribed outcome is liable as a principal offender. However, it is clear that, in the context of no-fault offences, D is secondarily liable for causing P to commit a no-fault offence:

> **Example B8**
>
> D 'laces' P's non-alcoholic drink with the result that P unwittingly drives while in excess of the prescribed limit.

D is guilty of the no-fault offence of driving with excess alcohol[39] but as a secondary party and not as a principal offender.

B.22 As Professor Ashworth has observed, cases like example B8:

> represent the high-water mark of causal connection among the various types of accessorial conduct ... in which there is no meeting of minds between principal and accomplice.[40]

Nevertheless, if D procures P to commit a no-fault offence, it is at least understandable that D should be convicted of the offence as a secondary party rather than as a principal offender. After all, it is P who has committed the offence and it is inappropriate and inaccurate to describe D and P as joint principals.[41]

B.23 However, the courts have gone beyond this by extending 'procuring' as a basis of secondary liability to offences that do require proof of fault. The courts have done so in order to ensure that D is held criminally liable in cases where, although P has not committed an offence, D has acted reprehensibly. In cases where, by lies, threats or other underhand behaviour, D has brought about the commission by P of the conduct element of a principal offence, the courts have held that D can be convicted of the offence as a secondary party although there is no principal offender.[42]

B.24 The result is not necessarily unsatisfactory. As Professor Ashworth has commented:

---

[38]   *A-G's Reference (No 1 of 1975)* [1975] QB 773.

[39]   Above.

[40]   A J Ashworth, *Principles of Criminal Law* (4th ed 2003) p 423.

[41]   After all, only P has driven the motor vehicle. However, we believe that in such circumstances D ought to be convicted as a principal offender, albeit it not of the principal offence that P commits but of causing P to commit the offence – see Part 4 paras 4.28 to 4.37.

[42]   *Cogan and Leak* [1976] QB 217; *Millward* [1994] *Criminal Law Review* 527; *DPP v K and B* [1997] 1 CR App R 36.

[D] has done all that he or she intended to do in order to further [P's] crime and, considered in isolation, D is surely no less culpable than if [P] had been found guilty.[43]

However, whatever the practical benefits, the outcome represents a significant dilution of the derivative theory of secondary liability and is achieved only by affording an enhanced scope to what was already an anomalous form of secondary liability.

Secondary liability for a more serious principal offence than that committed by P

B.25 As we suggested above,[44] a logical application of the derivative theory of secondary liability is that D's liability cannot exceed that of P. This was accepted by the Court of Appeal in *Richards*.[45] It can, however, lead to the result that, in example B1 above, D is guilty of manslaughter and not murder despite intending that P should kill V.

B.26 Accordingly, in *Howe*,[46] the House of Lords disapproved *Richards*. However, identifying the precise basis of D's liability for a more serious offence than that committed by P is problematic. On one view, in relation to the more serious offence, P does not act as a fully informed individual and, therefore, in relation to that offence, is an innocent agent. On the other view, D cannot properly be convicted of the more serious offence on the basis of innocent agency because P is not a *wholly* innocent agent.

B.27 The view that P is an innocent agent in relation to the more serious offence is particularly difficult to sustain in cases of homicide where the reason why P is convicted of manslaughter rather than murder is because of provocation or diminished responsibility:

Example B9

D encourages P to murder V. P does so. On being charged with murder, P successfully pleads provocation.

P is convicted of the lesser offence, manslaughter, despite satisfying the fault element of murder. In relation to the offence of murder, P cannot be accurately described as an innocent agent. At the same time, however, it is difficult to justify convicting D of murder on the basis that he or she has procured P to commit murder because, in killing V, P acted as a fully informed individual.

---

[43] *Principles of Criminal Law*, (4th ed 2003) p 435.

[44] Para B.10.

[45] [1974] QB 776.

[46] [1987] AC 417.

THE CONDUCT ELEMENT OF SECONDARY LIABILITY

Modes of participation

B.28   The present law is to be found in section 8 of the Accessories and Abettors Act 1861 and section 44 of the Magistrates' Courts Act 1980. The former applies to indictable offences, the latter to summary offences. Both provisions provide that a person who 'aid[s], abet[s], counsel[s] or procure[s]' the commission of an offence 'shall be liable to be tried, indicted and punished as a principal offender'.

B.29   By virtue of the wording of section 8 and section 44, an indictment or charge is not legally defective merely because it does not specify whether a person has committed an offence as a principal offender or by having aided, abetted, counselled or procured its commission. However, in *Maxwell*[47] the House of Lords said that wherever the prosecution is in a position to do so, the indictment or charge should make clear the factual basis of the case alleged against each defendant.[48]

B.30   If the prosecution case is that the defendant has committed an offence otherwise than as a principal offender, the indictment or charge can, but does not have to, contain all four words 'aid, abet, counsel or procure'. Provided that the evidence establishes that D's conduct satisfies one of the words, that is enough. If the indictment or charge only refers to some of the words, the prosecution must prove that D's conduct fits the word(s) used.[49]

The meaning of "aid, abet, counsel or procure"

B.31   Disregarding procuring, it is generally accepted that these specified modes of involvement cover two types of conduct, namely the provision of assistance or encouragement.[50] The nature of the assistance or encouragement may take any form provided that it occurs before or during the commission of the principal offence.[51] Professor Sir John Smith has observed:

---

[47]   [1978] 1 WLR 1350.

[48]   In *Mercer* [2001] EWCA Crim 638, [2001] WL 542166 it was held that there is no violation of Article 6(3) of the European Convention on Human Rights and Fundamental Freedoms where the prosecution alleges that the accused was a party in a joint criminal venture but cannot specify his or her precise role.

[49]   It is not uncommon for the particulars of the offence to refer to all four words but for the statement of the offence to be confined to the particular mode of participation alleged. For an example see *JF Alford Transport Ltd* (1997) 2 Cr App R 326.

[50]   In *JF Alford Transport Ltd* (1997) 2 Cr App R 326 the Court of Appeal said that the trial judge had been right to direct the jury that aiding and abetting meant assisting and encouraging.

[51]   In *A-G's Reference (No 1 of 1975)* [1975] QB 773 the Court of Appeal was of the view that each of the words 'aid, abet, counsel or procure' should be given its ordinary meaning, each representing a different mode of participation. This runs counter to the earlier view, namely that the words were technical terms. On this view, 'aid and abet' did not purport to describe the nature of D's conduct but denoted that he or she was present at the commission of the principal offence. By contrast, 'counsel or procure' again did not describe the nature of D's conduct but denoted that he or she was not present at the commission of the principal offence. See J C Smith, "Aid, Abet, Counsel, or Procure" in *Reshaping the Criminal Law, Essays in Honour of Glanville Williams* (ed P R Glazebrook) (1978) p 120.

We still use the old language of aiding, abetting, counselling or procuring but these are technical terms. What they mean in practice is "assists or encourages". Before the law relating to felonies was abolished in 1967 we used to distinguish between the principal in the second degree, who was present at the commission of the crime, and the accessory before the fact, who was absent; but that is no longer necessary, because modern cases established that the same principles apply whether the person who assists or encourages is present or absent.[52]

B.32 However, it is doubtful if all cases of 'procuring' can be properly described as involving the provision of assistance or encouragement. In *A-G's Reference (No 1 of 1975)*[53] D added alcohol to P's drink without P's knowledge. As a result, D committed the offence of procuring P's no-fault offence of driving with excess alcohol. In examples like this one, to describe D's conduct as assisting or encouraging P to commit the offence, despite its obvious attraction, nevertheless disregards the fact that it was not P's intention to commit any offence.[54]

Voluntary presence at the scene of an offence

B.33 It is clear that words and gestures can constitute encouragement. A more difficult question is whether voluntary presence, unaccompanied by any words or gestures, at the scene of an offence can constitute encouragement. There are two types of case. One is where an offence, of which D has no forewarning, takes place in D's presence:

Example B10

D is sitting on a bus. Another passenger P starts to assault the driver, V. D decides to stay in his seat and observe.

D's conduct in remaining in his seat is not a positive act. If D has encouraged P, it can only be by virtue of omitting to remove himself from the scene. However, under English law, D can be a secondary party to an offence by virtue of an omission in only very limited circumstances. No citizen is under a general duty to intervene to prevent the commission of an offence or to remove him or herself from the place where an offence is being committed.[55]

B.34 The second type of case is where D voluntarily goes to a place knowing or believing that an offence is being or will be committed. Having arrived at the place, D does no more than observe the offence being committed:

---

[52] "Criminal Liability of Accessories: Law and Law Reform" (1997) 113 *Law Quarterly Review* 453, 453.

[53] [1975] QB 773.

[54] For our recommendation, see Part 4, para 4.37.

[55] *Smith v Baker* [1971] RTR 350.

> **Example B11**
>
> D goes into a room where he knows that P is raping V. D stays to watch.[56]

B.35 The relevant authorities are difficult to interpret because they do not always distinguish clearly what are three discrete issues, namely D's act of voluntarily going to a place believing that an offence is being or will be committed, D's state of mind in doing so and the effect of D's conduct on the mind of P. In this section, we are concerned with only the first issue.

B.36 The authorities suggest that voluntarily going to a place knowing or believing that an offence is being or will be committed is an act which is *capable* of constituting encouragement. Ultimately, however, whether D by doing so has encouraged P is a question of fact for the jury to determine.[57]

Omissions

B.37 In general, the common law is more likely to impose criminal liability for an act rather than an omission. There are public policy reasons for this but, in addition, there are issues relating to causation and whether certain verbs imply action and, therefore, exclude liability for omissions.

B.38 The starting point is that, in general, an omission to act does not fix D with secondary liability:

> **Example B12**
>
> P, a prospective suicide bomber, sends a letter to D who is P's spiritual adviser. P says that he intends to board a crowded train and detonate a bomb. P says that if D thinks that it would be wrong to do so, D should so advise. On the other hand, if D approves of the action, D should do nothing. P concludes by saying that if he hears nothing within 10 days, he will assume that D endorses P's proposed action. There is no response from D and P commits the atrocity. On searching D's home, the police find P's letter opened with comments in the margin in D's handwriting.

D is not a secondary party to murder because his lack of response is an omission. It matters not that D's status and position is such that he exerts a potent influence, albeit not a power of control, upon P and that the omission is intended to encourage P.

B.39 The general rule reflects the reluctance of the common law to impose criminal liability for omissions. Arguably, however, there are two categories of cases which are exceptions to the general rule.

---

[56] The facts of *Clarkson* [1971] 1 WLR 1402.

[57] *Coney* (1882) 8 QBD 534; *Allan* [1965] 1 QB 130; *Clarkson* [1971] 1 WLR 1402.

FAILURE TO DISCHARGE A LEGAL DUTY

B.40   If D is under a legal duty to act, failure to discharge the duty is capable of constituting assistance or encouragement.[58] Examples are a security guard who deliberately omits to lock a door to enable burglars to enter the premises and a store detective who deliberately ignores acts of theft committed by customers. In each case, the duty to act emanates from their contract of employment.[59]

B.41   A legal duty to act can also arise from a personal relationship. An example is that of parent and child. If a parent deliberately withholds food from the child intending that the child should starve to death, the parent commits murder as a principal offender. Secondary liability, based on an omission, of a parent for the death of or injury to his or her child is more difficult. In *Russell and Russell*,[60] Lord Chief Justice Lane said:

> Generally speaking, parents of a child are in no different position from any other defendants charged with a crime. To establish guilt against either, the Crown must prove at the least that the defendant aided, abetted, counselled or procured the commission of the crime by the other. The only difference in the position of parents, as opposed to others jointly indicted, is that one parent *may* have a duty to intervene in the ill-treatment of their child by the other when a stranger would have no such duty.[61]

B.42   In *Russell and Russell*, it was alleged that the parents were parties to a joint venture. In the absence of a joint criminal venture, there is academic disagreement as to whether a parent's failure to protect his or her child is capable of 'aiding and abetting' an offence against the child. Professor Sir John Smith thought that it was.[62] By contrast, Professor Glanville Williams rejected that view, both on principle and because there is no English authority to that effect.[63]

B.43   Even if Professor Smith's view correctly reflects English law, it will not always be the case that a parent will be secondarily liable for not taking steps to protect his or her child. If, for example, D's husband is about to place their child into a bath of scalding water and threatens D that if she tries to intervene he will shoot her, it might be thought to be inappropriate to characterise D's non-intervention as assistance or encouragement. On the other hand, if D were in a position to intervene without danger to herself, a jury could properly conclude that her non-intervention 'aided and abetted' the offence.

---

[58]   Simester and Sullivan, *Criminal Law Theory and Doctrine* (2nd ed 2003) p 204 suggest that where there is a failure to take reasonable steps to discharge a legal duty, the failure in itself constitutes assistance and not merely evidence of encouragement.

[59]   In each example, the fact that the burglars and the customers may be unaware of D's assistance is irrelevant.

[60]   (1987) 85 Cr App R 388.

[61]   Above, p 393 (emphasis added).

[62]   Commentary on *Gibson and Gibson* [1984] *Criminal Law Review* 615, 616. The case is fully reported at (1984) 80 Cr App R 24.

[63]   "Which of you did it?" (1989) 52 *Modern Law Review* 179.

B.44   The common law has recognised that if D fails to exercise an entitlement to control the actions of P, he or she may be liable for an offence that P commits as a result. Thus, in *Du Cros v Lambourne*[64] it was proved that D's car had been driven dangerously at a time when D and P were both in it. However, it could not be proven whether it was P or D who was driving. D's conviction was upheld because, even if not the driver, he was a secondary party as he had the power to prevent P driving or continuing to drive in a dangerous manner.

B.45   In *Webster*[65] D was convicted of being a secondary party to causing death by dangerous driving. During a journey, he allowed P to drive his car knowing that P had consumed alcohol. One basis of the prosecution's case was that D was aware that P was driving the car dangerously at a high speed and failed to intervene. The Court of Appeal quashed D's conviction because the jury had not been directed that they had to consider not only whether D knew P was driving dangerously but also whether D had had an opportunity to intervene before it was too late.

B.46   The entitlement to control exception is significant because it represents a potentially extensive departure from the general rule. It has been applied to the licensee of a public house who allowed customers to drink alcohol outside the permitted hours,[66] to the supervisor of a learner driver[67] and to a company for omitting to take steps to prevent its drivers from falsifying their tachograph records.[68]

B.47   However, the ambit of the exception is unclear and it is questionable whether it is a general principle. If D holds a party at his or her home and knows that one guest is about to rape another guest, is D liable if he or she, although able to intervene, decides not to? Alternatively, in the middle of the night, D is awoken by screams in his or her garden. D gets up and sees that P is about to assault V. Although able to intervene safely and effectively, D goes back to bed. Does it make any difference that, in the former case, P is an invitee whereas in the latter P is a trespasser? The common law provides no clear answer to these questions.[69]

Causation, connection and secondary liability

Introduction

B.48   In this section we consider what effect, if any, D's assistance or encouragement must have in relation to P's commission of the principal offence if D is to incur liability for the offence as a secondary party.

---

[64]   [1907] 1 KB 40.

[65]   [2006] EWCA Crim 415, [2006] 2 Cr App R 6.

[66]   *Tuck v Robson* [1970] 1 WLR 741.

[67]   *Rubie v Faulkner* [1940] 1 KB 571.

[68]   *J F Alford Transport Ltd* [1997] 2 Cr App R 326. However, on the facts the conviction was quashed because of the trial judge's misdirection to the jury. See also *Gaunt* [2003] EWCA Crim 3925, [2004] 2 Cr App R (s) 37 where D, a manager, failed to take steps to prevent his employees, P, racially harassing another employee, V.

[69]   For our answers and recommendations, see Part 3, paras 3.39 to 3.41.

D's conduct need not cause P to commit the principal offence and need not make any difference to the outcome

B.49 Apart from 'procuring', D's conduct need not cause P to commit the principal offence in the sense that 'but for' D's conduct, P would not have committed the offence.[70] However, according to Professor K J M Smith, although D's conduct does not have to cause P to commit the principal offence in the 'but for' sense:

> It has always been implied in the concept of complicity that [D's] involvement ... did make some difference to the outcome and as a consequence of this, accessories have been implicitly linked to the harm element in the principal offence.[71]

B.50 However, it is clear that D can be convicted as a secondary party despite the fact that his or her assistance or encouragement has made no material difference to the 'outcome':

Example B13

P has made up his mind to murder V. He plans to do so by stabbing V with his kitchen knife. However, D, who has his own reasons for wanting to see V murdered, provides P with an identical kitchen knife. P uses D's knife to murder V.

D's act of assistance has made no material difference to the outcome but D is guilty of murder. What matters is that D's assistance or encouragement has some impact on the course of conduct that ends in the commission of the offence. In this example, D's assistance does have such an impact because V is killed with D's knife and not with P's.

---

[70] In the nineteenth century, Stephen thought that 'counselling' incorporated a requirement of 'but for' causation – *Digest* (4th ed) Art 39. Dicta in *Assistant Recorder of Kingston-upon-Hull ex parte Morgan* [1969] 2 QB 58, 61 can be interpreted as support for Stephen's view. However, in *Calhaem* [1985] QB 808 the Court of Appeal held that there did not have to be any causal connection between the counselling and the commission of the offence. See also *Bryce* [2004] EWCA Crim 1231, [2004] 2 Cr App R 35.

[71] Professor K J M Smith "The Law Commission Consultation Paper on Complicity: Part 1 – A Blueprint for Rationalism" [1994] *Criminal Law Review* 239, 244.

B.51 The authorities speak of there having to be "a connection"[72] between D's conduct and P committing the principal offence. In *A-G v Able*,[73] Mr Justice Woolf said that that there has to be a "sufficient" connection.[74] However, the precise nature of this *sufficient* connection is elusive. It is best understood, at least where D's conduct consists of assistance, as meaning that D's conduct has made a contribution to the commission of the offence. This is why D is guilty of murder in example B13. D, by providing P with the knife which P used to murder V, has contributed to the outcome. By contrast, if P had decided to use his own knife to murder V, D would not have been guilty of murder because his assistance would have made no contribution to the commission of the offence.[75]

B.52 P does not have to know that he or she is being assisted by D:

Example B14

P plans a robbery intending to use his own gun. D is aware of this. The day before the robbery, D notices that P's own gun is missing from the drawer. Without telling P, he places his own gun, a similar kind to P's, in the drawer for P to use. P commits the robbery using D's gun.[76]

D is guilty of robbery.[77]

ENCOURAGEMENT

B.53 In example B14, D provided assistance. Cases where D encourages but does not assist P are more difficult to analyse. In contrast to assistance, encouragement must have the capacity to act on P's mind and P must, therefore be aware of D's encouragement.[78] Thus, D cannot be convicted of an offence as a secondary party if he or she shouts encouragement to P if P is deaf and therefore unaware of the encouragement.

---

[72] *Calhaem* [1985] 1 QB 808, 813.

[73] [1984] 1 QB 795.

[74] Above, p 812.

[75] However, under the recommendations in the first report, D would be guilty of the inchoate offence of intentionally assisting or encouraging P to commit murder.

[76] The example is provided by Simester and Sullivan, *Criminal Law Theory and Doctrine* (2nd ed 2003) p 200.

[77] See also *State v Tally* (1894) 102 Ala 25 where D, who knew that P was planning to murder V, prevented T from warning V. This facilitated the killing of V by P who was unaware of what D had done. The fact that D's conduct can clearly assist P without P being aware of it calls into question Lord Chief Justice Widgery's assertion in *A-G's Reference (No 1 of 1975)* [1975] QB 773, 779 that, "aiding and abetting almost inevitably involves a situation in which [D] and [P] are … in contact so that each knows what is passing through the mind of the other".

[78] *Caelham* [1985] 1 QB 808.

B.54   However, as with assistance, D can be liable as a secondary party even if D's encouragement makes no difference to the outcome, for example if P has already irrevocably made up his or her mind to commit the principal offence.[79] The focus is not on whether D's encouragement made a difference to the outcome but whether the encouragement was proffered in circumstances where P could have been aware of the encouragement.

Presumed encouragement

B.55   A useful tool for analysing the current law is to construct a presumption of encouragement. Although it is not explicit, the case law appears to presume that where D acts in a manner that is capable of encouraging P, P was aware of the encouragement and, further, that it operated on P's mind, thereby contributing to the commission of the principal offence. Thus, if D, seeing P with a knife in his hand chasing V, shouts out 'stab him' and P does so, it is presumed not only that P heard D's words but also that they operated on P's mind and, thereby, contributed to the commission of the offence.

B.56   The presumption is clearly demonstrated where the conduct that is alleged to constitute the encouragement consists of D's voluntary presence at the scene of an offence:

Example B15

D, a critic, attends a concert. One of the performers is P. By performing at the concert, P is committing an offence because he does not have a work permit. D is aware of this.[80]

D's presence at the concert has made little difference to the outcome but it is presumed, by virtue of D being part of an audience for whom P is playing, that P is inspired to perform by D's presence as part of the audience.

B.57   In this manner, joint criminal ventures are examples of presumed actual encouragement. In many joint criminal ventures, P is also assisted by D. However, even if P is not assisted by D, P is presumed to have been encouraged by D as a result of D being a party to an agreement with P to commit an offence or as a result of D and P sharing a common intention to commit an offence.

B.58   On one view, the presumption extends beyond the agreed offence to any collateral offence that P commits in the course of the joint criminal venture. On this view, in relation to the collateral offence, P is presumed to have derived actual encouragement from D's decision to participate in the joint criminal venture:

---

[79]   As in *Giannetto* (1997) 1 Cr App R 1 where the Court of Appeal noted, without disapproval, the trial judge's direction that D could be convicted of murder if, on P saying that he was going to kill D's wife, D had patted P on the back and said "Oh goody".

[80]   The facts are those of *Wilcox v Jeffery* [1951] 1 All ER 464.

> **Example B16**
>
> D and P agree to cause less than serious harm to V by punching and kicking him. In the course of the assault, P produces a knife and fatally stabs V. P's intention was to kill V. D knew that P had the knife and, fearing that he might use it, had prior to the attack stressed to P that he was not to use it.

There is a presumption that, in murdering V, P was encouraged by D's participation in the punching and kicking of V. The presumption is not negated merely by evidence that D expressed opposition to the use of the knife.

Why does the law presume that P is aware of D's encouragement and is in fact encouraged?

B.59   In some jurisdictions, the courts have held that D can be convicted of an offence as a secondary party without the prosecution having to prove:

     (1)   that P was aware of D's acts or words of encouragement provided they were communicated or conveyed in circumstances where P could be aware of them; or

     (2)   that P was in fact encouraged by D's conduct.[81]

B.60   In the Supreme Court of Victoria, Justice Redlich sought to justify this conclusion:

> It would impose an impossible burden on the prosecution, who would rarely be in a position to place evidence before a jury as to the effect of [D's] conduct on [P's] state of mind.[82]

B.61   English law has not been prepared to dispense with the dual requirements that P must have been aware of D's encouragement and must have been encouraged by it. However, in its presumption of actual encouragement, English law reflects the concerns of Justice Redlich and also those of Chief Justice Eichelbaum who, in delivering the judgement of the New Zealand Court of Appeal, said:

> … where violence is inflicted or sexual offending perpetrated in the presence of others, it would be a manifest nonsense to require proof that [P] were aware of the encouragement provided by each individual.[83]

Rebutting the presumption

B.62   In cases other than those involving joint criminal ventures, the presumption is rebuttable. If D can adduce evidence that realistically suggests that P might not have been aware of D's encouragement or might not have been encouraged by it, the prosecution must prove that D was aware of it and was in fact encouraged by it. Professor Keith Smith provides this example:

---

[81]   *Schriek* [1997] 2 NZLR 139; *The Queen v Lam (Ruling No 20)* [2005] VSC 294.

[82]   *The Queen v Lam (Ruling No 20)* [2005] VSC 294 [77].

[83]   *Schriek* [1997] 2 NZLR 139, 150.

> **Example B17**
>
> D comes across P and V in the middle of a fierce argument. D, a congenital troublemaker, urges P to punch V. Just before striking V, P tells D 'to mind his own business'.[84]

The presumption that D's words of encouragement made a contribution to P's assault on V is rebutted by the evidence of what P said to D.

B.63   The presumption can be rebutted even if there is a meeting of minds between P and D:

> **Example B18**
>
> D encourages P to murder V. P attends a football match at which, unknown to P, V is present. There is a riot in the course of which P murders an unknown person who turns out to be V.[85]

D is not an accessory to V's murder because the act of P was not done "within the scope of [D's] authority or advice."[86] It was pure coincidence that the victim turned out to be V.

B.64   However, where D and P are parties to a joint criminal venture, the presumption is irrebuttable in the sense that, whilst part of a joint criminal venture the parties are encouraging each other by their continuing agreement. As a result, rebuttal of the presumption is tied to withdrawal from the venture. For this, D must withdraw voluntarily and effectively from the joint criminal venture before P commits the agreed offence or a collateral offence. Whether D has withdrawn from a joint criminal venture is a question of fact dependent on all the circumstances of the case. In the absence of an effective withdrawal, the presumption is irrebuttable in such cases.

---

[84]   K J M Smith, "The Law Commission Consultation Paper on Complicity: (1) A Blueprint for Rationalism" [1994] *Criminal Law Review* 239, fn 26.

[85]   The example is taken from the Court of Appeal's judgment in *Calhaem* [1985] QB 808, 813.

[86]   Above. In *Calhaem* the Court of Appeal upheld D's conviction for 'counselling' P to murder V. At his trial, P had testified that, although hired by D to murder V, he originally had never intended to murder V. He said that he did so only when V screamed and he panicked. The court held that the murder of V had been done within the 'scope of the authority or advice' of D.

Criticisms of the presumption

B.65 Although the presumption of actual encouragement is a useful construct through which to rationalise the case law in this area, it has several drawbacks. The most notable of these can be demonstrated by its application to collateral offences committed pursuant to a joint criminal venture. For example, in example B16, D agreed to become part of the joint criminal venture with P to commit less than serious harm to V, knowing that P might murder V. On these facts, a case can be made for the proposition that D, as well as P, should be liable for V's murder in the event that P murders V. However, to base this liability on a presumption that P was *encouraged* by D to commit murder fails to reflect the reality of the situation.[87]

Procuring

B.66 Where D's contribution consists of 'procuring' P to commit an offence, there is authority that there has to be a causal link between D's conduct and P's commission of the principal offence. In *A-G's Reference (No 1 of 1975)*[88] the Court of Appeal said:

> To procure means to produce by endeavour. ... Causation here is important. You cannot procure an offence unless there is a causal link between what you do and the commission of the offence ....[89]

Thus, the prosecution must prove that P would not have committed the offence but for D's conduct.[90]

THE FAULT ELEMENT OF SECONDARY LIABILITY

Introduction

B.67 The law relating to the fault element of secondary liability is complex and difficult. Professor Sir John Smith has commented:

> In the nature of things the [state of mind required of D] must differ from that of [P]. The definition of the offence specifies the state of mind with which the act causing the actus reus must be done. [P] does the act but [D] does not. ... . [D's state of mind] relates to what [P] does and the state of mind with which he does it.[91]

---

[87] Due to the various problems with the presumption of actual encouragement, we recommend an alternative approach in Part 3, paras 3.47 to 3.58.

[88] [1975] QB 773.

[89] Above, 779 to 780.

[90] It is true that in *Blakely and Sutton v DPP* [1991] RTR 405 the Divisional Court thought that D 'procured' a result if he or she contemplated it as a possible consequence of his act. However, the observation was not necessary to the decision.

[91] Commentary on *Smith* [1988] *Criminal Law Review* 616, 618.

B.68   In addition, it is necessary to consider D's state of mind in relation to his or her acts of assistance or encouragement. Given that D's state of mind is relevant to his or her conduct, to P's conduct and to P's state of mind, it is not surprising that from the case law it is difficult to pinpoint the precise fault element of secondary liability. No single case sets out a general test and the cases from which a general test may be inferred are inconsistent.

D's state of mind in relation to his or her own conduct

Intending the act of assistance or encouragement

B.69   D must intend to do the act of assistance or encouragement.

> **Example B19**
>
> D, following a day's grouse shooting, forgets to return his shotgun to the secure cupboard where he keeps his firearms. P, finding the shotgun in D's kitchen, uses it to murder V.

D is not guilty of murder because, although his conduct has assisted P to murder V, he did not intentionally leave the shotgun where P could find and use it to kill someone.

Intention to assist or encourage

B.70   According to Mr Justice Devlin:

> … an indifference to the result of the crime does not of itself negate abetting. If one man deliberately sells to another a gun to be used for murdering a third, he may be indifferent whether the third man lives or dies, and interested only in the cash profit to be made out of the sale, but he can still be an aider and abettor. To hold otherwise would be to negative the rule that mens rea is a matter of intent only and does not depend on desire or motive.[92]

B.71   Yet, he also said that D had to have the "intention to aid".[93] This suggests a distinction between intending to aid (or encourage) and intending that the principal offence should be committed. In our view, although D must intend to do the act that assists or encourages P, it is generally not necessary that he or she should act in order to assist or encourage P. Were it otherwise, D would not be liable in cases where he or she rendered assistance or encouragement under duress. Yet, it is clear that in such cases, D can be convicted of the principal offence despite not acting in order to assist or encourage P.[94]

---

[92] *NCB v Gamble* [1959] 1 QB 11, 23. Professor Glanville Williams famously described the judgment of Mr Justice Devlin as "a specimen of extraordinarily poor judicial thinking" - "Complicity, Purpose and the Draft Code – Part 1" [1990] *Criminal Law Review* 4, 15.

[93] [1959] 1 QB 11, 20.

[94] *Howe* [1987] AC 417.

B.72 According to Professor Dennis, D intends to assist or encourage if D acts in order to render assistance or encouragement.[95] This can, but need not, involve a wish or desire on the part of D that the principal offence be committed. Accordingly, for Professor Dennis, it is possible to reject the view that D must share with P a common intent that the principal offence should be committed while still maintaining that D can and must act in order to assist or encourage P.

B.73 Support for Professor Dennis can be found in a number of authorities which speak of D having to intend to encourage purely in the sense of acting in order to render encouragement.[96] Nevertheless, our view is that the authorities, properly interpreted, do not support Professor Dennis.

B.74 The recent decision of the Court of Appeal in *Bryce* is not inconsistent with our view. The court contrasted an intention to aid with an intention to hinder or obstruct, holding that the latter is inconsistent with the former,[97] something that had already been recognised over 50 years earlier by Lord Chief Justice Goddard.[98] *Bryce* does not, however, support the wider proposition that, absent an intention to hinder or obstruct, D must act *in order* to render assistance or encouragement. Accordingly, the preferred view is that the prosecution only have to prove that D acted in order to assist or encourage P if there is an evidential basis supporting a claim that D acted in order to hinder or obstruct P or, arguably, if D is said to have encouraged P by nothing more than his or her voluntary presence during the offence.

D's awareness of the capacity of his or her conduct to assist or encourage

B.75 Although D does not have to act in order to assist or encourage P, D must at least believe that his or her conduct is *capable* of assisting or encouraging P. The more difficult issue is whether, beyond capability, D must also believe that his or her conduct *will* assist or encourage P?

---

[95] I H Dennis, "The Mental Element for Accessories" in P F Smith (ed) *Criminal Law, Essays in Honour of J C Smith* (1987) 40. Professor Dennis' article provoked an intense debate between himself and Professor Sullivan – see G R Sullivan, "Intent, Purpose and Complicity" [1988] *Criminal Law Review* 641, [1989] *Criminal Law Review* 166; I H Dennis, "Intention and Complicity: A Reply" [1988] *Criminal Law Review* 649, [1989] *Criminal Law Review* 168. See also Glanville Williams "Complicity, Purpose and the Draft Code – Part 1" [1990] *Criminal Law Review* 4.

[96] Most of these cases involve a defendant's voluntary presence at the scene of an offence. The issue is whether such presence, without more, can be construed as encouragement – *Coney* (1882) 8 QBD 534; *Clarkson* [1971] 1 WLR 1402. Recently, in Bryce [2004] EWCA Crim 1231, [2004] 2 Cr App R 35 the Court of Appeal has held that there must be an intention to assist (or encourage).

[97] The case was unusual in that it was evidence adduced by *the prosecution* that formed the basis of the defence submission that D's intention was to hinder or obstruct.

[98] *Wilcox v Jeffery* [1951] 1 All ER 464. D's conviction for encouraging P's offence by attending a concert at which P gave an unlawful performance was upheld but Lord Goddard indicated that it might well have been different if D had booed or otherwise voiced opposition to the performance.

> **Example B20**
>
> D sells P some poison. D believes that P is going to murder V and that there is a 50% chance that P will use the poison to murder V. In the event, P does use the poison to murder V.

D's state of mind falls short of a belief that his act of assistance will assist P to commit murder but he does believe that his act is capable of assisting P to do so.

B.76 The case law is inconclusive.[99] Some authorities suggest that it suffices if D believed that his or her conduct was *capable* of assisting or encouraging P[100] while others suggest that D's belief must be that his or her conduct *is* encouraging P[101] or "will probably (or possibly and desirably) ..." assist P.[102] Our recommendations will resolve this confusion.[103]

D's attitude towards the commission of the principal offence

B.77 It does not follow from the mere fact that D encourages or assists P to commit an offence that D does so in order that the offence should be committed. Admittedly, as a general rule, if D *encourages* P to commit an offence, this will be with a view to the offence being committed. D will not usually encourage P to commit an offence if D is indifferent as to whether it is committed. For this reason, in joint criminal ventures where D and P are mutually encouraging each other, it will usually be D's purpose that the agreed offence should be committed.[104] The same is not true of assistance. In example 1B, the shop assistant who sold P a baseball bat did not do so in order that P should commit an assault.

B.78 The general consensus amongst commentators is that the preponderance of authority supports the view that the prosecution does not have to prove that D assisted or encouraged P intending that the principal offence should be committed.[105] The strongest support for this view is the passage from the judgement of Mr Justice Devlin in *NCB v Gamble* cited in paragraph B.70 above.

---

[99] The issue has generally received little scrutiny by the courts particularly in cases of joint criminal venture where the focus instead has been on D's state of mind in relation to the commission of the principal offence.

[100] *JF Alford Transport Ltd* [1997] 2 Cr App R 326, 334 to 335; *Bryce* [2004] EWCA Crim 1231, [2004] 2 CR App R 35.

[101] *Clarkson* [1971] 1 WLR 1402.

[102] *DPP for Northern Ireland v Lynch* [1975] AC 653, 698 by Lord Simon. This case was overruled in *Howe* [1987] AC 417.

[103] This is because intention that P will commit the conduct element of the principal offence will become the central consideration. See Part 3, paras 3.77 to 3.83.

[104] *Rook* [1993] 1 WLR 1005 is an example of an exception to the general rule - see paras B.119 and B.120 below. *Rook* is a case that, for the wrong reasons, has influenced the law of secondary liability in recent years.

[105] *NCB v Gamble* [1959] 1 QB 11; *DPP for Northern Ireland v Lynch* [1975] AC 653 (overruled by *Howe* [1987] 2 WLR 568); *Clarke* (1985) 80 Cr App R 344; *Rook* [1993] 1 WLR 1005; *JF Alford Transport Ltd* [1997] 2 Cr App R 326; *Bryce* [2004] EWCA Crim 1231, [2004] 2 Cr App R 35. One authority suggests that cases of 'procuring' are no different – *Blakely and Sutton v DPP* [1991] RTR 405 in which D's intention was that P should *not* commit the principal offence.

D's state of mind in relation to the principal offence

Knowing the essential matters of the principal offence

B.79   Suppose that D sells some petrol to P. P uses the petrol to make a petrol bomb which P then throws into V's house intending to destroy it and to kill V. P succeeds in doing both. P is guilty of arson and murder. By selling the petrol to P, D has intentionally done an act that has assisted P to commit both offences. However, the law does not hold D liable merely because D, by selling petrol, has deliberately done an act that has in fact assisted P to commit the offences. What is critical is D's state of mind both in relation to P's subsequent use of the petrol and to P's own state of mind in using the petrol.

B.80   There is a range of possibilities. D may have believed that P intended to use the petrol for an innocent purpose in which case D is not guilty of either arson or murder. Alternatively, D may have believed that P intended to use the petrol in order to destroy V's property and to kill V. If so, under the present law, D is guilty of both arson and murder. The difficulties start when D's state of mind lies between those two extremes. D may have suspected that P possibly intended to use the petrol in order to destroy V's property and to kill V. Alternatively, D may have believed that P probably intended to do both. Another alternative is that D may have believed that P did intend to use the petrol to destroy V's property but at a time when it was unoccupied. Another possibility is that D believed that P would set fire to V's house while it was occupied but merely in order to frighten V. D may have formed that belief because D thought that P would use the petrol to make only a small petrol bomb whereas P makes a much larger one. These examples do not exhaust the possibilities.

B.81   In this section, we attempt to provide an account of what knowledge or belief D must have in relation to the commission by P of the principal offence. The starting point is a statement of Lord Chief Justice Goddard in *Johnson v Youden*:

> Before a person can be convicted of aiding and abetting the commission of an offence he must at least *know the essential matters* which constitute that offence.[106]

This seemingly simple statement raises a number of difficult issues particularly where D's assistance precedes the commission of the principal offence.[107] There are two central and overlapping issues:

(1)   what are the 'essential matters' of the principal offence?

(2)   what state of mind is denoted by 'know'?

---

[106] [1950] 1 KB 544, 546 (emphasis added). See also *Ackroyd's Air Travel Ltd v DPP* [1950] 1 All ER 933, 936; *Ferguson v Weaving* [1951] 1 KB 814.

[107] However, these issues can also arise where D's encouragement or assistance occurs simultaneously with P's commission of the principal offence – *Carter v Richardson* [1974] RTR 314; *Webster* [2006] EWCA Crim 415, [2006] 2 Cr App R 6.

The 'essential matters' of the principal offence

B.82   A criminal offence can consist of one or more of three external elements: conduct, the circumstances in which the conduct takes place and the consequences of the conduct. Although, an offence can comprise all three elements, not all three are integral to the definition of every offence. Whether one, two or all three elements are part of the definition of an offence varies a good deal. It might be thought that, for D to be convicted of a principal offence, all the external elements of *that* offence would be 'essential matters' of which D must have knowledge.

THE CONDUCT ELEMENT OF THE PRINCIPAL OFFENCE

B.83   Whether the conduct element of the principal offence is always an essential element of which D must have knowledge depends on how the decision of the Court of Criminal Appeal in *Bainbridge*[108] is interpreted. D provided P with cutting equipment which P used to commit the conduct element of burglary, namely to break into a bank as a trespasser and thereafter appropriate property. D said that he thought that the equipment would be used to perpetrate conduct that did not constitute the conduct element of burglary, namely the handling and cutting up stolen property. The trial judge directed the jury that D could be convicted of burglary only if he knew that P intended to use the equipment to break into a bank and steal property from the bank. He also directed that, if D did have that knowledge, it was legally irrelevant that D did not know the date and location of the burglary. D was convicted of burglary and on appeal his conviction was upheld.

B.84   This suggests that the conduct element of the principal offence, but not its details, is an essential element of which D must have knowledge. However, Lord Chief Justice Parker, approving the trial judge's direction to the jury, said there must be "knowledge that a crime of the *type* in question was intended".[109] In the view of some commentators, Lord Parker's reference to 'type' has opened up the prospect of D being convicted of an offence the conduct element of which was different from the offence that he or she believed P was intending to commit:

Example B21

D provides a stolen credit card to P believing that it is P's intention to use it to obtain property by deception. Instead, P uses the card to commit burglary by slipping the latch on V's door, entering V's property and stealing V's stereo recorder.[110]

On one view, obtaining by deception and burglary are offences of the same 'type' because they are offences of dishonesty and each involve an intention to permanently deprive the victim of his or her property. On this view, the fact that their respective conduct elements are different is of no consequence.

---

[108] [1960] 1QB 129.

[109] Above, 134.

[110] The example is taken from Smith and Hogan, *Criminal Law* (11th ed 2005) 188.

B.85   However, while acknowledging that the word 'type' is not free from ambiguity, we believe that commentators may have read too much into its use by Lord Parker. His judgment has to be seen in the context of the trial judge's summing up. The trial judge had directed the jury that the defendant "must know the type of crime that was in fact committed. In this case it is a breaking and entering of premises and the stealing of property from those premises".[111] Lord Parker, approving the direction, said:

> In his reference to the felony of the type intended it was, as he stated, the felony of breaking and entering premises and the stealing of property from those premises.[112]

In our view, it is arguable that, far from endeavouring to expand the scope of secondary liability, Lord Parker was seeking to restrict it. On this view, in referring to 'type', he was emphasising that D should be held liable for a principal offence only if he or she knew that it was conduct falling within the definition of *that* offence, the one that P was intending to perpetrate.

B.86   The fact that D knew that P intended to perpetrate the conduct element of the principal offence does not in itself render D liable for the offence. Different offences can share the same conduct element:

Example B22

In return for payment, D acts as a lookout while P takes V's car without V's consent. D believes that P intends to use the car for some 'joyriding' and will then return it. In fact, P takes the car and sells it to X.

There are two relevant offences: taking a motor vehicle without the consent of the owner[113] and theft (of a motor vehicle).[114] The conduct (and circumstance) element of each offence is identical – appropriation of a motor vehicle. However, the offences are distinguished by their different fault elements – theft requires a dishonest intention to permanently deprive whereas taking without consent is merely dishonest borrowing.

---

[111] [1960] 1 QB 129, 132.

[112] Above, 134.

[113] Contrary to the Theft Act 1968, s 12(1).

[114] Contrary to the Theft Act 1968, s 1(1).

B.87   Some commentators imply that in example B22 it is an open question whether, in the light of *Bainbridge*, D can be convicted of theft even though D did not believe that P intended to permanently deprive V of the car. This assumes that *Bainbridge* is capable of supporting the proposition that offences are of the same type merely because they share a common conduct element. Again, we believe that this is to read too much into Lord Parker's judgment. This is because, just as the conduct element of an offence is an essential matter of which D must have knowledge, so too is P's state of mind in perpetrating the conduct element. In example B22, P's state of mind is to intentionally deprive V of his property. D has no knowledge of P's state of mind and, therefore, cannot be convicted of theft. However, D can be convicted of taking a motor vehicle without the authority of the owner because in this instance the greater offence (theft) includes the lesser.

B.88   Accordingly, properly interpreted, *Bainbridge* is authority for the following propositions of law:

> (1)   it is not enough that D knows that P is intending to do 'something' unlawful;
>
> (2)   D must know that P intends to do an act that falls within the definition of the conduct element of the offence that P in fact commits but does not have to know the details of the act;[115] and
>
> (3)   the fact that D does know that P intends to do an act that falls within the definition of the conduct element of the principal offence does not in itself render D liable.

Variation in the details of the conduct element[116]

B.89   *Bainbridge* establishes that D does not have to know the details of the act that constitutes the conduct element. Thus, if D sells P some petrol believing that P will use the petrol to make a petrol bomb with which to commit arson, it matters not that D has no idea which property P will set fire to.[117] Likewise, D may be liable if he or she encourages P to attack V with a broken beer glass but, instead, P does so with a broken beer bottle.

B.90   However, besides *Bainbridge*, there is an earlier line of authority that suggests that if D, in providing encouragement or assistance, *specifies* a particular victim or item of property, that victim or item of property becomes an essential matter. On this view, if P does an act that falls within the conduct element of the principal offence but in relation to a different victim or item of property from that stipulated by P, the variation in performance is something over and above a matter of detail. It becomes a matter of substance:

---

[115] Previously *Lomas* (1913) 9 Cr App R 220 had been authority for the view that where D provided assistance in advance of the commission of the principal offence, he or she had to know the details of the planned offence.

[116] For our discussion and recommendations on this topic in Part 3, see paras 3.153 to 3.166.

[117] If D believes that P will commit arson against either property x or property y but is not sure which, D will be liable whichever of the two properties P in fact targets. If D believes that P will commit arson in respect of property x and also believes that there is a real possibility that P will also commit arson in respect of property y, D is guilty of each arson should P commit both – *Reardon* [1999] *Criminal Law Review* 392.

If a man command another to commit a Felony on a particular Person or Thing, and he does it on another; as to kill A and he kills B or to burn the house of A and he burns the house of B or steal an Ox, and he steals a Horse; or to steal such Horse, and he steal another; ... the Commander is not an Accessory because the Act done varies in Substance from that which was Commanded.[118]

Although, in this passage, Hawkins does not attach importance to whether or not the variation was deliberate, it has come to be accepted that this is a crucial factor. Accordingly, if D hands a broken beer glass to P so that P can attack V1 but, instead, P uses the glass to deliberately attack V2, D is not an accessory to the assault.[119]

B.91 By contrast, D's liability is unaffected by an *accidental or mistaken* change of victim or outcome:

Example B23

D hands P a broken beer glass so that P can attack V1. P, intending to strike V1, *accidentally* strikes V2 with the glass.

P is guilty of malicious wounding[120] by virtue of the doctrine of transferred malice and so too is D.[121]

B.92 It is unlikely that *Bainbridge* was intended to qualify this preceding line of authority, not least because in *Bainbridge* D did not specify any particular property. However, the exact scope of the variation in performance rule remains unclear. If D encourages P to steal V's Rolls Royce, is D liable if, instead, P deliberately steals V's Bentley? If D urges P to steal V's priceless painting by Constable, is D liable if, instead, P deliberately steals V's slightly less valuable painting by Turner? The authorities suggest that D is not liable. If this is the case, D will incur no criminal liability in circumstances where it might be thought that he or she ought to:

---

[118] W Hawkins, *A Treatise of the Pleas of the Crown*, vol 2 (8th ed 1824) ch 29, s 21. See also M Hale, *The History of the Pleas of the Crown*, vol 1 (1800) p 616 to 617.

[119] *Leahy* [1985] WL 310719 (Crown Court); *Reardon* [1999] *Criminal Law Review* 392.

[120] Depending on P's state of mind, P would be guilty of wounding with intent to cause grievous bodily harm contrary to the Offences against the Person Act 1861, s 18 or unlawful and malicious wounding contrary to the Offences against the Person Act 1861, s 20.

[121] *Saunders and Archer* (1573) 2 Plowd 473. Transferred malice is a common law doctrine whereby, if D satisfies the external elements of an offence accompanied by the requisite fault element, D is guilty of the offence even though the occurrence of the external elements are unexpected (but in a way which is immaterial to the definition of the offence). However, the institutional writers based their opinion not on the doctrine of transferred malice but on the fact that the offence actually committed by P was "in the ordinary course of things the probable consequence" – Foster, *Crown Law*, p 370.

> **Example B24**
>
> D, a racist, pays P £500 to set fire to the local Afro-Caribbean community centre. P, finding blanket security at the centre, instead sets fire to a local public house that is frequented by people from the centre.

Being a racist, D is unlikely to be disappointed that the public house has been burned down.[122]

THE CIRCUMSTANCE ELEMENT OF THE PRINCIPAL OFFENCE

B.93   The circumstance element of the principal offence is always an essential matter of which D must have knowledge:

> **Example B25**
>
> D sells petrol to P believing that P is going to make a petrol bomb with which to set fire to P's isolated country cottage, with a view to making a false insurance claim. P does use the petrol to make a bomb but instead uses it to set fire to the house of his enemy, V.

P is guilty of arson.[123] Arson is an offence that consists of three elements: conduct (an act or omission which creates a fire), consequence (damaging or destroying property) and circumstance (the property belongs to another person). D believed that P would perpetrate the conduct element of the offence and that the consequence element would ensue. However, because D believed that P would set fire to his own property, D did not believe that the circumstance element of arson would be satisfied. As a result, D is not guilty of arson.

B.94   The circumstance element of an offence is an essential matter even if it is a no-fault offence.[124] A no-fault offence is one that P can commit even though he or she is not at fault in relation to the circumstance element:

> **Example B26**
>
> P is a learner driver. Shortly before leaving home for his driving lesson, he has an orange juice at home. Unknown to P, his eight-year-old son had poured some vodka into the orange. While on his lesson under the supervision of his instructor D, P has a minor collision another vehicle. P is breathalysed and is found to be slightly over the limit.

P is guilty of driving with excess alcohol despite not knowing and having no reason to know that he was over the limit. By contrast, D is not liable for P's offence because D did not know that P was over the limit.

---

[122] An unreported Crown Court case suggests that D is liable even where the variation in performance is deliberate – *Dunning and Graham* (December 1985).

[123] Contrary to Criminal Damage Act 1971, s 1(1) & (3).

[124] *Callow v Tillstone* (1900) 83 LT 411.

B.95   The position with regard to the consequence element of the principal offence is more complicated. The general rule is the same as for the circumstance element, namely that the consequence element is an essential matter of which D must have 'knowledge'.[125] However, consider the following example:

Example B27

D holds V so that P can punch V. The intention of D and P is merely to give V a black eye.[126] Unfortunately, the impact of the punch causes P to fall over. He strikes his head against the kerb and sustains an injury from which he dies.

P is guilty of (unlawful and dangerous act) manslaughter. P's act was dangerous because it would have been obvious to any reasonable person that a punch to the face would subject V to the risk of some harm, albeit not serious harm. D, although not at fault in relation to the consequence, is also guilty of manslaughter because in this example the consequence is not an 'essential matter'. Why is this?

B.96   As we explained in the first report,[127] P can be guilty of some offences that have a consequence element despite not being at fault in relation to the defined consequence. These are constructive liability offences and they include some of the most serious offences, for example, murder, manslaughter, unlawful and malicious wounding and causing death by dangerous driving. They are the counterpart of no-fault offences where P can be convicted despite not being at fault in relation to the circumstance element. We noted above[128] that for the purposes of secondary liability the circumstance element is always an essential matter of which D must have knowledge. The common law could have adopted a similar position in relation to D's liability for constructive liability offences. Instead, however, the starting point of the common law is that the consequence element of a *constructive liability* offence is not an essential matter of which D must have knowledge.

---

[125] We refer to 'knowledge' because that was the concept employed by Lord Goddard in *Johnson v Youden* when he said that D had "to know the essential matters". However, the concept of 'knowledge' is inapposite in relation to consequences. A person intends or foresees a risk of a consequence.

[126] Thereby committing the offence of assault occasioning actual bodily harm, contrary to Offences against the Person Act 1861, s 47.

[127] Paras 5.107 to 5.108.

[128] Para B.93 above.

B.97   For the purpose of determining D's liability, distinguishing no-fault offences and constructive liability offences in the way that the common law does is not indefensible. Typically, where an offence comprises a conduct element and a circumstance element, the conduct element consists of an activity that in itself the law has no reason to punish. Examples are driving, selling meat, having sexual intercourse and going through a ceremony of marriage. The criminal law intervenes if the conduct is perpetrated in specific circumstances - driving with excess alcohol, driving while disqualified, selling meat that is unfit for human consumption, having sexual intercourse without the consent of the other and 'marrying' when already married. While there may be strong policy reasons for holding P criminally liable for some offences even though P is not at fault in relation to their circumstance element, it would be a significant further step to hold D likewise liable.

B.98   By contrast, offences of constructive liability, consisting of a conduct and consequence element, are offences where the conduct element in itself merits the attention of the criminal law. Unlawful and dangerous act manslaughter is an example. In example B27, P's act of punching V is conduct that the law has every reason to punish. On one view, the law is severe in holding D responsible for a consequence, V's death, the risk of which D did not foresee and which could not reasonably have been foreseen. However, that is not a legitimate reason for exonerating D from responsibility for V's death. D intentionally assisted P to perpetrate conduct that D knew involved wrongdoing (an assault), and if P is to be held responsible for that conduct so too should D.

B.99   However, the principle that the consequence element of a constructive liability offence is not an essential matter causes acute problems in cases where P's actions are different from those which D had intended or anticipated and P's state of mind in perpetrating those actions is also different from what D had anticipated. This issue has invariably arisen in the context of the law of homicide:

> **Example B28**
>
> D and P agree to inflict less than serious harm on V by punching him. In the course of the assault, P pulls out a knife which D was unaware that P had. P fatally stabs V.

We consider how the courts have addressed the issue of whether D is liable for the consequence – V's death - after explaining what is meant by D having to 'know' the essential matters.[129]

P'S STATE OF MIND IN RELATION TO THE PRINCIPAL OFFENCE

B.100   If P, in order to be convicted of the principal offence, is required to have a particular state of mind, P's state of mind is an essential matter of which D must have knowledge:

---

[129] Paras B.124 to B.132 below.

> **Example B29**
>
> D and P share a flat. D drives P to the local supermarket. D waits in the car. A little later, P emerges from the store carrying bags of food. D drives them home. P did not pay for the food but D believed that he did.

In order to be convicted of theft, P must 'dishonestly' appropriate property belonging to another. In example B29, P has done so. However, D is not guilty of theft because, although he intended that P should perpetrate the conduct element of theft, D believed that P would pay for the food.

'Knowledge' of the essential matters[130]

NO JOINT CRIMINAL VENTURE[131]

B.101 In *Johnson v Youden* Lord Goddard said that D must "know" the essential matters of the offence that P commits. We have suggested that, apart from the consequence element of a constructive liability offence, "the essential matters" of an offence comprise its external elements together with P's state of mind. If this is correct, "know" should mean that:

   (1)   in relation to the conduct element, D believes that P intends to perpetrate the conduct element;

   (2)   in relation to the circumstance element, D believes that, if P perpetrates the conduct element, he or she will do so in the circumstances proof of which is required for conviction of the offence;

   (3)   in relation to the consequence element, D believes that, if P perpetrates the conduct element, he or she will do so with the consequences proof of which is required for conviction of the offence.

B.102 The following example illustrates (3):

> **Example B30**
>
> P tells D that he wants to borrow D's rifle so that he can shoot at and cause grievous bodily harm to V. D, who has his own reasons for placating P, gives his rifle to P. However, D does so believing that, given the distance between P and V combined with P's poor eye sight, P will miss the target. In the event, P's shot hits V causing grievous bodily harm.

---

[130] In this section, we distinguish 'non joint ventures' from joint ventures. We do so because we believe that the rules for each are not identical. We are conscious that Graham Virgo, a respondent to our consultation paper *A New Homicide Act for England and Wales?* (2006) Consultation Paper No 177, was extremely critical of our view that, in cases where there is no joint venture, D must intend or believe that the principal offence will be committed. We stand by that view which we note is similar to that of Professor Andrew Simester, "*The Mental Element in Complicity*" [2006] Law Quarterly Review 578. We acknowledge that there are cases that support Graham Virgo but, as we hope to show, these authorities are inconsistent and unsatisfactory.

[131] For our discussion and recommendations on this topic in Part 3, see 3.70 to 3.122.

P is guilty of causing grievous bodily harm with intent.[132] Although D believed that P would perpetrate the conduct element of the offence, he did not believe that the consequence element would materialise. Accordingly, applying *Johnson v Youden*, D is not guilty of the offence.[133]

B.103   Following *Johnson v Youden*, the courts twice considered the liability of licensees of public houses who were charged with aiding, abetting, counselling or procuring their customers to commit the strict liability offence of consuming intoxicating liquor outside permitted hours.[134] In each case, D's conduct was contemporaneous with the commission of the principal offence. In each case, the Divisional Court held, that to be liable, D had to know that customers were consuming alcohol outside the permitted hours.

B.104   In *Bainbridge*,[135] the Court of Criminal Appeal applied *Johnson v Youden* in a case where D's assistance was antecedent to the commission of the principal offence. The trial judge directed the jury that D was guilty of burglary if he knew that P would use the cutting equipment that D had provided to break into a bank. In dismissing D's appeal, Lord Chief Justice Parker said:

> … there must be not merely suspicion but knowledge that a crime of the type in question was intended, and that the equipment was bought with that in view.[136]

B.105   In the CP, the Commission said that this aspect of *Bainbridge* was "troublesome":

> It is too narrow in that the requirement of knowledge, taken literally, would exculpate [D] who, because of his suspicions, was in effect reckless as to whether the principal crime was committed.[137]

B.106   In *Maxwell*[138] D drove P to the vicinity of an inn. D believed that there was to be an attack, not necessarily on the inn, involving violence in which persons would be endangered or premises seriously damaged. D was uncertain whether the attack would be perpetrated by bomb, bullet or other means but he knew that there would be some form of attack. In the event, P threw a pipe bomb containing explosive into the inn. Fortunately, no one was injured. D was convicted of being an accessory to two offences under the Explosive Substances Act 1883.[139] The House of Lords upheld D's conviction.

---

[132] Contrary to Offences against the Person Act 1861. It is not a constructive liability offence.

[133] It would be different if it had been D's *intention* that V should suffer grievous bodily harm. D is liable for an intended consequence even if he or she believes that it is unlikely to materialise.

[134] *Thomas v Lindop* [1950] 1 All ER 966; *Ferguson v Weaving* [1951] 1 All ER 412.

[135] [1960] 1 QB 129.

[136] Above, 134 by Lord Chief Justice Parker.

[137] Para 2.72.

[138] [1978] 1 WLR 1350. D and P were not parties to a joint criminal venture because they did not form or share a common intention to commit an offence.

[139] Section 3(1)(a): doing an act with intent to cause by explosive substances an explosion of a nature likely to endanger life or cause serious injury to property; s 3(1)(b): possessing an explosive with similar intent.

B.107   *Maxwell* establishes that if D believes that P intends to commit at least one of a number of offences but has no belief as to which one P will commit, D can be convicted of the offence that P does commit if that offence is one of those that D believed that P might commit:

Example B31

In return for payment, D drives P to the vicinity of V's house. D does so in the belief that P will commit murder, robbery or burglary but is unsure which one P will commit. In the event, P murders V.

D is guilty of murder because murder falls within the range of offences that P believed might be committed. Had P instead committed criminal damage, D would not have been liable for the offence because criminal damage was not amongst the offences that D believed might be committed.

B.108   *Maxwell* is of limited scope. It does not establish a general test based on foresight that P might commit an offence. It leaves unaltered the *Bainbridge* rule that P must believe that an offence will be committed. It refines that rule by establishing that, if D believes that an offence will be committed but cannot be sure which offence, he is liable for the offence that P commits provided that the offence is one that D believed might be committed.

The subsequent case law

B.109   Although the House of Lords on two occasions[140] has approved *Johnson v Youden*, subsequent cases suggest that D can be convicted of the principal offence even if his or her state of mind falls short of a belief that P:

   (1)   intends to perpetrate the conduct element; or

   (2)   will do so in the circumstance proof of which is required for conviction of the offence; or

   (3)   will do so with the consequence proof of which is required for conviction of the offence.

However, in our view, these authorities[141] are not only inconsistent with each other but also reliant on cases of joint criminal venture where different principles apply. In addition, the courts' observations were unnecessary to the decisions.[142]

---

[140] *Churchill* [1967] 2 AC 224, 236 to 237; *Maxwell* [1978] 1 WLR 1350.

[141] *Carter v Richardson* [1974] RTR 314; *Blakely and Sutton v DPP* [1991] RTR 405; *Reardon* [1999] *Criminal Law Review* 392; *Webster* [2006] EWCA Crim 415, [2006] 2 Cr App R 6.

[142] *Carter v Richardson* [1974] RTR 314; *Blakely and Sutton v DPP* [1991] RTR 405; *Webster* [2006] EWCA Crim 415, [2006] 2 Cr App R 6.

B.110   In *Carter v Richardson*[143] the issue was D's state of mind in relation to the *circumstance* element of the principal offence. D was the supervisor of P, a learner driver. The magistrates found as a fact that D knew that P had been drinking alcohol and was over the prescribed limit. Accordingly, they convicted D of driving with excess alcohol by virtue of having aided and abetted P to commit the offence. The magistrates' finding of fact was sufficient to dispose of P's appeal because the finding was that D knew that P was in excess of the prescribed limit. However, the Divisional Court upheld the conviction on the ground that it sufficed that D believed that P's blood alcohol was *probably* in excess of the prescribed limit.

B.111   The offence at issue in *Carter v Richardson* – driving with excess alcohol – was a no-fault offence. We explained above[144] that, in determining D's liability, the circumstance of a no-fault offence is an essential element of the offence even though P can be convicted without being at fault in relation to the circumstance. It is possible to accord *Carter v Richardson* a restricted interpretation, namely that, in relation to *no-fault* offences, it relaxes the requirement that D must know or believe that the circumstance element of the principal offence is or will be satisfied.[145]

B.112   In *Blakely and Sutton v DPP*,[146] D 'laced' P's non-alcoholic drink because she did *not* want P to drive when in excess of the prescribed limit. Her intention was to inform P of what she had done but, unfortunately, P, in excess of the prescribed limit, drove off before she could do so. It was a case, therefore, where D intended to bring about the circumstance element of the offence but not the conduct element. D was convicted of driving with excess alcohol by virtue of having *procured* P to commit the offence. The Divisional Court quashed her conviction on the basis that it was possible that the magistrates had applied an objective test of recklessness.[147] That was sufficient to dispose of the appeal. However, McCullough J went on to say that in cases where D's conduct precedes the commission of the principal offence, it had to be proved that D "contemplated that his act would, *or might*, bring about or assist the commission of the principal offence".[148]

---

[143] [1974] RTR 314.

[144] Para B.94.

[145] It has to be said that support for this restricted interpretation is not to be found in the judgment of Lord Chief Justice Widgery.

[146] [1991] RTR 405.

[147] In other words, the magistrates convicted on the basis that D ought to have realised that there was a risk that, as a result of what she had done, P might drive in excess of the prescribed limit.

[148] *Blakely and Sutton v DPP* [1991] RTR 405, 414.

B.113   In *Reardon*[149] P shot two men in the bar of a public house and carried them out into the garden. P returned to the bar and asked D for the loan of D's knife saying that he needed it to finish off one of the men who was still alive. The medical evidence showed that both men died from a stab wound inflicted with D's knife. D was convicted of murder as an accessory to both killings. Both convictions were upheld on the ground that the jury must have found that D intended to assist one murder but had also foreseen that there was "at least the strong possibility" that two murders would be committed. Professor Sir John Smith commenting on the decision said that:

> ...it appears to decide that the principles applicable to an accessory who shares a common purpose with the principal are equally applicable to an accessory who does not.[150]

The judgment was unreserved and is based on authorities[151] which were concerned with D's liability in cases where D was a party to a joint criminal venture where different principles apply.

B.114   In *Bryce*[152] the Court of Appeal said that it suffices if D "contemplates" the commission of the principal offence in the sense of realising that "it is a real possibility that it will be committed".[153] This was stated as a general proposition applying to both non-joint criminal ventures and joint criminal ventures. However, the Court of Appeal relied on *Rook*[154] which was a case of joint criminal venture. Further, the judgment of the Court wrongly cites *Bainbridge*[155] as authority for the proposition that D aids P to commit an offence if D provides P with assistance realising that "there is a real possibility"[156] that it will be used to commit an offence of a particular type.

---

[149] [1999] *Criminal Law Review* 392.

[150] Above, 393.

[151] *Chan Wing-siu* [1985] AC 168; *Powell and Daniels, English* [1999] 1 AC 1.

[152] [2004] EWCA Crim 1231, [2004] 2 Cr App R 35. Curiously, the Court of Appeal thought that the case was not a joint criminal venture.

[153] Above, [58].

[154] [1993] 2 All ER 955.

[155] [1960] 1 QB 129.

[156] [2004] EWCA Crim 1231, [2004] 2 Cr App R 35 [49].

B.115 In *Webster*,[157] D was giving P and V a lift home in D's car. During the journey, D allowed P to drive the car. P drove the car erratically and at excessive speed as a result of which it left the road. V was killed. D was charged with aiding and abetting P to cause death by dangerous driving. In evidence D said that he knew P had been drinking alcohol. The Court of Appeal quashed D's conviction because the trial judge had directed the jury that D was guilty if, at the time that he allowed P to drive, he recognised, or it would have been obvious to him, that it was dangerous to let P drive. That was an incorrect direction because it focused on the wrong issue. Clearly, if D knew that P had been drinking alcohol, he knew that there was a danger in letting P drive. It did not follow, however, that D knew or believed that P would or might in fact drive dangerously.

B.116 That was sufficient to dispose of the appeal. However, the Court of Appeal held that, in order to convict D, it had to be proved that D foresaw that P was *likely* to drive in a dangerous manner. The Court of Appeal referred to *Blakely and Sutton v DPP*, seemingly without appreciating that in that case the Divisional Court had suggested that the correct test was one based on foresight of a possibility.

B.117 The result is that on several occasions the courts, without the need to, have departed from *Johnson v Youden*. As a result, there are now at least four different tests for determining D's liability– contemplation of a probability, a strong possibility, a real possibility and a likelihood. The following example reveals the problems caused by the more recent case law:

Example B32

P asks D for the details of V's address. P refuses to say why he wants V's address but D believes it might be because P wants to have sexual intercourse with her. D also believes that, if so, should V not consent to sexual intercourse, P might compel her to have intercourse with him. Anxious to secure favour with P, D provides him with V's address. In the event, V refuses to consent to intercourse and P rapes V.

With regard to the conduct element of rape, penetration, D's liability appears to depend on determining whether he foresaw it as a possibility, a real possibility, a strong possibility or a likelihood and, having done so, deciding which of the recent 'authorities' to apply. The same is true of the circumstance element, V's lack of consent, save that, if *Carter v Richardson* is not confined to no-fault offences, D would be liable only if he believed that it was 'probable' that V would not consent.

---

[157] [2006] EWCA Crim 415, [2006] 2 Cr App R 6.

JOINT CRIMINAL VENTURES[158]

Liability for the agreed offence

B.118   It might be thought that the issue of D's 'knowledge' in relation to P committing the agreed offence would be academic. If D and P are parties to an express agreement to commit an offence, it will usually be D's intention that the offence be committed. D will believe that P or another party to the venture will perpetrate the conduct element of the offence in the circumstances and with the consequences proof of which is required for conviction of the offence. The same is true where D and P's shared intention to commit the agreed offence is inferred from their conduct rather than an express agreement.

B.119   However, in *Rook*[159] D, exceptionally, did not intend that the agreed offence should be committed. D participated in a plan to murder V. However, at his trial D testified that it was never his intention that D should be killed. Instead, D said that his intention was, having been paid, to absent himself on the day of the murder in the (mistaken) belief that, because of his absence, P would desist from murdering V. The trial judge directed the jury that D was guilty of murder if he had foreseen that P would probably murder V. The Court of Appeal held the direction was too generous to D. D was guilty of murder if he foresaw that there was a real or substantial risk that P might murder V.

B.120   As the next section demonstrates, prior to *Rook* the courts had already held that D could be convicted of a collateral offence committed as an incident of a joint criminal venture if D had foreseen a real risk of P committing the offence. Accordingly, in holding that D could be convicted of the agreed offence if he or she foresaw a real risk of P committing it, *Rook* was not extending the law. Unfortunately, however, subsequent cases, in which D and P have not been parties to a joint criminal venture, have accorded *Rook* a significance that it does not merit. It has been interpreted as authority for the view that, irrespective of whether D and P are parties to a joint criminal venture, D can be convicted if he or she foresaw a real risk that P would commit the principal offence.

Liability for a collateral offence

B.121   In *Rook*, the Court of Appeal, without needing to, applied the decision of the Privy Council in *Chan Wing-siu*.[160] In that case, D was a party to a joint criminal venture to commit robbery. In the course of the robbery, V was murdered. It was unclear who had murdered V. The trial judge directed the jury that D was guilty of murder if he had contemplated that one of the parties to the joint criminal venture might attack V intending to cause V serious bodily harm. The Privy Council upheld D's conviction.

B.122   Subsequently in *Hui Chi-Ming v R*, Lord Lowry, delivering the opinion of the Privy Council, stated:

[158] For our discussion and recommendations on this topic in Part 3, see 3.123 to 3.169.

[159] [1993] 2 All ER 955.

[160] [1985] 1 AC 168.

... [D], in order to be guilty, must have foreseen the relevant offence which [P] may commit *as a possible incident of the common unlawful enterprise* and must, with such foresight, still have participated in the enterprise.[161]

B.123 Taken together, *Chan Wing-siu* and *Hui Chi-Ming* establish that if D foresees that P might commit murder as an incident of a joint criminal venture, D is guilty of murder should P commit murder as an incident of the venture. However, there is no reason why the principle should be restricted to cases where the collateral offence is murder:

Example B33

D and P agree to commit a burglary at V's premises. D foresees that if V disturbs them, P may rape her. V does disturb them and, as D feared, P rapes her.

D is guilty of rape.

COMPLICITY AND THE LAW OF HOMICIDE

B.124 The problem which the courts have grappled with can be stated simply: if P and D are parties to a joint criminal venture which, as far as D is concerned, does not have as its object the intentional killing of V,[162] to what extent if any, should D be held responsible for V's death in the event that P kills V? The courts have struggled to provide a satisfactory answer.

B.125 In practice, prior to *English*,[163] the question fell for consideration in two ways:

(1) the offence that P and D agreed to commit, for example burglary or assault occasioning actual bodily harm, did not involve the use or threatened use of *serious* violence against V. Further, D did not foresee that P might do an act intending to kill or cause serious bodily harm to V. However, in the course of the venture, P did such an act ("the lethal act") and V died:

Example B34

D and P agree to inflict less than serious harm on V by punching him. In the course of assaulting V, P pulls out a knife, which D was unaware that P had, and fatally stabs V. P is charged with murder, and D is charged with manslaughter.

---

[161] [1992] 1 AC 34, 53 (emphasis in original)

[162] If the agreed offence involves the use of violence which is *intended to kill* V, there is no difficulty. Should P kill V, P and D are each guilty of murder. This would be so even if the method that P employed to kill V was one that D had not foreseen and involved exceptional cruelty which sickens D.

[163] [1999] 1 AC 1.

The issue was whether D should be convicted of manslaughter or completely exonerated from liability *for V's death*.[164] On one view, it might be thought that if, in example B27, D is guilty of manslaughter, he also ought to be guilty of manslaughter in example B34.

(2)   The offence that P and D agreed to commit (the agreed offence) did not involve the use or threatened use of serious violence against V. However, D did foresee that P might do an act intending to kill or cause serious harm to V. In the course of the venture, P did such an act and V died:

Example B35

D and P agree to commit burglary at V's premises. D foresees that if V disturbs them, P might attack V intending to kill or cause serious harm to V. D implores P not to use any violence against V. As D feared, V does disturb them and P murders her.

The issue was whether, despite not satisfying the fault element of murder, D should be convicted of murder because he foresaw that P might murder V. If not, should D be convicted of manslaughter?

The authorities prior to 1997

B.126   Reflecting (1) and (2) above, two parallel but distinct lines of authority, each unsatisfactory, developed. In relation to (1), the Court of Appeal was unable to adopt a consistent line. In some cases, the court upheld D's conviction for manslaughter[165] while in others it quashed D's conviction.[166]

B.127   In relation to (2), as noted above, in *Chan Wing-sui*[167] the Privy Council held that foresight that P might attack V intending to kill or cause serious harm rendered D liable for murder if P did so and killed V. However, subsequently, the Court of Appeal vacillated in cases that called for consideration of *Chan Wing-sui*.[168]

---

[164] Regardless of whether D was liable for V's death, D would be liable for the offence that he or she had agreed with P to commit (assuming that it had been committed).

[165] *Smith (Wesley)* [1963] 1 WLR 1200; *Betty* (1963) 48 Cr App R 6; *Reid* (1976) 62 Cr App R 109; *Stewart and Schofield* [1995] 1 Cr App R 441. In all these cases, D knew that P was armed with a weapon.

[166] *Davis v DPP* [1954] AC 378; *Anderson and Morris* [1966] 2 QB 110; *Lovesey and Peterson* [1970] 1 QB 352; *Dunbar* [1988] *Criminal Law Review* 693.

[167] [1985] AC 168.

[168] It was distinguished in *Barr* (1989) 88 Cr App R 362 and *Smith* [1988] *Criminal Law Review* 616 (not a case of homicide). These two authorities were declared by the House of Lords in *Powell and Daniels* [1999] 1 AC 1 to have been wrongly decided. It was applied in *Ward* (1986) 85 Cr App R 71; *Slack* [1989] QB 775; *Wakely* [1990] *Criminal Law Review* 119 and *Hyde* [1991] 1 QB 134.

Powell and Daniels, English[169]

B.128　On one view, the rule established in *Chan Wing-siu*, namely that D is guilty of murder if, participating in a joint criminal venture, he or she foresees that P might attack V intending to kill or cause serious bodily harm to V, is severe on D. On this view, it is particularly severe if D foresees that P might attack V not with the intention of killing V but with the intention of causing serious but non-lethal harm to V. The problem arose in 1997 in the conjoined appeals of *Powell and Daniels, English*.[170]

B.129　In *Powell and Daniels* D and P went to V's house to buy drugs. On arrival, P shot and killed V. The trial judge directed the jury that D was guilty of murder if D foresaw that P might intentionally kill or cause serious harm to V. D was convicted of murder as a secondary party. The House of Lords, following *Chan Wing-siu*, upheld D's conviction.

B.130　In *English*, D and P agreed to attack V by assaulting V with wooden posts. As far as D was concerned, the shared intention was to cause injury to but not to kill V. In the course of the attack, P pulled out a knife, which D maintained he was unaware that P had, and killed V. The trial judge, in accordance with *Hyde*[171] directed the jury that they could convict D of murder if he had foreseen that P might attack V intending to kill or cause serious injury to V. As such, the direction enabled the jury to convict D irrespective of what particular act he foresaw P might perpetrate provided that they were sure that D had foreseen that P might attack V intending to kill or cause serious bodily harm. D was convicted of murder.[172]

B.131　It was possible that, following the judge's direction, the jury convicted D on the basis that he had intended or foreseen that P might attack V with a wooden post (but not a knife) intending to cause V serious bodily harm (but not to kill V). The certified question for the House of Lords assumed that it was on that basis that the jury had convicted D. The House of Lords quashed D's conviction. In doing so, Lord Hutton made it clear that D is liable if he or she foresaw the act causing V's death as a possible incident of the joint criminal venture unless he or she had dismissed the risk as negligible.

B.132　Lord Hutton, delivering the leading speech, said that he agreed with the submission made on behalf of English that:

> ... to be guilty under the principle stated in Chan Wing-siu v R [D] must foresee an *act* of the *type* which [P] committed, and that in the present case the use of the knife was *fundamentally different* to the use of a wooden post.[173]

---

[169] [1999] 1 AC 1.

[170] Above.

[171] [1991] 1 QB 134.

[172] It is not known whether the jury found that, in stabbing V, P intended to kill V or merely intended to cause serious bodily harm.

[173] *Powell and Daniels, English* [1999] 1 AC 1, 28 (emphasis added).

D was not guilty of murder because although he had intended or foreseen that P might attack V intending to cause serious harm, the act that killed V was 'fundamentally different' from the act that D had anticipated. P's lethal act was outside the scope of the joint criminal venture. Since it was outside the scope of the venture, not only was D not guilty of murder but, according to Lord Hutton, he was also not guilty of manslaughter.

The issues arising from Powell and Daniels, English

DISTINGUISHING ACTIONS FROM THE INTENTIONS WITH WHICH THEY ARE DONE?

B.133   In *Van Hoogstraten,*[174] Sir Stephen Mitchell said that "...foresight defines the scope of the joint [criminal venture]". In that regard, he set out a two-step test to determine whether D is liable for the killing of V by P. First, the task of the trial judge is to identify correctly the act of P that caused V's death. It is then for the jury to determine whether or not D foresaw that P might do that act. If the jury is not sure that D did so foresee, they should acquit D of both murder and manslaughter.

B.134   Secondly, and by way of contrast, if the jury is sure that D *did* so foresee, the extent of D's liability for V's death will then depend on whether the jury is also sure that D foresaw that P might do the act with the necessary intent for murder. If they are sure, the verdict is murder. Otherwise, D is guilty of manslaughter.

B.135   In *Van Hoogstraten,* P was convicted of murder for shooting V in the head at point blank range. D was convicted of manslaughter. However, D's conviction was quashed and a re-trial ordered. At the re-trial, the prosecution intended to allege that D had hired P to put pressure on V through terror by firing a loaded firearm not at V but in the vicinity of V. However, the prosecution was not alleging that D intended or foresaw the possibility of death or injury to V.

B.136   At a preparatory hearing, Sir Stephen ruled that the act which caused V's death was the deliberate discharge of a loaded firearm deliberately aimed at V. With the prosecution having already conceded this point, it was found that this was not an act that any reasonable jury could conclude had been foreseen by D. Accordingly, D could not be liable for V's death. In *Attorney-Generals Reference (No 3 of 2004)*[175] the Court of Appeal upheld Sir Stephen's ruling but on a different basis. Agreeing with Sir Stephen that the crucial question was identifying the act that caused V's death, the court said that the answer was to be found by applying the 'fundamentally different" test. The court stated, incorrectly, that Sir Stephen had applied that test and had properly ruled that the act that caused V's death was fundamentally different from that foresee by D.

---

[174] 2 December 2003, unreported.

[175] [2005] EWCA Crim 1882.

B.137 Sir Stephen's approach had much to commend it, not least because it simplifies the task of the jury. The jury is not required to consider whether the act that caused V's death was 'fundamentally different' from that foreseen by D, but only whether it was foreseen by D as a possibility. Nevertheless the approach of the Court of Appeal is a more accurate reflection of Lord Hutton's speech in *English.* Although some passages suggest that Lord Hutton was endorsing an undiluted test of foresight, the preferred view is that he was not. Accordingly, following *English,* if the act of P that caused V's death was not foreseen by D, D is not criminally responsible for V's death provided that the lethal act was 'fundamentally different' from that foreseen by D. If the lethal act was not 'fundamentally different', the mere fact that it was not foreseen by D will be of no avail.

THE SCOPE OF THE 'FUNDAMENTALLY DIFFERENT' ACT RULE

B.138 Under the *Chan Wing-siu* principle, there are a number of different ways in which D can be convicted of murder in the event of P killing V:

(1)   D foresaw that P might kill V intending to kill V, and P does kill V with that intent. In principle, both D and P have committed murder;

(2)   D foresaw that P might kill V intending to cause V serious bodily harm. An example would be if D foresaw that P might knee-cap V intending to cause serious harm but not to kill. Nevertheless, D realised that the knee-capping might result in V's death. P intentionally kills V in some other way. In principle, both D and P have committed murder; and

(3)   D foresaw that P might cause serious harm to V intending to cause serious harm to V. P intentionally kills V. In principle, both D and P have committed murder.

B.139 In *English,* the issue of D's liability for a "fundamentally different" lethal act was confined to (3). Subsequently, the Court of Appeal in *Rahman*[176] has held that in (1), D cannot take advantage of the "fundamentally different" rule. Thus, if D foresees that P might kick V to the head intending to kill V and, instead, P murders V by stabbing V, D is guilty of murder. By contrast, the Court of Appeal also said that in (2), D can take advantage of the "fundamentally different" rule.[177]

---

[176] [2007] EWCA Crim 342.

[177] The fundamental difference rule will also apply to cases where the question is whether D is guilty of *manslaughter,* or of no homicide offence. An example would be where D foresaw that P might cause less than serious harm to V intending to cause less than serious harm to V and P killed V. There is no doubt that on such facts D can take advantage of the 'fundamentally different act' rule: *Attorney General's Reference (No 3 of 2004)* [2005] EWCA Crim 1882.

The relevance of P's state of mind in perpetrating the lethal act

B.140   In Attorney General's Reference (No 3 of 2004)[178] the prosecution submitted that *as a matter of law* a lethal act perpetrated by P cannot be 'fundamentally different' if the only difference between it and the act foreseen by D was P's state of mind in perpetrating it. The Court of Appeal rejected the submission.

B.141   Does it follow that P's state of mind in perpetrating the lethal act is a factor that the jury is entitled to take into account in deciding whether the act is 'fundamentally different'? In *Gilmore*[179] the Court of Appeal of Northern Ireland said that it was 'conceivable that in some cases the nature of the principal's [state of mind] may change the nature of the act committed by him....'[180] However, in *Van Hoogstraten,* Sir Stephen Mitchell said that attention should at first be focused on the act that caused death than rather than upon the state of mind of P.

B.142   In *Rahman*[181] D was convicted of murder following a direction by the trial judge that D was guilty of murder if he foresaw that in the course of attacking V, P might produce and use a knife intending to kill or cause serious harm to V. On appeal, it was submitted that the jury should have been directed that when considering whether the lethal act was 'fundamentally different' they should take into account that P's intention was or may have been to kill and not merely to cause serious harm.[182]

B.143   The Court of Appeal rejected the submission. Lord Justice Hooper referred to *Attorney General's Reference (No 3 of 2004).*[183] He said that in that case what made the act 'fundamentally different' from that foreseen as a possibility by D was not that P had deliberately discharged the firearm at V intending to kill. Rather, it was the deliberate discharge of the firearm *at V* rather than in the vicinity of V.

---

[178] [2005] EWCA Crim 1882.

[179] [2000] 2 Cr App R 407.

[180] Above.

[181] [2007] EWCA Crim 342.

[182] Support for the submission can be found in dicta in *Anderson and Morris* [1966] 2 QB 110, 120 and in *Uddin* [1999] QB 431, 441. However, a similar submission had previously been rejected in *Roberts, Day and Day* [2001] *Criminal Law Review* 984.

[183] In which he had delivered the judgment of the Court of Appeal.

The relevance of the weapon used by P

B.144   In *English*, P and D agreed to attack V by hitting him with wooden posts. In the event, P used a knife to fatally stab V. The House of Lords was in no doubt that the use of the knife was a 'fundamentally different' act. Lord Hutton referred with approval to *Gamble*.[184] In that case P and D agreed to shoot V in the knees. Instead, P murdered V by slitting his throat. Beyond this, P fired four bullets into V's head. The bullets would have killed V had he not died from the slitting of his throat. Mr Justice Carswell, without employing the language of 'fundamentally different', held that D was not criminally responsible for V's death. Lord Hutton, although he thought it was debatable, through that the same result should follow had V died from the bullet wounds:

> ...if the weapon used by the primary party is different to but as dangerous as the weapon that the secondary party contemplated he might use, the secondary party should not escape liability for murder because of the difference in the weapon, for example, if he foresaw that the primary party might use a gun to kill and [he] used a knife to kill or vice-versa.[185]

B.145   The passage is puzzling. In *English*, the weapon used by P (a knife) was as dangerous as the weapon (wooden posts) that D had agreed should be used to attack V. In *Gamble,* the weapon used by P was a knife and according to Lord Hutton, such a weapon is as dangerous as a gun. Yet in each case, Lord Hutton was of the view that P's act was 'fundamentally different'. Perhaps he meant no more than that if D had foreseen that P may use a particular weapon to *kill* V, D cannot rely on the fact that P used a different weapon to kill V.

[184] [1989] NI 268.

[185] [1999] 1 AC 1, 29.

B.146   Assuming that D did not foresee that P might attack V intending to *kill,* if P kills V by employing a weapon that D did not contemplate, or by using it in a way that D did not contemplate, it will be a question of fact whether the use of the weapon was a 'fundamentally different' act. There has been very little in the way of guidance for juries.[186] The case of *Gilmore*[187] illustrates the problem. D had driven P to the house knowing that the house was occupied and that P intended to petrol bomb it. However, D believed the petrol bomb to be much smaller than was the case. D believed that the bomb would damage the property and cause fear to the occupants but would not harm them. P, aware of the size of the petrol bomb, threw it into the house. The occupants were killed. P and D were convicted of murder. The Court of Appeal of Northern Ireland quashed D's conviction for murder in the light of D's belief in the size and impact of the bomb. However, it substituted a conviction of manslaughter because the act carried out by P (the throwing of a petrol bomb into an occupied property) was the very act contemplated by D. The fact that the bomb used was much larger than the one contemplated by D was beside the point.[188]

The most recent guidance

B.147   The most recent decision is that of the Court of Appeal in *Rahman*.[189] Lord Justice Hooper said that the proper approach is reflected in the four following questions:

> "1. What was P's act which caused the death of V? (eg, stabbing, shooting, kicking, beating).[190]
>
> 2. Did D realise that one of the attackers might do <u>this</u> act? If yes, guilty of murder. If no go to the next question.
>
> 3. What act or acts did D realise that one of the attackers might do to cause V really serious injury?
>
> 4. Is this act or are these acts which D realise that one of the attackers might do, of a fundamentally different nature to P's act which caused the death of V? If yes, not guilty of murder. If no, guilty of murder."

B.148   The provision of this guidance is welcome.[191] However, the guidance brings into focus two further weaknesses within the current law.

---

[186] The current Judicial Studies Board direction refers without any elaboration of an act that is 'fundamentally different'.

[187] [2000] 2 Cr App R 407.

[188] In *Van Hoogstraten*, Sir Stephen Mitchell doubted the correctness of *Gilmore*. This is because, employing Sir Stephen's approach, the definition of the 'relevant act' is likely to have included the fact that the petrol bomb was very large and that it would be thrown with the intention to kill. If the relevant act was defined in such terms, the defendant in *Gilmore* is likely to have escaped liability for manslaughter as well as murder. This comparison not only demonstrates the central importance of the definition of the 'relevant act', but also how different interpretations would effect a defendant like the one in *Gilmore*.

[189] [2007] EWCA Crim 342.

[190] On this view, the focus is on the physical act of P and not on P's intention in doing the act (our footnote).

B.149 In one respect the law may now be too harsh on D. This may happen when the act done by P is the one D anticipated, but P intends that act to be lethal, whereas D anticipated only that P might intend it to cause serious harm. In such a case, D will be guilty of murder in spite of the fact that he or she did not anticipate the use of lethal force.

B.150 Contrariwise, in one respect the law may be too generous to D. This may happen when the act done by P is not the one anticipated by D, yet D appreciated not only that P might act with the intent to do serious harm, but also that V might die as a result. In such a case, D may escape liability for murder, in spite of the fact that he or she did anticipate the use of lethal force if, for example, P uses a weapon that D did not anticipate P using.

B.151 In both such cases, it is not clear that the 'fundamental difference' rule produces the right results.

NO LIABILITY FOR NOT ONLY MURDER BUT ALSO MANSLAUGHTER

B.152 *English* clearly decides that if the act that caused V's death was fundamentally different and therefore one for which D is not responsible, as well as being not guilty of murder, D is not guilty of manslaughter. There is no halfway house as far as liability for V's death is concerned.[192] The decision opens up the prospect of D escaping all liability for V's death even in cases where D's intention was that V should suffer serious, albeit non-lethal, harm. Lord Hutton made no reference to the line of authority[193] which had previously held that, if D is a party to a joint criminal venture involving the use or threatened use of unlawful violence against V, D can be convicted of manslaughter even though he or she had not foreseen the lethal act. The status of that line of authority is, therefore, uncertain.[194] However, subsequent cases have confirmed that D is not guilty of either murder or manslaughter.

[191] We have already pointed out that we believe this guidance is more generous to the accused than the guidance provided in *Powell and Daniels*, para B.139 above.

[192] D may be convicted of other offences, for example causing grievous bodily harm with intent, assault occasioning actual bodily harm and conspiracy to cause such harm.

[193] *Anderson and Morris* [1996] 2 QB 110, n 158.

[194] *Crooks* [1999] NI 226; *Uddin* [1999] QB 431; *A-G's Reference (No 3 of 2004)* [2005] EWCA Crim 1882.